WORDS TO LIVE BY

BOOKS BY RABBI SIDNEY GREENBERG

Inspirational Essays:

Adding Life to Our Years
Finding Ourselves
Hidden Hungers
Say Yes to Life
Lessons for Living

Anthologies:

A Treasury of Comfort
The Bar Mitzvah Companion (Co-Editor)
Light from Jewish Lamps
A Treasury of the Art of Living
Teaching and Preaching: High Holiday Bible Themes
  Volume I: Rosh Hashanah
  Volume II: Yom Kippur
A Treasury of Thoughts on Jewish Prayer

Youth Prayer Books:

Siddurenu (Co-Editor)
High Holiday Services for Children
Sabbath and Festival Services for Children
A Contemporary High Holiday Service (Co-Editor)
The New Model Seder (Co-Editor)
Junior Contemporary Prayer Book for the High Holidays (Co-Editor)

Prayer Books:

Contemporary Prayers and Readings for the High Holidays, Sabbaths, and
  Special Occasions
Likrat Shabbat: Workship, Study, and Song for Sabbath and Festival Evenings
  (Co-Editor)
The New Mahzor for Rosh Hashanah and Yom Kippur (Co-Editor)
A Minyan for Comfort

WORDS TO LIVE BY
Selected Writings of
Rabbi Sidney Greenberg

edited by Arthur Kurzweil

JASON ARONSON INC.
Northvale, New Jersey
London

10 9 8 7 6 5 4 3 2 1

Library of Congress Cataloging-in-Publication Data

Greenberg, Sidney, 1917–
    Words to live by : selected writings / by Sidney Greenberg :
  edited by Arthur Kurzweil.
        p. cm.
    ISBN 0-87668-706-0
    1. Jewish sermons, American. 2. Jewish meditations.
  I. Kurzweil, Arthur. II. Title.
  BM740.2.G73   1990
  296.4′2 – dc20
                                                                90-40486
                                                                CIP

Manufactured in the United States of America. Jason Aronson Inc. offers books and cassettes. For information and catalog write to Jason Aronson Inc., 230 Livingston Street, Northvale, New Jersey 07647.

This book is dedicated to
two of my very dear friends,
loyal members of Temple Sinai

the late
LOUIS E. WAXMAN
who never learned the word "impossible"
and
LILIAN R. WAXMAN
who is always available to help

* * * * * * * * *

The publication of this book
was made possible
by their children

Barry & Elsa Waxman
Elaine & Marvin Samson

CONTENTS

PART III LIVING AT OUR BEST

PART VI LIVING AS A JEW

PART VII REACHING FOR THE HIGHEST

PART VIII   A SHEAF OF PRAYERS

FOREWORD

The term *maggid,* which literally means "one who relates," is often used in an informal way to refer to a teller of stories. A century or two ago, however, *maggid* was a title given to a great teacher who was known for his masterful ability as a preacher.

But a true maggid is more than that. It has been said that the maggid is not merely a master preacher but rather someone who can speak on a vast number of levels simultaneously, thereby reaching each of his listeners on precisely the level that defines their present situation. There is a story told of just such a maggid, who was invited to speak before an audience in the synagogue. Before the formal presentation, the maggid mingled with the congregation, speaking for at least a moment or two with each person individually. With every encounter, the maggid asked if the congregant had a favorite passage in the Torah, and when the maggid finally got up to speak, he managed to include each and every passage that was told to him, prompting everyone to feel that the maggid was speaking directly to him. It was not, of course, that this maggid merely took the Torah passages to weave a sermon. With each brief encounter, the maggid did indeed hear the words spoken, but the transmission between the maggid and the congregants was more profound: the maggid was able to see through the windows of their souls.

Another term that has been used for centuries among the Jewish people is the title of *darshan,* also denoting a preacher. In the Middle Ages, the darshan was the expert preacher, and his status was of an official nature; whereas the rabbi of the community would typically be occupied with matters of law, the darshan was the preacher, the teller of parables, "the one who relates."

Rabbi Sidney Greenberg is a maggid and a darshan. His colleagues refer to him precisely as a "master preacher" and he has been called, by many rabbis throughout the United States, the top preacher of the American Rabbinate. Having served as a spiritual leader within the Jewish community for a half century, Rabbi Greenberg has helped to raise a new generation of American rabbis who have had him as a role model and have reaped the benefit of his instruction.

Since time immemorial, Jews have been aware of the potential power to be found within words, and the value of the form known as the sermon has been a vital element within Jewish life. It is interesting to note that the *Encyclopaedia Judaica* offers a lengthy discussion regarding the sermon, pointing out that it has always been the chief means of instruction among the Jews and that "the importance of the sermon can hardly be overestimated."

If the sermon cannot be overestimated, then surely this book, which is essentially a collection of the best sermons by a great maggid of our generation, is an important publishing event. And while it is an undeserved honor for me to have been a part of the selection process, looking for the best among the best of a rabbi who has taught among the Jewish people for 50 years, my participation offered me a most remarkable experience of seeing, firsthand, the true nature of the maggid: Once the contents of this book had been chosen, the manuscript was read by many, many people – not only the readers who are typically asked by a publisher to review a manuscript and who are considered experts in their fields, but also the typesetter, the proofreader, the secretary, the editorial assistant, and others. And like the definition of the maggid of old, the manuscript touched each and every person without exception in a way that one rarely witnesses. Be they scholars or laypeople, experts or beginners, Jews or non-Jews, young or old, they seemed to think that the book was written for them, that this great maggid was speaking to each of them directly and individually.

Of course, they were correct. For Rabbi Sidney Greenberg is a maggid, a vessel of the Almighty, through whom sparks of Divine wisdom flow, to nourish and to sustain us.

Arthur Kurzweil

ACKNOWLEDGMENT

The passages in this volume have been selected, with the exception of several newspaper columns, from books that I have authored during close to a half-century of teaching and preaching. By way of acknowledging my genuine indebtedness to the publishers who made possible the appearance of those books, and, therefore, this one, I list them together with the names of the volumes for which they were each responsible:

Jonathan David Publishers – *Adding Life to Our Years*
Finding Ourselves
Crown Publishers Inc. – *Say Yes to Life*
Hartmore House – *A Treasury of Comfort*
Hidden Hungers
Lessons for Living
Prayer Book Press of Media Judaice – *Likrat Shabbat*
Mahzor Hadash
A Minyan of Comfort
Siddur Hadash

I am especially grateful to my good friend, colleague, and co-editor of my liturgical works, Rabbi Jonathan D. Levine, who is the publisher of Hartmore House and Prayer Book Press. His editorial skill is especially evident in the last chapter, "A Sheaf of Prayers."

Arthur Kurzweil, editor of this volume, has earned my special appreciation by generously putting at my disposal his great wealth of publishing experience. Working with him has been an immensely enriching experience.

The appearance of this volume is timed to coincide with the launching of my congregation's Jubilee Celebration. For 48 of those 50 years I have been Temple Sinai's spiritual leader, their first full-time rabbi. Most of the pages of this book originated as spoken messages to this congregation. For the unfailing encouragement and enthusiastic support I have always received, I want to register my deepest thanks.

My wife and helpmate in the rabbinate is very much part of this book, even as she has been an enormously blessed influence in the life of Temple Sinai. Few congregations are privileged to enjoy the boundless caring and dedication from the rabbi's wife that Hilda has brought to Temple Sinai and its members. They and I are profoundly indebted to her.

Gert Silnutzer, my faithful and competent secretary, was indispensable to the appearance of *Words To Live By*. She addressed the myriad details that the publishing of a book involves with rare humor and uncommon efficiency. I want her to know how warmly I appreciate her loyalty.

Above all, I express my gratitude to Him who, in the words of our prayer book, "graciously grants us intelligence and endows us with understanding." It is also He who has kept me alive, sustained me, and enabled me to reach this day.

Sidney Greenberg
Temple Sinai
Dresher, Pennsylvania
July 1990–Tammuz 5750

I

LIVING EACH DAY

*God is waiting for us to stop waiting and to begin to do
now all the things for which this day was made.*

The Unforgivable Error

One of the first lessons taught in Homiletics at the Jewish Theological Seminary is that a rabbi never reads simply for pleasure. A rabbi must always be wearing sermonic spectacles because ideas waiting to be preached lurk in the most unsuspected places. If Shakespeare could find "sermons in stones" why should we not be able to find sermons in the morning newspaper or even in a mystery story?

A case in point is one of Agatha Christie's tales. Her detective hero Hercule Poirot says to his good friend Captain Hastings: "It is your destiny to stand beside me and prevent me from committing the unforgivable error."

"What do you call the unforgivable error?" the captain asks.

Poirot answers: "Overlooking the obvious."

When we stop to reflect upon the detective's answer we realize that overlooking the obvious is indeed if not "the unforgivable error" at least a very widespread human error. In an age when we have walked on the moon and conducted space flights to explore planets hundreds of millions of miles away, our attention has been focused on distant horizons, while we too frequently overlook the crucial matters so close at hand.

But "the unforgivable error" of overlooking the obvious is not a product of the space age. A Torah portion talks of it long ago. We find Hagar and her son Ishmael dying of thirst in the wilderness of Beer-

Sheba. In despair she places her child under one of the shrubs and sits some distance away. "For she thought: 'I cannot look on as the child dies.' And sitting thus at a distance she wept loudly. . . . Then God opened her eyes and she saw a well of water; and she went and filled the bottle with water, and gave the lad drink."

Let us note carefully what the Torah tells us about Hagar's deliverance. God did not create a well in answer to her desperate prayers. The well had been there all along. Her source of salvation and survival was close at hand. What God did for Hagar was to open her eyes so that she saw the well, the obvious she had overlooked.

I often wish that God would do for us what He did for Hagar — simply open our eyes to the unnumbered glories that surround us, the manifold blessings which sustain us; His "miracles which attend us daily, morning, noon and night."

If only we could see the obvious, what an effective antidote that would be to our gnawing discontent, our insatiable ambitions, our quiet desperation, our restless nights, our parched days. The fly in the ointment gets all our attention while we remain unmindful of the ointment. So preoccupied are we with what we lack that we are unmindful of what we possess.

Helen Keller was most sensitive to this common human failing and there is a special poignancy to the words she wrote in *The World I Live In.* "I have walked with people whose eyes are full of light but who see nothing in woods, sea or sky, nothing in the city street, nothing in books. . . .

"It were far better to sail forever in the night of blindness with sense and feeling and mind than to be thus content with the mere act of seeing.

"They have the sunset, the morning skies, the purple of distant hills, yet their souls voyage through this enchanted world with nothing but a barren stare."

The famous choreographer Agnes de Mille suffered a serious illness and after a long hard road to recovery she wrote about what illness had taught her. "I had a destroyed body," she wrote, "but I got a new way of looking at things. . . . My life pattern had been broken, the habits smashed. . . . The fight back to health has brought me a new sense of awareness. I think it's very invigorating to call a sharp halt to life and pay attention to what's going on and what we are doing. I believe we could learn a great deal and could take joy and power in matters which usually go totally unnoticed."

When we overlook the obvious we not only miss the beauty and the blessings which are close at hand, we also lose sight of the opportunities for fulfillment which we already possess. How often we delude ourselves into believing that if only circumstances were different, if we lived elsewhere, if we had a different environment, O how happy we could be. When we get into the mood of "if only" we would do well to ask ourselves whether we are not making the unforgivable error.

Among the Hasidim they tell the tale of poor Rabbi Eizik of Cracow. He had a recurring dream that under the bridge which leads to the king's palace in Prague there was a great treasure. If he would journey there and dig he need never know poverty any more.

Rabbi Eizik made the journey, found the bridge but he did not dare to try to dig because the bridge was guarded day and night. Finally the guard who had observed him asked what he was doing all this time near the bridge. Rabbi Eizik told him of the dream which had brought him here.

Whereupon the guard burst into laughter. "You have faith in dreams! If I believed in dreams I would have had to go to Cracow, because long ago I dreamed that there was a treasure buried beneath the kitchen stove of some Jew named Rabbi Eizik."

Rabbi Eizik took his shovel, returned home and dug up the treasure beneath his own stove. With the money he built a *Shul* which they called *Rabbi Eizik's Shul.*

One Day at a Time

We took a coffee break on the turnpike and decided that things would go faster at the counter. The nameplate on her uniform read "Tex," and her smile was warm and friendly. The patrons were few, and she had lots of time to pour out her heart, together with the two cups of coffee.

She hadn't always been a waitress. She was a housewife raising two young boys when her husband was killed in an accident. Suddenly her whole world caved in. In addition to her own sense of loss and desolation, there was the awesome responsibility of being father and mother to her sons.

She was gripped by panic and a paralyzing sense of helplessness. How would she manage all those stark, frightening years that stretched bleakly ahead of her? How would she care for herself and the two boys?

For the longest time she sat at home brooding and worrying. "Then one night," she said, "as I tossed sleeplessly, it came to me. I realized that I didn't have to solve all my problems all at once. All I had to do was to get through one day at a time. And for one day I could be strong enough, smart enough, and tough enough. That thought helped me to see it through."

What happened to the boys? Today one is a physician, the other is in medical school; and Mama serves the counter trade.

Tex poured out a lot of wisdom with her coffee. I've had occasion to pass along her advice in all kinds of difficult circumstances, and I have even kept some for personal use.

In times of trouble and tragedy, we deepen our anxiety and our pain if we try to look too far ahead. The climb seems so steep, the road is strewn with so many hurdles, we simply don't see how we're going to make it. But if we can look just one day ahead and try to muster sufficient courage and faith for that one day, we usually find that our inner resources are equal to the demand.

"The hero," wrote Emerson, "is no braver than an ordinary man, but he is brave five minutes longer." In this sense we can all strive for heroism—to be brave not for a lifetime, not for years or even for months—but just for five minutes longer.

It is worth noting that in the beloved twenty-third psalm the Bible says: "Yea though I *walk* through the valley of the shadow of death." We can neither fly over the valley, detour around it, nor run through it. We have to walk. One heavy step at a time. One lonely night at a time, one empty day at a time. Then somehow, in God's goodness, the days become weeks, the weeks add up to months, and the months turn into years.

But we cannot live years at a time. As Tex said—one day at a time. And if we do indeed persevere, patiently but resolutely, breaking time into manageable little pieces, we often discover the surprising truth captured by the anonymous poet:

> These things are beautiful beyond belief:
> The pleasant weakness that comes after pain,
> The radiant greenness that comes after rain,
> The deepened faith that follows after grief,
> And the awakening to love again.

We Wait Too Long

Watch the faces of people who celebrate a birthday, an anniversary, a new year, and see if you do not detect a certain wistfulness in their expressions, a measure of tentativeness in their joy. They seem to follow the biblical advice to "rejoice with trembling."

Life's arithmetic is not simple. Every addition is also a subtraction. When we add a year to those we have already lived, we substract a year from those remaining to be lived. So the privilege of reaching another milestone is accompanied by the sobering reminder of life's relentless flight.

There is therefore an added sense of urgency to the advice Teddy Kollek, Jerusalem's dynamic mayor, gives in his autobiography, *For Jerusalem A Life*. He recommends an Eleventh Commandment: "Thou shalt not be patient."

At first blush this bit of advice flies in the face of one of the most universally admired virtues – patience. "He that can have patience," wrote Benjamin Franklin, "can have what he wills."

And yet as we reflect on Kollek's words, they seem to contain a pungent wisdom that can serve as a much-needed antidote to our too-human tendency to procrastinate. The truth about us is that in too many vital areas of life we wait too long.

We often wait too long to do what must be done today, in a world that gives us only one day at a time, without any assurance of tomorrow. While lamenting that our days are few, we act as though we had an endless supply of time.

We wait too long to discipline ourselves and to take charge of our lives. We feed ourselves the vain delusion that it will be easier to uproot tomorrow the debasing habits we permit to tyrannize us today and that grow more deeply entrenched each day they remain in power.

We wait too long to show kindness. F. Scott Fitzgerald, the laureate of "the lost generation" created by World War I, wrote to a friend in a time of sadness, "Pray, do write to me. A few lines soon are better than a three-decker novel a month hence."

We wait too long to speak the words of forgiveness that should be spoken, to set aside the hatreds that should be banished, to express thanks, to give encouragement, to offer comfort.

We wait too long to be charitable. Too much of our giving is delayed until much of the need has passed and the joy of giving has largely been diminished.

A magazine cartoon shows two old women draped in rags shivering over a meager fire. One asks, "What are you thinking about?" The other answers, "About the nice warm clothes the rich will be giving us next summer."

We wait too long to be parents to our children – forgetting how brief is the time during which they are children, how swiftly life urges them on and away. We wait too long to express our concern for parents, siblings, and dear ones. Who knows how soon it will be too late?

We wait too long to read the books, to listen to the music, and to see the art waiting to enlarge our minds, to enrich our spirits, and to expand our souls.

We wait too long to utter the prayers that are waiting to cross our lips, to perform the duties waiting to be discharged, to show the love that may no longer be needed tomorrow. We wait too long in the wings when life has a part for us to play on the stage.

God, too, is waiting – waiting for us to stop waiting, and to begin to do now all the things for which this day and this life have been given to us.

Commonplace Blessings

Water plays a prominent role in the weekly biblical portion called *Hukat*. The absence of water in the wilderness of Zin leads to an angry confrontation between the people and their leaders – Moses and Aaron. Moses finally brings water out of a rock, but not before he loses his temper and bitterly castigates the people.

Later in this same portion, we read of the discovery of a well – an event that was celebrated in a song of thanksgiving (Numbers 21:17,18).

All this over ordinary water – not oil, not champagne, not any magical elixir. These events remind us to be aware of the commonplace blessings we so frequently overlook.

The people of Jerusalem who lived through Israel's War of Independence in 1948 do not take water for granted. They remember what it was like to live for months in a state of siege when the pipeline that brought water to Jerusalem was cut. A friend who experienced those horrible days once said to me: "Only after I learned what it means to be without water did I understand why our ancestors were ready to revolt against Moses. Water is life."

Another example: An Israeli soldier was cleaning up a mess hall with instructions to return untouched food to the kitchen and to discard partly eaten food. He placed one partly eaten piece of bread with the untouched bread. A sergeant told the soldier to discard that bread. The soldier refused. The order was repeated, and still the soldier refused.

Finally the sergeant threatened: "I'm going to repeat that order once more. If you refuse to obey it I shall have you court-martialed."

The soldier held up his two misshapen hands and said: "You see these 10 fingers, they were all broken in Buchenwald when the Nazi guard caught me stealing a moldy piece of black bread in the kitchen. I tried to steal that miserable crust of bread because I was crazed by hunger. I was ready to kill for a piece of bread. To me bread is holy. Don't ask me to throw away a piece of bread. I can't do it."

The sergeant's order was not repeated.

We take water and bread for granted, as we do our eyes, ears, hands, legs, hearts, minds. But let one of these be threatened, and we realize how precious it is. One of my favorite Hebrew prayers helps keep us from taking our blessings for granted: "We thank You for our lives which are in Your hand, for our souls which are in Your care, for Your miracles which are daily with us, and for Your wondrous kindness at every moment – morning, noon and night."

This Is the Day

One of my favorite biblical verses, a verse that becomes dearer to me as I grow older, proclaims a truth of which we should be reminded as we greet each new day: "This is the day that the Lord has made; on it let us rejoice and be glad" (Psalms 118:24).

The recognition that each day is another gift from God, that each day is an occasion for joy and gladness, can go a long way toward making us aware of the extraordinary privilege of being alive right here and right now. This awareness can in turn inspire us to live each day more intensely, more fully.

Too much of our living is done in the past or in the future while we neglect the present. But yesterday is a canceled check and tomorrow is a promissory note. Only today is cash at hand for us to spend. "This is the day. . . ."

Margaret Storm Jameson, the British novelist, has spoken directly to this theme:

> I believe that only one person in a thousand knows the trick of really living in the present. Most of us spend fifty-nine minutes an hour living in the past, with regret for lost joys, or shame for things badly done (both utterly useless and weakening) – or in a future that we either long for or dread. Yet the past is gone beyond prayer, and every minute we spend in the vain effort to anticipate the future is a moment lost. There is only one world, the world pressing against you at this minute. There is only one minute in which you are alive, this minute – here and now. The only way to live is by accepting each minute as an unrepeatable miracle. Which is exactly what it is – a miracle and unrepeatable.

When our daughters were young and we would start out on a trip, one of them was in the habit of asking about five minutes after we left, "Daddy, are we almost there?" A few minutes later she would ask, "When are we going to get there?" This is a question that is typical of too many of us. When are we going to get there? We are so anxious to get there that we don't enjoy the journey. And we forget that life is a journey and not a destination.

We are always looking ahead to something in the future. We are preparing for graduation, for a profession; we are working to pay off the mortgage; we are looking forward to the children's being independent; we're saving for that new home or the new car. And we wonder when we are going to get there. And then one day it suddenly dawns upon us that we've been there all along and that we should have enjoyed the journey a lot more. We should have paid more attention to some of the lovely scenes that we were passing en route. We should have lived more in each today.

One of the people whom I have known for many years retired from his business. I remember how eagerly he looked forward to retirement and how zealously he applied himself to making his retirement possible and comfortable. An extraordinary amount of sacrifice and self-denial went into the planning for this retirement. But when I spoke with him later I had the depressing feeling that retirement turned out to be a lot less fun than he had imagined it would be. And I could not help wondering, too, how many todays he missed for this tomorrow, which was finally today.

This is part and parcel of the problem of constantly asking, "When are we going to get there?" When we get there, we may find that there is no "there" there and all the while we were missing the fun of the journey. We were always going to live tomorrow, and in the meanwhile all those precious, irretrievable todays slipped away.

Life is a journey, not a destination, and happiness is not "there" but here; not tomorrow, but today. Let's not live by the edict of the White Queen in *Alice in Wonderland:* "Jam yesterday and jam tomorrow but never jam today." Today is not a parenthesis between yesterday and tomorrow. Good things can happen, do happen, and should happen today, if we make sure that they happen; if we learn how to live today.

"This is the day the Lord has made; on it let us rejoice and be glad."

Making Today Count

"You shall count from the day following the day of rest . . . seven full weeks shall be counted . . ." (Leviticus 23:15–16).

The 49 days that separate Pesah from Shavuot are counted days. Beginning with the second night of Pesah and on each evening for the following seven weeks we recite a blessing as we count each day by number. When the seven weeks are completed we usher in the Festival of Shavuot, the Festival of Weeks.

The 33rd day of *Sephira,* of counting, is observed as a special day, a day of rejoicing, because on this day, according to tradition, a plague that had ravaged Rabbi Akiva's pupils was stayed.

This tradition of counting days for so long a time cannot help but convey to us the importance of each day of our lives, and the importance of making each day count. Almost inevitably we hear in this practice an echo of the prayer of the Psalmist: "Teach us to count our days so that we may acquire a heart of wisdom."

How do we make each day count?

A highly charged executive, we are told, wanted to inspire his employees to be prompt in discharging their duties and completing their assigned tasks. So all around his office and factory, he placed a number of large signs reading: "Do It Now!"

The results, unhappily, were scarcely what he had hoped for. Within two weeks his cashier disappeared with some $10,000; his head bookkeeper left town with his most efficient secretary; every office worker asked for a raise; the factory people called a strike; and the office boy joined the Marines.

Despite the unanticipated consequences of his advice, the executive dispensed some wise counsel that we need to hear and to follow. So many of us postpone the business of living. We're so busy preparing for some future goal that we forget to live in the present.

Dr. William Moulton Marston, a psychologist, asked 3,000 people this brief question: "What do you have to live for?" He was shocked to find that ninety-four percent of his respondents were simply enduring the present while they waited for the future.

They were waiting for "something" to happen – waiting for children to grow up and become independent; waiting to pay off the mortgage; waiting for the day when they could take a long deferred trip; waiting for the leisure that retirement would bring. While they were waiting, life was passing them by, unenjoyed and unappreciated.

Too often, too many of us overlook the poet's simple truth:

> "I have no Yesterdays,
> Time took them away;
> Tomorrow may not be,
> But I have today."

Having stated this all-too-obvious truth, we then discover, as our unhappy executive did, that we have not necessarily solved our fundamental human dilemma. The question immediately confronting us is: "How shall we use today?" The way we answer this question determines the very texture of our lives.

In Genesis we read different answers given to this crucial question by Esau and his father Isaac at separate junctures in their lives.

For Esau, that moment came when he was asked to trade his birthright for a bowl of lentil soup. There was surely ample other food available, but Esau wanted only the lentil soup. He wanted what he wanted, when he wanted it. He did not believe in delayed gratification. Why should he? "Behold, I am going to die," he reasoned, "so of what use is my birthright to me?" (Genesis 25:32).

He surely used today – to appease his stomach, to gratify his physical needs. If he had to surrender his birthright in the process, so what? You can't eat a birthright. In his attitude and actions he anticipated Isaiah's hedonistic contemporaries whose self-indulgent motto was: "Let us eat and drink, for tomorrow we die."

Isaac's response to his human fragility and life's unpredictability was quite different. "I am old now," he said to Esau, "and I do not know how soon I may die . . . Go bring me something to eat so that I may bless you before I die" (Genesis 27:24).

Isaac was also going to use today – to be a source of blessing to others.

It may very well be that our tradition dealt quite harshly with Esau precisely because he trivialized life, reducing its awesome grandeur to the gratification of the stomach, dehumanizing it by forgetting that he also had a soul that needed nourishment.

Esau's descendants are legion. We live in an age when the media excite our appetite for instant gratification, instant relief from pain, instant rise to fame. Multimillion-dollar lotteries also stimulate our fantasies about instant riches. Underneath it all, like an uninvited skeleton at the wedding feast, lurks the ominous possibility of the instant destruction of the human race in a nuclear holocaust.

At such a time, the temptation to use today mindlessly and carelessly and selfishly is more than many can resist. And yet resist it we must – for our own salvation and for the preservation of all that makes us worth saving.

Eldad Ran was killed in Israel's War of Independence at the age of 20. Before he died, he left us a legacy containing wisdom that belies the youthfulness of its author. He wrote: "Lately I've been thinking about what the goal of life should be. At best, man's life is short. . . . The years of life do not satisfy the hunger for life. What then shall we do during this time?

"We can reach either of two conclusions. The first is that since life is so short, we should enjoy it as much as possible. The second is that precisely because life is short . . . we should dedicate life to a sacred and worthy goal . . . I am slowly coming to the conclusion that life by itself is worth little unless it serves something greater than itself."

Shortcuts to Distant Goals

A modern American was overheard offering a crisp prayer: "Dear God, please grant me patience. And I want it right now."

He was a faithful reflection of our assembly-line, speed-addicted "now" generation. We want what we want when we want it. We want it yesterday, today at the very latest; certainly not tomorrow. *Instant* is a key word in our vocabulary.

The frenetic pace of contemporary life shows through some of the verbs we use to describe our daily actions. We leap out of bed, we gulp our coffee, we bolt our food, we whiz into town, we dash to the office, we tear for home, and we drop dead. We travel at twice the speed of sound and half the speed of sense.

There is, for us, an especially crucial message in the biblical passage that tells of the way the Israelites traveled when they went out of Egypt. "God did not lead them by way of the land of the Philistines, although it was nearer; for God said, 'The people may have a change of heart when they see war, and return to Egypt.' So God led the people roundabout by way of the wilderness at the Sea of Reeds" (Exodus 13: 17–18).

Notice what the Bible is telling us. God deliberately avoided leading the Israelites on the shorter road. He took them on the long road because in His divine wisdom He knew that the short road to freedom could also become the quick road back to slavery. And so He led them "roundabout." Thus they – and we – were given the inescapable message: Beware of shortcuts to distant goals.

Happiness in marriage is a distant goal. There was a time when young people were warned that if they married in haste they would repent at leisure. This is no longer true. More and more young people are repenting in haste. They are too impatient to make the adjustments that marriage inevitably entails. They cannot wait to learn the tolerance that marriage always demands. They don't have the time to achieve the understanding that never comes quickly. They have not been taught that while love may come suddenly, happiness is a distant goal to which there is no shortcut.

The development of character is a distant goal. Goethe, the nineteenth-century German poet, once revealed the truth in this matter when he said, "Life is a quarry out of which we are to mold and chisel and complete a character." Notice all those time-consuming verbs. Character is distilled out of our daily confrontation with temptation, out of our regular response to the call of duty. It is formed as we learn to cherish principles and to submit to self-discipline. Character is the sum total of all the little decisions, the small deeds, the daily reactions to the choices that confront us. Character is not obtained instantly. We have to mold and hammer and forge ourselves into character. It is a distant goal to which there is no shortcut.

A genuine faith in God is a distant goal. We do not believe in instant conversions or spontaneous spiritual combustion. Like Jonah's gourd, that which grows in a day perishes in a day. A genuine faith in God, an appreciation of the wealth of our heritage and its noble beauty, have to be acquired slowly, painstakingly, in regular daily doses.

Religion is a quiet dimension of daily living; it is not a spectacular explosion. Its symbol is the soft eternal light, not the dramatic firecracker.

Predicting the Future

The future has been defined as something everyone reaches at the rate of 60 minutes an hour, whatever he does, whoever he is. But there has always been a vast curiosity to know the future before we get there.

Every day 50 million Americans read that special section in 1,200 newspapers to learn what the planets have in store for them. Astrology is a busy occupation in American to day – 10,000 people are working at it full-time and 175,000 part-time.

We consult the stars, the tea leaves, the palm readers, the crystal balls in an effort to part the curtain that veils the future. A cartoon shows a young girl reading her diary to a friend, and she says: "This is one book where I wish it were possible to peek in the back and see how it comes out."

Even our ancestor Jacob attempted for a fleeting moment to unravel the secrets hidden in the womb of time. We read in the synagogue that portion where the dying patriarch says to his children: "Come together that I may tell you what is to befall you in the days to come" (Genesis 49:1). As we read further , however, there are no predictions of things to come. And our sages pointed out that "Jacob wanted to fortell the future but the Divine presence departed from him." God apparently did not want the future to be revealed. Why not?

If you and I knew what was going to happen tomorrow and the day after and on all the tomorrows that are to be, wouldn't life lose its zest and its excitement? Wouldn't a terrible boredom set in as we played out mechanically the roles that had been predetermined for us?

And if we knew in advance all the heartbreak and the disappointments, the blasted hopes and the broken dreams, the small sorrows and the inconsolable griefs that awaited us – could we find the courage to venture into the future at all?

But the most compelling reason no one can predict the future is that the future does not exist. You and I are not robots. We have freedom of will to determine the shape of tomorrow by what we do today.

James Truslow Adams put his finger on the truth when he said that while an astronomer can predict precisely where every star will be at 11:30 tonight, he can make no such prediction about his young daughter.

What the future has in store for us depends largely on what we place in store for the future. Not the stars, nor the cards , but our own actions will determine the shape of things to come.

Every Day Is Examination Day

In a tribute to Albert Einstein, George Bernard Shaw once drew a distinction between "empire builders" and "universe builders." Napoleon, he said, was an empire builder, but empires are notoriously perishable. Einstein was a universe builder whose discoveries would endure as long as people hungered for truth.

Another universe builder was Abraham, of whom we read in the early chapters of Genesis. It is to him we are indebted for the incandescent truth that one invisible God is the Creator of the universe and the Father of every human being.

This truth did not come cheap. The Bible tells us that "God tested Abraham." The Jewish Sages taught that Abraham was tested no fewer than ten times.

Again and again when a burden was laid upon him, when a risky assignment was given to him, when a luring temptation was placed before him, Abraham felt himself being tested. Each trial was an opportunity to demonstrate to himself and to God, the stuff of which he was made.

Is this the secret of his radiant life? Is this the attitude we need if our lives are to be the meaningful adventures we know they can be? Must we, too, learn to regard life as a classroom and every experience as a quiz whose purpose it is to determine not what we know but what we are?

In James Agee's sensitive posthumously published novel, *A Death In The Family,* a father tries to comfort his daughter whose husband was killed in an auto accident. The unsophisticated father reveals genuine homespun wisdom and insight. He tells her that he realizes how little anyone can help her. She must work this thing out alone. He also points out "that nobody that ever lived is specially privileged; the axe can fall at any moment, on any neck, without any warning. . . .

You've got to keep your mind off pitying your own rotten luck and setting up any kind of howl about it." He reassures her that she will come through this as millions like her have come through it before. And then the father says these words: "It's a kind of test, Mary, and it's the only kind that amounts to anything. When something rotten like this happens, then you have your choice. You start to really be alive or you start to die. That's all." Note well those words: "It's a kind of test, Mary."

Our Sages correctly observed: "There is no creature whom the Holy One, blessed be He, does not test." We are all tested. We are always tested. Whether we are aware of it or not, life is constantly springing little quizzes on us.

Every day is examination day. As husbands we are tested and as wives we are tested. As children we are tested and as parents we are tested. The doctor confronting his patient is having his dedication tested. The lawyer consulting with his client is having his integrity tested. The rabbi preparing his sermon, the writer at his desk, is each having his honesty tested. The teacher preparing a lesson is having his or her devotion tested. The businessman on the telephone, the carpenter building a shed, the mechanic under the car, the painter on the scaffold – each is having his character tested.

When our neighbor has been bruised our kindness is tested. When we have been blessed our generosity is tested. When we have been hurt our forgiveness is tested. When we have hurt our humility is tested. Trouble tests our courage. Temptation tests our strength. Friendship tests our loyalty. Failure tests our perseverance. Success tests our gratitude.

No day is free from its full quota of tests. Indeed the uses to which we put each day, the purposes to which we dedicate it, the deeds with which we fill it – constitute perhaps the supreme test of all. An advertisement in the London *Times* read: "Some months to kill. Executive, 28, requires income for the assassination." To pass the daily quiz which the Father of all administers to us we must look upon time not as something to be killed but as something to be cherished. The prayer of the Psalmist is an excellent preparation for this test: "Teach us to number our days."

To look upon life as a test means to bring to it at every time the finest of which we are capable, to keep ourselves always in top moral condition, to realize the enormous possibilities for good or for ill

inherent in each situation regardless of how unspectacular, or humdrum, or even ominous it may appear.

Ralph Waldo Emerson put this truth in striking words: "It is one
of the illusions that the present hour is not the critical, decisive hour.
Write it on your heart that every day is the best day of the year. No
man has earned anything rightly until he knows that every day is
doomsday. Today is a king in disguise. . . . Let us not be deceived, let us
unmask the king as he passes."

II

ADDING LIFE
TO OUR YEARS

*For all its brevity life is long enough to find fulfillment,
to matter, to choose a path. The number of our years
may be beyond our control but their quality
and texture depend on us.*

Adding Life to Our Years

One of the unquestionably great scientific achievements of the modern age has been the prolongation of the human life span. A brief glance at the comparative statistics of the life expectancy of men and women as it is today and as it was a mere half century ago is sufficient to drive home the happy truth that our life expectancy has been dramatically expanded in a remarkably short time.

But somehow, at Yizkor time, these statistics do not overly impress us. In our heart of hearts we feel life's brevity. How quickly the past year seems to have sped by! It does not feel like twelve months since last Yom Kippur. Indeed, all the years seem to be flying at jet speeds these days. Mothers under the wedding canopy whisper, "It seems like only yesterday I was rocking her to sleep." A father after his son's graduation murmured to me recently: "I just couldn't believe it when I saw him claim his diploma. I was still thinking I'd have to lead him up by the hand." The years, like everything else nowadays, are travelling at accelerated speeds.

In many a heart too, there is a void left by the recent passing of a loved one. Last year we exchanged greetings. This year we're saying Yizkor. And many had so many unlived years! Statistics on the prolongation of human life offer little solace here.

If these personal reflections are not poignant enough we open our prayer book and a series of striking similes hammer home the awareness of life's brevity and transitoriness.

On each of the High Holy Days we repeat the passage which begins with the words: "Man's origin is the dust and his destination is the dust." And as for the interval between these two climaxes the passage goes on to make quite vivid its fleetingness. "Man's life may be compared to a broken potsherd, a dried up blade of grass, a flower that fades, a shadow which passes, a cloud which evaporates, dust which floats and a dream which vanishes." Scarcely a slow motion picture of the human adventure!

The contrast is completed by setting our limited days against the eternity of God. "Thy years have no measure nor is there any end to the length of Thy days." Compared to the everlastingness of God, our lives are but a faint tick on the clock of eternity.

But if we pause to examine carefully those very similes which the Prayer Book uses to convey the sobering fact of life's brevity, I think we can find a significant difference between them and it is in this difference that I think we may also find an insight into the problem of handling life's brevity. If science is concerned with the problem of adding years to man's life, Judaism is concerned with adding life to man's years. And a clue to the kind of life Judaism would have us pour into our years may be found in a second unhurried look at the passage in the Prayer Book.

Let us take first the two phrases – "the shadow which passes" and "the flower that fades." To be sure they both suggest vividly life's brief duration. But as we examine them further we discover a profound difference between them.

What does the word " shadow" suggest to us? A shadow is something which has no independent existence. The form it has at a particular moment depends upon the shape of the object upon which the light is falling and upon the angle at which the light is striking the object. At 3 o'clock the shadow has one shape, at 5 o'clock another and when the light disappears, the shadow must likewise disappear. The expression "chasing shadows" has become in the English language a symbol of futility. For who can grasp that which has no substance, is merely a darkened reflection of something else?

How different is the picture which the word "flower" conveys. Oliver Wendell Holmes said: "The Amen of nature is always a flower." "Flowers," said Henry Ward Beecher, "are sent to do God's work in unrevealed paths and to diffuse influence by channels that we hardly suspect." Wilberforce wrote, "Lovely flowers are similes of God's goodness." To Goethe flowers were "the beautiful hieroglyphics of nature with which she indicates how much she loves us."

Now, the shadow and the flower are both fleeting but it makes all the difference in the world whether we make of our lives flimsy shadows or beautiful flowers.

All of us know people who resemble one or the other. Many show no more independence of mind and thought than the formless shadow. Whatever thought they possess, whatever action they perform is merely a reflection of someone else's judgement, a response to someone else's urging. They take no trouble to form their own opinions or to plot their own course. There are many whose opinions reflect the last rumor they heard, their actions are an expression of the current rage. Pale, lifeless imitators, they possess neither color of their own, nor direction, nor purpose.

This, incidentally, is what dictatorship, whether of the right or left, tries to do to its subjects. It tries to strip them of their individuality, rob them of their ability to think for themselves. They must be guilty of no independent thinking. The dictator or the party will do the thinking, they will reflect the party line. Deviation is not to be tolerated. Hence the goose-stepping, the slogan chanting, the lavish parades, the thought control.

The sad part is, that what dictatorship imposes, some free people deliberately choose. Unwilling to pursue the discipline of study and thought which alone can produce independence of mind, they pick up the contemporary slogans and prejudices and become part of the anonymous mob. The extent of their contribution to society can be only too well imagined.

Then, of course, there are those who, like the lovely flower, possess their own uniqueness and individuality, who enrich the landscape of which they are a part; those, who by their own goodness and gentleness, "do God's work in unrevealed paths" and make it easy for us to believe in the basic goodness of all men.

That is the kind of influence many of those whom we remember this day had upon us. Many of us are fortunate enough to be able to remember a father or a mother or a brother or a mate of whom we could say as did Matthew Arnold of his father, who was a teacher, the headmaster of Rugby. . . .

> "And through thee I believe
> In the noble and great who are gone,
> Pure souls honor'd and blest
> By former ages, who else . . .

Seemed but a dream of the heart,
Seemed but a cry of desire.
Yes! I believe that there lived
Others like thee in the past . . .
. . . souls tempered with fire
Fervent, heroic and good
Helpers and friends of mankind."

"Small souls," it has been finely said, "help the world by what they do, great souls, by what they are." They are the living flowers in the human garden.

Yes, the shadow passes and the flower fades but it makes all the difference in the world whether we make of our lives flimsy, formless shadows or beautiful, lovely flowers.

Let us contrast further two other similes in the passage: "dust that flies," . . . "a dream that vanishes." Again, they both convey the sense of life's brevity but at this point the similarity ends. For the contrast between dust and dreams is literally as great as between earth and heaven.

What are the qualities of dust? Dust is an irritant. If it gets into the eyes or invades the nose or throat it brings distress and discomfort.

Unfortunately, many lives are like dust which flies. They possess a unique capacity for irritating people. There are some people who have the unhappy faculty of bringing out the worst within us. They may be the ones who are always criticizing you for your own good, never suspecting for a moment that an occasional compliment may also be for your good. They never weary of rehearsing their own good fortune in such a way as to excite your envy rather than your joy. They are people whose train of thought is utterly without any terminal facilities and when they have an hour to kill usually decide to spend it with someone who hasn't. After they are gone they usually leave us muttering with exasperation: "I don't know why but he always rubs me the wrong way. He always gets my dander up." Some people bring happiness *wherever* they go. These people bring happiness *whenever* they go. They irritate and distress.

Dust has another unattractive characteristic. When it is not flying about doing its irritating work it has a tendency to settle and it settles on the lowest level it can find.

How many of us do just that—settle on the lowest level we can find? Especially in our choice of leisure activities is the tendency to settle on the lowest possible level exceedingly strong. It seems that just as there is a physical law of gravity which pulls an object down so is there a social law of gravity which tends to pull us humans down. And we have to be especially careful against this downward drag. If we want to test our own resistance to this social tendency, let us ask ourselves a series of questions.

If we have a choice between a pulp novel and a serious book, which do we choose?

If we have a choice between a regular Tuesday night game and a Tuesday night study group, which do we choose?

If we have a choice between conversation and gossip, between a television program and a Friday Night Service, which do we choose?

In contrast to dust which irritates and sinks there is the dream which inspires, which elevates, which points to new horizons, which opens up new frontiers.

The motto which Theodor Herzl chose for his novel was: "If you will it, it is no legend." And he closed with this warning: "But if you do not will it, then it remains a legend which I have recited. Dreams and action are not as widely separated as many believe. All acts of men were dreams at first and become dreams again."

Every worthwhile human achievement, if traced back far enough, began as a dream. Youth Aliyah began as a dream in the heart of Henrietta Szold.

A reborn Israel began as a dream in the heart of the prophet Isaiah.

The freedom we enjoy began as a dream in the heart of a slave people in Egypt.

The medicines which heal us, the discoveries which sustain us, each began as an uplifting, inspiring dream.

There are many whose whole lives "are such stuff as dreams are made on." They bring upliftment, they evoke the very best within us, they challenge us to new achievement, they unfold before us new hope, new possibility, new opportunity. In his autobiography, "As I Remember Him," Hans Zinser speaks of his father "whose love enclosed me while he lived and whose hand I have felt caressingly on my head throughout my life whenever I was in need of comforting."

Yes, the dust floats away and the dream vanishes, but it makes all the difference in the world whether we make our lives like dust, irritating and sinking or like dreams soothing and uplifting.

Thus we can re-read that whole passage in the Prayer Book and see actually a series of alternatives. We can make our lives like the potsherd with its jagged edges, which is an obstacle on the human pathway, or like grass which clothes the earth, feeds the animal and, thus, sustains man. We can make our lives like the cloud which blots out the sun or like the caressing wind that softly brings relief.

Yes, life is brief, but we determine its quality. Indeed, precisely because it is brief we must be very discriminating as to what we put into it. We are like the man leaving on a journey with a small leather pouch. Shall he fill it with mud when he can take along diamonds? Shall we fill our days with pettiness and greed when close at hand are kindness and generosity? Shall we degrade or uplift, discourage or inspire, stagnate or grow?

We cannot determine what the New Year will bring to us but we have the more important choice–what we bring to the New Year. Shadows or flowers, dust or dream, what shall we make of our lives?

George Bernard Shaw's declaration might well serve as a watchword for the New Year: "Life is no brief candle for me. It is a sort of splendid torch which I have got hold of for a moment and I want to make it burn as brightly as possible before handing it on to future generations."

To Live All the Days of Our Lives

Some years ago a religious sect adopted as its motto these words: "Millions now living will never die." Whereupon one observer remarked, "Yes, but the tragedy is that millions now living are already dead but do not know it."

The rabbinic teachers may have been pointing in the same direction in their comment on the biblical narrative that tells of the death of the two sons of Aaron, Nadav and Avihu. The sages said that the young men had suffered a peculiar kind of death: "Their souls were consumed; their bodies remained intact."

Had the sages filled out the coroner's report, it might have read: "Biologically sound, spiritually dead." The ancient rabbis confirmed here a moral verdict that they rendered more explicitly in another passage: "The wicked even in life are considered dead."

Much has been written on the question of when true biological death sets in. When the heart stops beating? When the brain stops functioning? But what is the status of the human being when the soul shrivels and the spirit withers?

At a time when there is growing popular interest in a belief in life after death and a widely publicized book is entitled *Life After Life,* should we not each give more attention to the question "How about life during life?" Are we truly and fully alive, not only biologically, but spiritually as well?

Sinclair Lewis was a professed atheist. Once he engaged in a public debate in Kansas City on whether or not God exists. He finished his presentation with the dramatic challenge: "If there is a God, let him strike me dead now." He waited a few moments, nothing happened, and he marched triumphantly off the platform.

The following morning the *Kansas City Times* printed an editorial response to Lewis. Of course, it said, God did strike Lewis dead even though he did not seem to be aware of it. His spiritual demise was reflected in his despair about the value of life, in his cynical contempt for people, in his sneering egotism, and in his waning literary powers. It was another case of a human being who was biologically sound, spiritually dead.

A colleague once blessed his young grandson in these words: "My child, may you live all the days of your life." To live all the days of our lives is to live fully, with our whole being, with heart and mind and spirit. It means cultivating all our God-given resources for inner growth. It means being alive to the beauty of the world and to the wonder and the miracle of being part of it. It means becoming ever more sensitive to the abiding joys of sharing, the extravagant rewards of loving, the bountiful harvests of believing.

It means, in the words of the Hebrew prophet, "to act justly, to love mercy, and to walk humbly with your God" (Micah 6:8).

What Time Is It?

A Jewish tourist stops an Israeli on Ben Yehudah Street in Tel Aviv and the following conversation ensues:

"Can you please tell me the time?"

"I'm sorry, I don't have a watch."

"You don't have a watch? How do you know what time it is?"

"During the day, if I want to know what time it is, I ask someone."

"But what do you do at night?"

"For that I have a Shofar, a ram's horn."

"A Shofar! How do you tell time with a Shofar?"

"That's simple. If I wake up in the middle of the night and want to know what time it is, I open my window and I blow the Shofar as loud as I can. A neighbor will always call out, 'Idiot! At 3:30 in the morning, you blow the Shofar!' Now I know what time it is."

In using the Shofar to find out what time it is, our legendary Israeli friend is giving a new twist to a hallowed Jewish practice. On Rosh Hashanah, Jews who are assembled in their overflowing synagogues will hear once again the sharp piercing sounds of the Shofar. When a Jew hears the calls of the Shofar, he knows what time it is. It is the most sacred time of the year, the time for taking moral inventory. It is the time for self-evaluation. It is the time for asking what have I made of the year that has come and gone, what will I make of the New Year that I have just welcomed.

On each of the High Holy Days we repeat a prayer that reminds us in vivid imagery how brief life is.

"We are like a fragile vessel, like the grass that withers, the flower that fades, the shadow that passes, the cloud that vanishes, the wind that blows, the dust that floats, the dream that flies away."

The longest life ends too soon; a faint tick on the clock of eternity. And yet, we do have enough time to make a difference in so many ways. For we can determine how we use each day, all the more precious for being numbered.

For all its brevity, life is long enough to find fulfillment, to matter, to choose a path. The number of our years may be beyond our control, but their quality and texture depend on us. Shadows or flowers, dust or dreams, what shall we make of our lives?

The Shofar is sounded and it is the time to ask the timeless questions.

We Are Each Indispensable
in Our Small Parts

If all people on earth have a set of common ancestors – Adam and Eve – and, therefore, a common point of origin, we would expect them all to be speaking a common language. How, then, does it happen that there is in fact a multiplicity of tongues in use throughout the world?

The Bible addresses itself to this unspoken question in the celebrated story of the misguided people who built the Tower of Babel. What was their goal? "Come let us build ourselves a city and a tower, with its top in Heaven, and let us make ourselves a name" (Genesis 11:4). They believed that if they built the tallest tower, a heaven-scraper, they would acquire instant fame. Instead, the Bible tells us, they were doubly punished. They suffered a confusion of languages wherein all they could do was babble unintelligibly, and they were scattered abroad on the face of the earth. What was their sin?

It was, I suspect, that they mistook bigness for greatness, quantity for quality, size for substance. This particular sin did not disappear with the tower builders: it is still alive and well among us.

We live in a time addicted to bigness – bigger industries, bigger bombs, king-size cigarettes and giant movie screens. One Hollywood producer said that he wanted a film that began with an earthquake and worked up to a climax. In our concern with bigness, we have forgotten that a poor film becomes only more tedious by being prolonged, and that a nation bent on enslaving others becomes only more dangerous as its power increases.

Greatness is a matter not of size but of quality, and it is within the reach of every one of us. Greatness lies in the faithful performance of whatever duties life places upon us and in the generous performance of the small acts of kindness that God has made possible for us. There is greatness in patient endurance; in unyielding loyalty to a goal; in resistance to the temptation to betray the best we know; in speaking up for the truth when it is assailed; in steadfast adherence to vows given and promises made.

God does not ask us to do extraordinary things. He ask us to do ordinary things extraordinarily well.

Let none of us believe that greatness has passed us by. If we wish it very much, it can be ours. Of each of us it can be said, as it was of an actor who had played minor roles for twenty-five years, "He was indispensable in small parts."

Each of us is indispensable in the part assigned to us by the Master Playwright. Each of us has a job to do that will remain undone if we do not do it. Each of us has love that only we can give. Each of us has compassion that will be denied to the world if we suppress it. We are each indispensable in our small parts and each part is gilded with a glory all its own.

Why Not Me?

"Never volunteer!" was the first bit of barracks wisdom usually passed along to the new army recruit by the veteran. A corollary of this advice was: "Don't stick your neck out."

This counsel is not confined to the military. A host of people who never wore the uniform have made "Never volunteer" the golden rule of their lives. This all-too-human trait prompted this lament from a colleague:

> There's a clever young fellow named SOMEBODY ELSE,
> There's nothing this fellow can't do.
> He's busy from morning 'till late at night
> Just substituting for you.
> You're asked to do this, or asked to do that,
> And what is your ready reply?
> "Get SOMEBODY ELSE, Mr. Chairman,
> He'll do it much better than I."

Some of us "never volunteer" because of shyness, others because of selfishness, and still others because of a sense of inferiority.

Whatever the reason for our relying on Somebody Else, we can be enormously encouraged by the bold example of the prophet Isaiah. There was a most unpleasant assignment on hand – to speak words of harsh rebuke to his own people. This was hardly a task to enhance his popularity among his neighbors.

And then he heard an insistent voice asking: "Whom shall I send, and who will go for us?" Isaiah answered simply: "Here am I; send me" (Isaiah 6:8-9).

There's something so reassuring in those simple words: "Here am I; send me." How they shore up our faith in our ability to respond to the challenge to rise above ourselves! Most of the good that gets done would remain undone if there weren't decent people responding: "Here am I; send me."

In Kibbutz Ashdot Yaakov, in the north of Israel, there is a shoemaker who holds two Ph.D. degrees from European universities. Why did he come to Israel some time ago?

"One day," he answers, "I was telling somebody about the need to 'conquer' the land around the Sea of Galilee, cleanse it of malaria, make it fruitful. Suddenly, I thought: 'Why not me?' So I went. And all my life I have kept on trying to ask myself, 'Why not me?'"

The glory of the human race are those who ask "Why not me?" when there is great work to be done—visiting the sick, comforting the bereaved, feeding the hungry, cheering the distressed, fighting for truth, protesting injustice, advancing worthy causes.

These people not only bring blessings; they are blessed. For unless we live in some measure for others, we hardly live at all.

Preparing for Old Age

I was once visiting at the home of a friend shortly after the death of her aged father. During the course of our conversation she made a wistful remark which bore heavy overtones of regret. "You know," she said, "we ought to give a lot more thought than we do to the problem of preparing for old age."

The bereaved daughter's remorseful remark constitutes a challenge to consider a problem which happily is facing an ever-increasing number of people in our country. One hundred years ago, the life expectancy in our country was age 30. Today it has risen to more than double that.

A reflection of this trend is to be found in the emergence of a new science called *geriatrics* which is concerned exclusively with the aging process and its attendant problems. Geriatrics, as I see it, is the answer of science to mankind's perennial prayer. We all want to live long but none of us wants to be old. Geriatrics I think tries to satisfy both seemingly contradictory desires simultaneously.

Now, we must admit at the outset that we cannot speak of "old age" without a number of qualifications. For one thing, when does old age begin? Well, that depends upon whose age we're talking about – our own or our neighbor's. Most of us tend to grow old about 15 years later than the people we know. When one U.S. Senator became a grandfather for the first time, he was asked how he liked his new status. "I love it," he answered like a doting grandfather. "But," he added wryly, "it is somewhat distressing to have to live with a grandmother."

Yes, "old age" is relative. When Earl Warren was appointed Chief Justice in 1953, one of the reasons given for the choice was "his relative youth" – 62. On that very day, the governor of Puerto Rico pardoned a prisoner on account of "his advanced age" – 63. In baseball, a player is old at thirty-five. For congregational committees in search of a rabbi, old age begins at forty – with the candidates. And Dr. John Erdman, a prominent surgeon, was more in demand at eighty-five than ever before in his life.

Moreover, we do not grow old evenly, the different parts of our body do not age at the same pace. A physician will tell us that a 60 year old man may have a 50 year old kidney, a 40 year old heart, a 70 year old liver and he may be trying to live a 30 year old life.

There is also, as we know, a difference between chronological age and emotional age. Some there are who are the perpetual adolescents, petrified youths, who fell in love with an earlier period of life and subconsciously vowed never to part from it. "O moment stay, thou art fair!" they exclaimed with Faust and at that point their growth became arrested.

Notwithstanding these reservations, for our purposes we can define old age as I once heard Walter Reuther define it – that time in life when we are too old to work and too young to die. How should we prepare for old age?

Visible Means of Support

Well, the first thing that comes to people's minds when we speak of preparing for our twilight years, is economic security. We think in terms of pensions, social security, retirement funds, annuities, insurance policies. These are the means we try to adopt to forestall the day when we might find ourselves lacking both physical resources and financial resources. And there is no minimizing the importance of such planning and the peace of mind it affords. It is wise indeed that we do our best to answer the prayer which we repeat regularly in the grace after meals: "Please, O Lord make us not dependent upon the gifts of human beings." "*Nit onzukummen zu mentchen*" is the way our grandparents prayed in their daily speech.

And yet in old age as in our youth, economic security is never a guarantor of contentment. "Money," it has been correctly observed, "is an article which may be used as a universal passport to everywhere except heaven and as a universal provider of everything except happiness." All of us know some aged people who certainly have much more than the modest food and comfort their diminished appetites require and yet they are disgruntled, complaining, miserable.

What else then ought we to bring to old age besides economic security?

The Untroubled Conscience

One of the most important things each of us should try to bring to old age is an unsoiled and untroubled conscience. At that stage in life when our physical power ebbs and we live more and more with our thoughts, let us make certain that we will not be tormented with the memory of evils perpetrated and hurts inflicted.

This, as we will recall, is the central theme of Sholom Asch's novel, *A Passage in the Night*. Isaac Grossman, a one-time immigrant, has made a fortune and controls an empire of hotels and theatres. We find him vacationing in Florida when the book opens. He has everything, it seems, that a man would need in old age. He has more money than he can use, he has prestige, he has the smug self-satisfaction which success often breeds, he has children and grandchildren. But he has no peace of mind. For weighing like a mountain on his heart is the searing memory of the Polish worker, Yan Kovalsky, from whom young Isaac Grossman took $27.00 years ago. That was the $27.00 Kovalsky had intended to use for the purchase of a second-hand suit for his daughter's wedding. That was the $27.00 Isaac had needed to begin him on a traveling salesman career which was eventually to lead him to his millions. It is this memory which haunts old Mr. Grossman now and fills him with an obsessive, almost pathological, compunction to try to find the man he had wronged many years ago and to make amends to him. But Yan Kovalsky is not to be found and Isaac Grossman goes from one frustrating quest to the other until his own children begin to suspect his sanity and have him committed to a mental hospital.

Here we may have an extreme example for Isaac's offense was only a single lapse and Judaism does believe in atonement. But what of those who pile ruthlessness upon dishonesty, to whom no relationship is sacred, no loyalty binding, no morals restraining, who are unmoved by sympathy, who rarely yield to a charitable impulse – how serene an old age do they have a right to expect?

Our Sages were exceedingly wise. When they wanted to indicate how the young years could be used with greatest profit, they said: "Well spent is our youth if it does not bring shame to our old age." For they understood well that the transgressions of youth are loans upon old age payable with interest about thirty years after date. Max Ehrmann's prayer touches upon a most vital need for our advancing years. "May my thoughts and actions be such as shall keep me friendly with myself."

God grant us in old age the blessing of an untroubled conscience.

The Unclosed Mind

In the third place, we ought to try to bring to old age an unclosed mind. Someone has said that "Some minds are like concrete; all mixed up and permanently set." The latter part is a danger to which we become more vulnerable as we grow older. It is tempting to develop a permanent mind set.

To shut the windows of the mind is to court mental and spiritual suffocation. Leonardo da Vinci who lived to a ripe old age and continued to paint masterpieces in old age declared, "Learning keeps the soul young and decreases the bitterness of old age." We must literally never stop going to school, broadening our horizons and expanding our knowledge. This after all is the distinctive Jewish contribution to mental hygiene. The unparalleled emphasis of Judaism upon study as a process which only death ought to terminate, spelled out more than a religious duty. It was the key to the fulfillment of the blessing the Torah confers upon its devotees. Thus did the Jew find in it "length of days and years of life" – meaningful days, throbbing years.

The Talmud tells a story about Judah bar Ilai, a second century sage, who deeply impressed a pagan in the market place by his radiant face. "This man" said the pagan, "must either be intoxicated or he has just discovered a hidden treasure." Rabbi Judah overheard him and said: "Stranger, I do not drink except when I must for ritual purposes. When I drink the four prescribed cups of wine on the Seder night, I have a seven-week headache which lasts until Shevuos. Neither have I found any treasure. I am a poor man."

"Then what makes your face shine so? How do you manage to look so youthful?"

"That is quite simple." Rabbi Judah answered: "I study all the time. I study the Torah and the quest for knowledge makes the face of a man shine."

As long as we keep our minds open and alert, as long as we are willing to try a new skill, entertain a new thought, develop a new friend, surrender an old prejudice – so long do we remain vital people, so long do we gain ground and move forward in the search for more abundant life.

God grant us in old age the blessing of the unclosed mind.

The Undaunted Spirit

Fourthly, we ought to try to bring to old age an undaunted spirit.

The plain fact is that very many of us are literally afraid of growing old. We picture ourselves in old age like "a marooned sailor watching the ship in which he once served disappearing behind the skyline." There are many symptoms of this fear. The fact that cosmetics is today a billion dollar industry is one of them. The billboards and daily newspapers carry advertisements which make old age appear not as a stage of life but as a betrayal of it.

William Lyon Phelps once wrote about the alarm with which we greet the first gray hair. He went on to say: "Now one really ought not to be alarmed when one's hair turns gray; if it turned green or blue, then one ought to see a doctor. But when it turns gray that simply means that there is so much gray matter in the skull that there is no longer room for it; it comes out and discolors the hair. Don't be ashamed of your gray hair, wear it proudly like a flag. You are fortunate in a world of so many vicissitudes, to have lived long enough to earn it."

Now, one does not necessarily have to share Dr. Phelps' passionate love for gray hair. If we happen to prefer another color, today I suppose we have a choice and if another color makes us more cheerful, we are each entitled to our personal preference. But Dr. Phelps is entirely correct in sounding the caution against permitting the advancing years to plant the seeds of fear in our hearts. There has been monotonous repetition and widespread acceptance of the erroneous conception that life reaches its climax in youth. Dr. Phelps recalls that when he was an undergraduate he heard a distinguished gentleman say to the students with emphasis: "Young gentlemen make the most of these four years; for they are the happiest years you will ever know." "That remark," he goes on to say, "was given to us with that impressiveness that so often accompanies falsehood. My classmates and I have been out of college nearly 40 years; most of us are happier now than then."

Consider what it would really mean if it were true that "youth is the happiest time of life." If that were truly so, then nothing would be sadder to look at than a young man of 25. For here we would see someone who had reached the very peak of existence, the absolute height and now could only expect decay, decline and descent into the valley. This would be the greatest insult to human personality.

If we are to face the advancing years with serenity and hope we must realize that God has arranged human life on an ascending scale and that every age has its unique satisfactions and joys, just like every hour of the day has its own charm and loveliness. Being a father is wonderful. Being a grandfather isn't bad either. Being a great-grandfather may be even more exciting. True, old age is physical autumn but it can be a spiritual springtime. This is probably what George Santayana had in mind when he said: "Never have I enjoyed youth so thoroughly as I have in my old age."

God grant us in old age the blessing of the undaunted spirit.

Faith in His Reasonableness

For the last, I have left what I consider to be the most precious freightage we must bring to old age – and that is faith in God and in the reasonableness of His work.

Prince Albert upon his death bed is reported to have said: "I have had wealth, rank and power. But if this were all I had, how wretched I should be now."

There must be a great emptiness in the heart of a man who comes into the twilight of his life without the assurance that his life is not to be wasted, erased from the black-board of life as though it never existed. How depressing it must be to believe that we have been plodding laboriously along the highway of life only to find that it leads to a dead end.

On the other hand, how soothing is the Jewish faith that "this world is only a vestibule before the palace of eternal life" or as Edwin Markham put it: "The few little years we spend on earth are only the first scene in a Divine Drama that extends on into eternity."

The belief in the indestructability of the human soul has been one of the most passionate and persistent affirmations of all men. Philosophers and physicians, sages and scientists, poets and peasants, are all included in the mighty assemblage who answer "present" when the roll is called among the believers that death is not the end. And the more we have learned about the mysterious universe in which we live, the more persuasive have become the intimations of our immortality.

God has not endowed us with a single craving without providing us with the means of satisfying it. Every natural desire is met by the great commissary of the universe. If we hunger, there is food. If we crave for love, there are human beings to gratify that need. Can it be that our yearning for immortality alone must remain unsatisfied? Does the universe which responds to our every other need, deceive us only here? Is God a cruel prankster? Our craving for immortality in a world which satisfies our every other fundamental need and yearning points to a God who, in the words of our Prayer Book, "implanted within us everlasting life."

Yes, we who believe in God cannot look upon His finest and most sensitive creation, the human being, as a "bit player" who speaks a brief stammering line on the earthly stage and then is doomed to eternal silence. Rather do we regard life here as a prologue to a magnificent drama written by the divine Playwright.

"Come grow old along with me
The best is yet to be.
The last of life for which the
first was made."

God grant us in old age the blessing of faith in Him and in His wisdom.

Prepare Now Invisible Means of Support

Someone has complained that about the time we learn to make the
most of life, the most of it is gone. It need not be so. Now is the time to
begin to prepare for old age. Old Koheleth, who seems to have known
only too well the path that leads to cynicism, placed a helpful marker
on our road of life when he advised: "Remember your Creator in the
days of your youth." Yes, we should give thought to preparing *visible*
means of support—but let us not forget to develop *invisible* means of
support. Now is the time to keep that conscience clear, that mind open,
that spirit courageous, that faith strong.

Time: Ally or Adversary?

The beginning of a New Year on the Jewish calendar focuses our
attention sharply on the relentless passing of time. Actually the first
day of Tishre slips is as quietly as does any other day of the year.

There are no special peals of thunder or bolts of lightning to
proclaim that a new year has begun. In fact, for nearly 100 percent of
the people on our planet it isn't a new year at all. But whenever one's
new year begins it is an occasion to reflect on the meaning of the time
and how we relate to it.

Is time an ally or an adversary?

The poet Yeats wrote: "I spit in the face of time that has
transfigured me." But Benjamin Franklin kept on his desk two boxes.
One box was marked: "Problems it will take time to solve." The other,
"Problems time has already solved." For Yeats time was an enemy, for
Franklin a friend.

Time is neither. It is neutral. It is what we do with time that
matters.

Will Rogers once told about a druggist who was asked if he ever
took time off to have a good time. The druggist said, no, he didn't, but
he sold a lot of headache medicine to those who did.

One thing we can say with certainty. Time moves steadily
ahead. Like manna, it cannot be hoarded. Nor can it be reversed. The
film of life cannot be rewound. Nor can it be halted in its flight.

Sometimes we come to a moment so exquisite that we understand the poet's plea: "O moment stay, thou art fair."

But we cannot stop time in its tracks.

What can we do with time? Many things. We can kill it, we can waste it, we can use it, we can invest it.

Prisoners serve time; musicians mark time; idlers pass time; speeding motorists make time; referees call time; historians record time; scorekeepers keep time.

Each day every one of us is given the identical amount of a fresh supply of time—24 hours of 60 minutes each. This is the only time we have—not a year, not a month, not a week. The moment pressing against us now, this day, is ours to use. Once it is gone it is irretrievable.

Horace Mann once put this announcement in a newspaper's lost and found column: "Lost somewhere between sunrise and sunset, two golden hours, each set with 60 diamond minutes. No reward is offered, for they are gone forever." Like money, time has a way of slipping through our fingers with nothing to show for it.

Often we complain about the speed with which time passes. We shouldn't. If last year passed quickly, it is an indication that it was a good year for us.

Last year did not hurry by for all. For those who lost a dear one, the time of mourning did not pass quickly. For those who paced hospital corridors, who waited for a loved one's return, who searched in vain for a job—for them time did not fly by. At a time of loneliness, grief, anguish, worry, a single night can be an endless eternity.

At whatever speed last year moved, it is gone. No, it is here forever, woven into the very texture of our lives.

What shall we do with the year we have just begun? Professor Abraham Joshua Heschel left us an important clue when he wrote: "Judaism is a religion of time, aiming at the sanctification of time."

Yes, we can sanctify time. Not only is Rosh Hashanah a holy day, and Yom Kippur and Shabbat, but every day is holy if we choose to sanctify it. Remember the weekday to keep it holy.

How does time become holy? It becomes holy when a part of it is given to others, when we share and care and listen. Time is sanctified when we use it—

> to forgive and ask forgiveness;
> to remember things too long forgotten and to forget things
> too long remembered;

to reclaim sacred things too casually abandoned and to
abandon shabby things too highly cherished;
to remember that life's most crucial question is – how are we
using time?

Yes, time flies but we are the navigators. More important than
counting time is making time count.

As we face the new year there is a special urgency to the prayer of
the Psalmist: "Teach us to number our days so that we may attain a
heart of wisdom."

Time: The Thoughtful Thief

Time has been called a thief. There is much truth in that designation.
Time robs us of our loved ones, steals the spring from our steps, the
bloom from our cheeks, the smoothness from our skins.

But, if Time is a thief, he is not without a core of compassion. For
everything he takes, he thoughtfully leaves something behind.

In place of loved ones, he leaves undying and enduring lessons.
The bloom he stole, Time replaced with lines he gently etched in
bright moments of shared laughter and somber moments of chastening
sorrow. If we can no longer run as quickly as we did yesterday, we can
stand today with greater poise. And while Time was stealing the
smoothness from our skins, he was giving us the opportunity to
remove the wrinkles from our souls.

Time does something else, too. Time converts knowledge into
wisdom, energies spent into experience gained. Time leaves us richer
for what we have had.

And Time thoughtfully permits us to use the fire of youth to drive
the engines of age. We can be young and old at the same time.

We can be young enough to believe in people, but old enough not
to expect more from them than we are prepared to give.

We can be young enough to enjoy pleasure, but old enough to
know that we miss the whole point of living if pleasure is all we
pursue.

We can be young enough to acquire a new idea and old enough to surrender an ancient prejudice.

We can be young enough to strive for success, but old enough to treasure the things that money cannot buy.

We can be young enough to want to be attractive, but old enough to appreciate the beauty that is manufactured inside ourselves.

We can be young enough to seek companionship, but old enough to appreciate solitude.

We can be young enough to crave happiness, but old enough to know that the harvest of happiness is usually reaped by the hands of helpfulness.

We can be young enough to want to be loved, but old enough to strive to be lovable.

We can be young enough to pray as if everything depended on God, but old enough to act as if everything depended on us.

III

LIVING AT OUR BEST

When we realize that we are not God we have a better chance of becoming human.

The Search for More Abundant Life

One of the distinctive, traditional synagogue practices is the public reading of a portion of the Torah, or Pentateuch. This is done no fewer than four times during the ordinary week. Should a Jewish festival occur during the week, the Torah would be read on those days too.

The most joyous of all Jewish festivals is Simchat Torah—"Rejoicing in the Torah." On that day the reading of Deuteronomy, the last of the Five Books of Moses, is completed; immediately thereafter we begin again the reading of Genesis, the first book of the Torah. Thus the reading of the Torah is never really finished. It continues uninterrupted.

And so does our obligation to study it. We are never relieved of that happy privilege.

Perhaps the greatest tribute to continuous Torah study was spoken by a first-century sage: "Turn it again and again, for everything is in it; contemplate it, grow gray and old over it, and swerve not from it, for there is no greater good" (Mishnah Abot 2:14).

Judaism is vitally concerned that we serve God with heart, soul, and might. But it has been no less insistent that we serve Him too with our minds—with minds that stay open and keep growing.

Someone has said that some minds are like concrete: all mixed up and permanently set. As we grow older, it is very tempting to develop a permanent mind set. But minds, like parachutes, are valuable only when open.

Make Warm Fuzzies – Today

"What did you do in school today?" I asked six-year-old Daniella.

"We made warm fuzzies."

"Warm fuzzies? What are warm fuzzies?"

"Well," she said slowly, trying to find words that even a grand-father could understand, "warm fuzzies are things that you say that make people feel good." And then, reaching into her schoolbag, she added, "Here are some of the warm fuzzies I got."

"You ar my best frend."

"You are veeree prittee."

"Yu I lik."

"I liek the prezint you gave mee."

Much later that evening I thought of the lesson Daniella's teacher had taught her class. How much easier life would be for all of us if we concentrated on handing out warm fuzzies to the people whose lives intersect our own in the course of any day. Mark Twain once said that he could live on a good compliment for two months. How long has it been since we gave a warm fuzzy to our children, our mates, the people who serve us, our brothers and sisters?

On the occasion of his ninety-fourth birthday, the late Will Durant was interviewed by the press. One of our most prolific authors, he wrote, with his wife, Ariel, an eleven-volume biography of man-kind, *The Story of Civilization*. In the interview, Durant was asked what piece of wisdom he would distill from a lifetime of reading and reflecting. "If you insist upon one brief answer," he said, "I say kindness. And that is, in my opinion, the finest, most successful method of behavior, not merely of a man to his wife, or vice versa, but of a man to his neighbor, of any individual to the individuals he meets."

Daniella says warm fuzzies. Durant says kindness.

How desperate is our need for kindness! So many of us hunger for it most of the time. One doctor has estimated that 90 percent of all the mental illness he has treated could have been prevented or cured by ordinary kindness. What an indictment against us! All around us there is emotional starvation, and we do not have the time or the thoughtfulness or the compassion to speak a kind word, perform a gracious act, pay a visit, drop a line, make a warm fuzzy.

Kindness is a universal language which even an animal can understand and even the mute can speak. The person who has not learned kindness remains uneducated no matter how many diplomas adorn his office walls or the number of degrees that follow his signature. The person who has learned to be kind has mastered the most vital subject in life's curriculum. His formal schooling may be meager, his familiarity with books not very intimate. If he has learned how to bring a ray of light where there is darkness, a touch of softness where life has been hard, a word of cheer to lift drooping spirits – that person is best equipped to live life as it should be lived.

In *The Summing Up*, W. Somerset Maugham tries to communicate the essence of what he learned in all his years. He too comes to the conclusion that the most important thing in life is kindness. And then he hastens to add that he is ashamed that he has reached so commonplace a conclusion. He would have liked to leave his readers with some sort of startling revelation or with a glittering epigram of sparkling originality. "It seems," he says ruefully, "I have little more to say than can be read in any copybook or heard from any pulpit. I have gone a long way round to discover what everyone knew already."

Daniella is learning the lesson early. Make warm fuzzies – today.

Unfinished Lives

The High Holy Days, taken in their entirety, constitute one continuous hymn in celebration of life. After each sounding of the shofar during Rosh Hashanah we repeat the passage which begins with the words: "Hayom harat olam, on this day the world was born." We celebrate the beginning of the life of the universe on Rosh Hashanah. The Torah reading on Rosh Hashanah deals with the birth of Isaac; the Haftarah recounts the birth of Samuel. The recurrent prayer which we offer again and again is "Zochraynu l'chayim – remember us to life." In our greetings during this season we wish each other to be inscribed in the Book of Life.

In the midst of this symphony celebrating life, the Yizkor service in its preoccupation with the dead, seems to strike a discordant note. It dramatically focuses our attention not on what lies ahead but on what has already been and will not be again. It deals not with our hopes but with our memories, not with our aspirations but with our anguish.

And yet, more deeply understood, even the Yizkor motif can be blended into a symphony of life. "To see life steadily and to see it whole," to use the words of the poet, means to see it in its entirety, to embrace the whole gamut of human experience and emotion. Life as we know it, is inseparable from death. Indeed, where there is no death there is no birth. Rocks do not die. From the moment of birth we move towards death. So that when we want to deal realistically with life, if we really want to tell it like it is, as the young people say today, how can we fail to deal with death?

And Yizkor is woven into the theme of life in another vital sense. At this point in the service, I often have the feeling that it is not only the living who pray "Zochraynu l'chayim – remember us to life." The dead, too, wish to be remembered to life. As long as we remember them we rescue them from oblivion and we prolong their life span. There is profound truth in the words of the poet, "To live in hearts we leave behind is not to die." We do indeed possess the magnificent power to confer immortality on those who have preceded us into the great beyond. And so in reciting Yizkor, in our preoccupation with the dead, we are at the same time conferring life.

And there is yet another way in which Yizkor is related to life. At the University of Oxford, I am told, over the entrance to the Department of Anatomy, there is an inscription which reads: "This is the place where death teaches life." In a very real sense, this is the place today and this is the moment when death teaches life, when our human frailty and inescapable mortality are dangled before us. Why? To what purpose this reminder? To depress us? No! To spur us on to use whatever time is ours as fully and as totally as we are capable. In the words of Kipling, this moment pleads with us to "fill the unforgiving minute with 60 seconds worth of distance run."

Some time ago there appeared the autobiography of the cele-brated American playwright, Lillian Hellman, who has made some rather impressive contributions to the American stage over the years. I think she has something like twelve plays to her credit and she is widely regarded as one of America's foremost dramatists. We would imagine that a life filled with so much creativity would be judged conspicuously "successful" in the finer sense of that much abused word. And yet, Lillian Hellman calls her autobiography "An Unfinished Woman" and she provides an explanation for that somewhat ambiguous title. "All I mean," she says in the book, "is that I left too much of me unfinished because I wasted too much time. However."

However. For her, life has been only partially lived. In retrospect, she realizes how much more she could have made of her gifts and her years.

This is the kind of thought that should shake us up at Yizkor time. Are we living unfinished lives? Usually we think of unfinished lives as lives interrupted by death on the battlefield or by a variety of killers, diseases, and accidents. But, as Lillian Hellman makes quite clear to us, we can live many years and then confront ourselves with the haunting regret that we are really unfinished people – a host of gifts undeveloped, an assortment of powers unused, a vast, incredible potential uncultivated, large chunks of time misused.

Lillian Hellman's complaint evokes poignant echoes in our hearts because the fact is that all of us live far below the level of our capabilities, we never quite reach our full dimensions. To be human is to be aware of greater things within our reach. Lewis Mumford has defined man as "the unfinished animal, the radically dissatisfied and maladjusted animal. . . . Man is the only animal who is not content to remain in the original state of nature."

Life for each of us is a finishing school in which we are called upon to work on the raw material with which nature endows us. The message of this day is to remind us what the main business of life is all about. When we pause to remember the lives unfinished because of death we are reminded too, of the danger that our lives may remain unfinished in life. How, then, are we to live fuller, more complete lives?

The High Holy Day prayer book offers us, I believe, a magnificent formula. On each of these days we are summoned to three basic disciplines. "T'shuvah – repentance, T'filah – prayer, and Tz'dakah – charity." Let us take a few moments to try to understand what these disciplines can do for us. And may I start first with "T'filah – prayer."

It is no secret that more and more of us are praying less and less. Prayer, meditation, reflection are widely neglected among us. The world in which we live and move is a noisy, busy place. The pace is hurried, the action feverish, the sounds deafening. A thousand activities are competing for our time. The ubiquitous hucksters are competing for our attention.

In the day by day pursuit of immediates we lose sight of ultimates. Preoccupied with means, we lose sight of goals. Caught up by things, we have no time for thoughts. The bulletin board of a synagogue recently sounded this word of caution: "If you are too busy to pray, you are too busy."

An issue of the *Reader's Digest* contains a perceptive article by Dr. Louis Finkelstein, past Chancellor of the Jewish Theological Seminary. His article carries the intriguing title, "Make an Appointment with Yourself." In it he reveals that at the Seminary there is a rule that anyone who is involved in meditation or study is not to be disturbed by the telephone, and the caller is advised by the secretary or telephone operator that the professor is not available. Frequently, he tells us, the callers are not too happy with the excuse, and he adds, "It is odd how likely we are to respect the privacy of people talking but not of one who is thinking."

He goes on to tell us how important it is for him to study some Talmud every morning because it keeps him in touch with some of the great minds of all times. In this period, regularly set aside for meditation, reflection and study, he finds great strength as well as wisdom. He reminds us of the celebrated incident in which Isaac Newton discovered the laws of gravity. We will recall that Newton was sitting under a tree when an apple detached itself from the tree and hit him on the head. The important thing about that experience is not that he was lucky to be hit by the apple but that he was, happily, alone and able to think about the implications of the falling apple.

One of the real perils of growing older is that we tend to think less and less. We feel that we know all the answers. We are old pros. We've been on this course before. And why bother thinking things through again when we have already thought about them once before? But unless we do indeed make an appointment with ourselves regularly and keep it faithfully and utilize it constructively, our lives remain terribly unfinished. A shrinkage takes place because we fail to catch a glimpse of something higher and something better and something deeper. The mind and soul become wrinkled. The function of prayer is not to enable us to acquire what we should like to possess, but rather to become what we are capable of being.

And so, the first discipline to which these days summon us, if we would lead fuller and more fulfilled lives, is the discipline of meditation and reflection.

In addition to T'filah, these days summon us to "T'shuvah, repentance." T'filah deals with our thoughts; T'shuvah is concerned with our deeds. If T'filah would have us reflect deeper, T'shuvah would ask us to act better. It summons us to perform at our highest human level.

Arthur Koestler in his book, *Act of Creation,* tells a very instructive anecdote taken from the life of Picasso. It seems that an art dealer in Paris bought a painting bearing the artist's signature and he wanted to have the painting authenticated by Picasso. The master looked at it and said quickly: "It's a fake." Two years later the same art dealer acquired another signed painting. Once again he showed it to the artist, and once again Picasso replied, "It's a fake." But this time the dealer protested heatedly. "Why I myself was present when you painted this canvas. With my own eyes I saw you do it." Whereupon Picasso shrugged and said, "I often paint fakes."

How often do you and I paint fakes, dear friends! Doctors and lawyers, plumbers and painters, doing shabby work because we will not give all that we possess; bringing so much less than our best to the task at hand. Too frequently we bring only a portion of ourselves to our husbands and to our wives. We are fractional parents and fractional children. As brothers and as sisters we hold back, giving marginal concern and divided attention.

How often are the words that we speak fakes – debased of any real currency, emptied of any real meaning. We use stock phrases of endearment with the most casual acquaintances. The salesgirl we just met becomes "dearie" and of course, everybody is "darling." We inquire into the health of people about whose health we don't have the slightest concern. Our "How are you?" is as perfunctory as the "Fine, thank you," which greets us in return. A bore is defined as a person who when you ask him how he feels, proceeds to tell you. The point of course, is that he is unsophisticated. He doesn't understand that we are not really interested. Words are spoken but there is no person behind the words, no genuine collateral to back up the verbal currency, and so it becomes debased, cheapened. In brief, fake.

There is a crying need for authentic people. We need the stamp of authenticity to back up our signatures, our gestures, our words. There aren't many Picassos around, but in whatever area we create, each of us can be the supreme artist by virtue of the fact that we bring to the task at hand the finest and the best of which we are capable. "To thine own self be true. And it must follow as the night the day, thou canst not then be false to any man."

T'shuvah is a summons to each of us to narrow the gap between our performance and our potential, between what we are and what we could become.

And there is a third discipline to which these days summon us. They ask us not only to reflect deeper and to act better but also to reach further. This is how I understand Tz'dakah which we translate literally as "charity." What is charity at bottom? It is a reaching out beyond ourselves; an enlargement of the area of our concern, a growing outward.

How marvelously the Torah captures the maturity of Moses in a single sentence: "And Moses grew up and he went out to his brothers." Growing up means growing out. It means going out of ourselves and reaching beneficently into the lives of others.

Here too, I often have the feeling that so many of us shrink as we grow older. We tend to become ingrown, to narrow the area of our concern, to contract it to include "me and mine" and sometimes not even "mine."

I read recently of a large home in the hills of New Hampshire. The passing years dealt harshly with the old house. The children were gone and the last echoes of laughter had faded with them. The old porch was rotted down from too much exposure and too little attention. One by one the outer rooms became unlivable as they remained unpainted and uncared for. The only ones left in this once impressive home were the old folks who kept retreating into the interior of the home as the process of disintegration proceeded all around them. As they retreated they dragged with them pieces and bits of furniture until at last they lived in one small room in the midst of a big, dilapidated house.

Isn't this a melancholy parable of what happens to so many lives who grow emptier and emptier, narrower and narrower until at last the only interest left is self-interest?

And then there are the others, the glory of the community, of a family, of a people for whom life is an ever expanding reaching out. As they grow older they realize that one of the great privileges in life is to be able to give. A Hasidic bit of wisdom reminds us that there are two hands in the matter of charity. Thank God if yours is the hand that gives. So highly do they cherish the privilege of giving that they refuse to give only through their wills. They want to have the pleasure of sharing while they are alive.

When Billy Rose decided to contribute his one million dollars worth of sculpture to the museum which now bears his name in the hills of Judea, this hard headed businessman gave the following explanation: "I decided to give it away while I was alive. It doesn't take much generosity to give things away when you are dead. I'd rather do it now, rather than have some thin-lipped banker give them away later on."

We live at a time when it is possible to reach further than ever before. A dollar of ours can travel thousands of miles in a day and our influence can reach into the farthest parts of the world.

The Jewish conception of Tz'dakah, this reaching out towards our fellow man, deals not only with tangibles. We have so much more to give than mere money, so much of which there is a desperate shortage in this world. We have friendship to give in a lonely world and encouragement to give to weary fellow travelers. We have a compliment to give to those who serve us constantly. We have a gracious gesture which we can give to all by way of saluting and respecting the basic dignity of every human being. We have forgiveness to give to those who have offended against us. We might even think of sacrificing a little stubbornness and a little false pride that prevent us from admitting that perhaps we aren't perfect. None of us is so poor that we have nothing to give. None of us is so rich that we are not in need of gifts.

Some time ago there was a novel called *Second Growth*. It didn't attract much attention and was not too widely read. But one of its scenes is worth recalling. It takes place in a small town in Vermont where opportunities for young people were quite limited. One of the teachers becomes interested in a young boy who shows a great deal of promise. She encourages him to leave the little town and to look elsewhere for greater educational opportunities. "I'd take this chance to go to college if I were you," she tells him. "There won't be much else we could teach you around here. You *would stay the same size all your life.*"

The risk of staying the same size all our lives is as great in a metropolis as in a little town. If we fail to utilize the vast resources available to us for growing and becoming finished people we do indeed remain stunted and arrested.

In America today there is a multi-million dollar industry which deals with diet food, diet drinks, weight-watchers, physical exercises, and recreational activities. All these testify to our justifiable fear of growing in the wrong places and in wrong ways as we grow older. What we need is the greater fear, much more justifiable, that in some vital ways we stop growing altogether. Where our human dimensions are concerned – the dimensions of the mind, heart and soul – we must not stay the same size all our lives.

This moment of this day urges us above all to become the very best and finest human beings we can become so that when the shadows lengthen and the night draws near we shall be comforted with the knowledge that we made the most of our best to complete our lives.

What Courage Can Accomplish

Hanukah, the joyous eight-day festival recalls the rededication of the Temple by the Maccabees after their victory over the armies of the Syrian King Antiochus, who had attempted to suppress and eradicate Judaism.

Of all the virtues that Hanukah celebrates, the most prominent among them is courage. We dwell upon the bravery of the vastly outnumbered Maccabees who dared to risk their very lives against an enormously superior foe. And if after almost 22 centuries the Jewish people are still here to light the Hanukah candles, it is due in no small measure to another kind of courage – the courage of men and women in every generation to persist in loyalty to their heritage in the face of unrelenting efforts to persuade or compel them to abandon it.

It is told that after the court philosopher finished his lecture on the possibility of miracles, his king challenged him: "Show me a miracle!" The philosopher answered simply: "Sir, the Jews." The crucial quality in the making of the miracle of Jewish survival has been courage.

Courage works miracles daily. And it is found in the most unspectacular places, among ordinary people and often in places of hardship and suffering.

Perhaps I am writing about courage because I have just finished reading *When Bad Things Happen to Good People,* by my friend and colleague, Rabbi Harold Kushner. When his son Aaron was 3 years old, the Kushners learned that this "bright and happy child, who before the age of 2 could identify a dozen different varieties of dinosaur," was suffering from a very rare and fatal disease called progeria – rapid aging.

Aaron would never grow taller than three feet, he would grow no hair on his head or body, he would develop the appearance in childhood of a shriveled old man and he would die in his early teens. Aaron did in fact die two days after his 14th birthday.

Rabbi Kushner's book addresses itself to the moral and theological questions raised by the suffering and early death of a child. How does a good God bring bad things, or permit bad things to happen to innocent people? How does faith in God survive such a crushing test? Rabbi Kushner deals with these questions in a humane and reassuring way.

I found especially moving his tribute to the courage of Aaron, who "managed to live a full life despite his limitations," who participated in all the games he could despite his strange appearance. That courage, the rabbi believes, even affected his friends and schoolmates. Physically, Aaron was terribly undersized, but his courage was giant-size.

Yes, indeed, courage is found in unexpected places and wears many faces.

Sometimes courage masquerades as hope and in the dark night of despair whispers assurance of a brighter tomorrow.

Sometimes courage appears in a house of mourning and counsels the bereaved to grit their teeth, clench their fists and face up to life's demands.

"Sometimes," says one of Sholom Aleichem's characters, "you have to go on living even if it kills you." And that takes courage.

Sometimes courage dresses up as stubborn loyalty during weeks, months and years of ministering to a brain-damaged child or a helpless parent.

Sometimes courage wears the mask of integrity and enables a person to resist the temptation to trade a long-range goal for a short-term profit, to surrender enduring principles for fleeting pleasures.

Of one thing we can be sure: No life will go very far before it needs courage, no life will reach very high without it.

A frightened, unemployed father of three children climaxed his tale of woe by sobbing. "If only you knew, Rabbi, what courage it takes just to get out of bed in the morning."

More than we suspect, it is courage that enables people to carry on day by day despite fear and anxiety, heartache and heartbreak, betrayal and disappointment, loneliness and lovelessness.

Only rarely does courage win public recognition and applause. "The most sublime courage I have ever witnessed," wrote Henry Wheeler Shaw, "has been among that class of people too poor to know they possessed it and too humble for the world to discover it." In this season of light and hope, the words of the poet Adam Lindsey Gordon shine with special brightness:

> "Life is mostly froth and bubble,
> Two things stand like stone;
> Kindness in another's trouble,
> Courage in your own."

The Judged and the Judges

In his essay "The Over-Soul," Ralph Waldo Emerson wrote: "Our faith comes in moments, our vice is habitual. Yet there is a depth in those brief moments which constrains us to ascribe more reality to them than to all other experiences." For us of the household of American Israel, the present exalted mood of the holy days constitutes such a moment of faith to which Emerson referred. All too infre-quently during the year do we find ourselves in this reverent attitude, yet who among us will deny that these are the greatest moments in our year? Now we are closer to the heart of the human enterprise, now we more nearly approximate the finest within ourselves, now we are engaged in life's most sacred dialogue, the human soul in communion with its God.

These are not only real moments. They are also solemn moments because in the picturesque language of the Prayer Book, we are standing before the divine bar of justice. Today, the Great Judge holds court and all His creatures pass in review. He reviews not only our deeds, He also pays attention to motives. "He searches the heart on the Day of Judgment." Who can pass such rigid moral scrutiny without genuine humility and deep remorse?

The truth of the matter is, of course, that we are judged not only on this Yom Hadin – this supreme Day of Judgment. Rabbi Yosi said: "Man is judged daily." Rabbi Nathan went further: "Man is judged every hour." And I should like to go a step further. We are not only judged constantly, but we are constantly judging. And on this Day of Judgment I should like to dwell upon these vital areas where we the judges are so prone to misjudge.

Consider in the first place, how prone we are to misjudge our fellowman. All too often we are superficial, impressed by externals, focusing attention upon what a man has, rather than what he is. We are like the beggar who approached a kindly looking gentleman and proceeded to make a moving plea for a contribution. When he had completed his woeful tale, the gentleman said softly: "My friend, I have no money, but I can give you some good advice." The beggar looked at him with contempt. "If you ain't got no money I reckon your advice ain't worth hearing." How many of us use the same reckoning, confusing a man's valuables for his value and his wealth for his worth.

In addition to being superficial in our judgment of others we are too frequently superficial, quick to impugn motives and misinterpret deeds. This is a sin from which, as this morning's Haftarah testifies, even the greatest are not exempt. We recall how the tormented Hannah came to the temple to pour out her embittered heart before God. She prayed silently, only her lips moving. And Eli, the high priest, misjudges her anguished movements and taunts her: "How long will you remain drunk? Go put away your wine." And Hannah answers, "No, my lord, I am a woman of a sorrowful spirit, I have drunk neither wine nor strong drink, but I poured out my soul before the Lord." Scripture charitably does not record how Eli felt when he heard that soft reply.

A somewhat similar type of incident is described in a modern poem by Rosa Zagnoni Marinoni which may hit a little closer home because it deals with the super-critical motorist. I have often wondered why our most primitive instincts come to the fore when we drive the most modern vehicle. The title of the poem is "Crushed Fender." The poet was driving one night down a narrow street in Milan when she crashed into another car.

> I hurled my ire against the guilty one:
> "You should be taught to signal as you turn!
> At least put out your arm!" I cried at him.
> "You could have caused our car to overturn!"
>
> At first the man was silent, then he spoke:
> "Sorry," he said, "to cause you such alarm.
> You did not see it, for the night is dark,
> But as I turned, I did put out my arm.
>
> Please take my license number and my name
> I hope you will forgive and understand.
> I was a soldier once, somewhere in France,
> My left arm is a stub. I have no hand."
>
> I could not speak. The words choked in my throat—
> I did not take his number, nor his name—
> I turned the car against the dull black night,
> My face averted to conceal my shame.

Those whom we misjudge do not usually get the opportunity to defend themselves. Would we therefore not do well to pray in the words of the Sioux Indians: "Great Spirit, help me never to judge another until I have walked two weeks in his moccasins." Ought we not to search diligently for the good in others, humbled by the realization that they may have to search even harder to find the good in us? It is this charitable motivation which prompted our sages to say—"Judge not your fellow man until you are in his place." Until we

understand his fears and his frustrations, his hopes and his hungers—
until we know all that, we ought not to judge for we are too liable to
misjudge.

Consider now in the second place, how prone we are to misjudge
ourselves. An old Yiddish folk expression has it that "No one will fool
you as well as you will fool yourself." If there is anyone we should
know well, it is ourselves. Yet modern psychiatry has underscored the
truth of the Yiddish expression. We do persistently delude ourselves.
Our basest acts often mask themselves to appear like noble deeds. We
throw the mantle of deception over our failures, so that others and not
we must assume the blame.

We did not get the promotion we had hoped for, not because our
work left something to be desired, but because "the boss had a grudge
against me. He knows I'm superior to him."

We do not succeed in establishing a harmonious relationship
with our mates, not because we have not really tried hard enough or
patiently enough, but because "She doesn't understand me. . . . He
doesn't understand me."

We do not respond to an appeal for funds from the synagogue,
the Seminary or the United Appeal even though we are financially able
to do so, not because we are too small to assume our Jewish obligations,
but because, "that's all they do, ask for money. Besides I don't like to be
asked."

We do not read a book of Jewish content from one year to the
next, not because the traditional Jewish love for learning has departed
from us, but because in this age of unprecedented leisure, "I just don't
have the time."

We who leave our homes three or four nights a week for social
and recreational purposes cannot get to services on Friday night, not
because we are spiritually indifferent, but because, "after a day's work
I'm just too tired."

We who pride ourselves on the attractiveness of our homes have
stripped them of the beautiful Jewish rituals and ceremonial objects,
not because we are careless custodians of a proud heritage, but because
they are old fashioned and our homes are modern.

Need we go on? If we were honest with ourselves we could find
impressive evidence of our tendency to misjudge ourselves.

Rabbi Yisroel Salanter, whose biography can now be read in
English, used to say that the Almighty created us with two eyes so that

with one we might observe the virtues of our fellowman, while with the other we ought to observe our own limitations and shortcomings. Unfortunately we have reversed the function of our eyes. The eye meant for detecting faults, we have trained upon our fellow man. This eye works so well that we can see faults in others where they do not exist. The eye designed for beholding virtue we have trained upon ourselves. This eye also works very well. It looks at weakness and sees strength.

Our reluctance to acknowledge our many failings is exceeded only by our tendency to exaggerate our few virtues.

It is told that the great Sarah Bernhardt was among some friends, when one of them remarked about the strange manner in which some young lady had been acting of late.

"I know why," explained the French actress. "Someone told her that she had a beautiful profile and ever since she has been trying to live sideways."

How many of us live "sideways." How we shriek for the spotlight upon our virtues. How much wiser we would be if we paid more attention to our weaknesses and tried to bring them to the level of our potential strength. The advice of Oliver Cromwell is especially relevant. "A portrait should include all the warts." Only as we have the honesty and the courage to see ourselves with our blemishes, can we outgrow the things that we should leave behind and draw closer to the things to which Rosh Hashanah calls us.

In the last place, on this day when we pray for life, let us consider the sad fact that very often we misjudge the purpose of life and its meaning.

To some degree, I believe that all of us have a share in the vulgarization of the human spirit, which was perhaps inevitable in an age which has seen wanton destruction of life through Nazi barbarism, world wars, and atomic bombs. As life became cheap, things became precious. That may be why we so often by-pass the lasting things for the latest things.

We sacrifice health for wealth and then try in vain to undo a bad bargain. We try to keep up to the minute and our interests become momentary. We have so many beautiful houses and an unprecedented number of broken homes. We have accelerated our traveling speed and lost our sense of direction. We have confused running after pleasure with the pursuit of happiness. We have added knowledge without increasing wisdom. We have overstuffed our bodies and starved our souls. We have been so concerned with making a living, we have paid little heed to making a life. We have made of the means of living, the goal of life.

A wealthy retired businessman on a pleasure trip in New Mexico, came upon an able-bodied Indian who was loafing idly during a working day. Our ambitious enterprising businessman was offended by such conspicuous inaction. Turning to the Indian he challenged him: "Why don't you try to get yourself a job?" "Why?" asked the Indian. "Well," said the other, "you could earn as much as $50.00 a week." "Why?" asked the Indian again. "Then you could earn a sum of money and even put some away in the bank." Once again the Indian asked simply, "Why?" "Well," continued the retired friend, "When you saved up enough money you could do as I did. You could retire and you would not have to work anymore." To this the Indian replied: "But I am not working now. Why should I go through all that trouble?"

The Indian's logic was unassailable. If all he would get out of his life's tasks was the ability ultimately to leave them, he had just as well not begin. Our society is filled with people who are making lush livings and lean lives. Are we among them?

Rosh Hashanah not only focuses attention upon these common errors of judgment, it also points to a pattern for eliminating them. "Through penitence, prayer and charity we eliminate our wrong verdicts, our misguided judgments." To our fellow man we should show *Tz'dakah,* charity. In the words of the poet Wordsworth, we must learn:

> What need there is to be reserved in speech
> And temper all our thoughts with charity.

For ourselves we need *T'filah*—which, while it is translated as "prayer," is derived in Hebrew from the root which means, "To judge oneself." That is the true function of prayer at its highest, self-judgment. We must judge ourselves honestly. We must tear away the cloak of rationalization, the mask of pretense, so that we can truly conquer our weaknesses.

For life we need *T'shuvah,* literally—"a returning" to a higher conception of life, the kind of life worth praying for. "Remember us to the kind of life which Thou O King desirest."

In judging life let us understand that:

Much as we need something to live with, we need even more, something to live for;

If our lives are not to become spiritual dust-bowls we need regular replenishment from the waters of study, reverence and unselfishness;

Happiness resides not in things but in ourselves;

There is no security like the untroubled conscience;

There is no adventure as exciting as the adventure of a mind and soul which never stop growing;

There is no better exercise for the spirit than bending down to help lift someone up;

The greatest endowment we give our children, is the example of an upright life;

The best portions of a good man's life are, as the poet said, "his little nameless unremembered acts of kindness and of love."

If this be our judgment of life, then our faith need not come in moments. It can be the steady quality of a life which will merit the blessings of the Divine Judge.

The Greatest Treason

The doctor examined the three-pack-a-day smoker and was distressed by the findings. "Look here," the doctor said, "you say you've been a heavy smoker for forty-two years. You see that building across the street? If you had saved all that money you spent on cigarettes, you might own that building today."

"Do you smoke, doctor?" the patient asked.

"No, never did."

"Do you own that building?"

"No!"

"Well, I do."

The doctor was correct in urging his patient to surrender a destructive habit, but instead of speaking to him about preserving his health and his life, he spoke about saving dollar bills. He spoke not with the medical authority of a physician, but with the prudence of a banker. He gave him good advice with a bad reason.

There are two lines by T.S. Eliot that the doctor would have done well to ponder:

> The last temptation is the greatest reason,
> To do the right deed for the wrong reason.

Eliot's lines are addressed not only to the doctor. Many of us could profitably reflect on them.

How many of us pray for the wrong reasons! We have a "slot machine" approach to prayer. All we have to do is insert a prayer and out will come instant fulfillment, immediate gratification, regardless of whether what we are asking for is moral, ethical, or possible, regardless of whether or not it clashes with the needs and hopes of others.

When what we ask for is denied us, we often abandon prayer as an exercise in futility. We forget that prayer at its highest involves praise and thanksgiving and that its primary concern is not getting but becoming. Our prayers are answered when they enable us to grow toward the person we are capable of being, and live as God would have us live.

How many of us perform our small acts of charity and goodness for the wrong reasons. We expect a kind deed to be rewarded by a kind fate, to preserve us from trouble and misfortune. More than once have I heard this melancholy verdict: "When my mother died, I stopped believing in God. She was such a good person, how could God let this happen to her?"

Goodness does not confer immunity to disease, disaster, or death. It does not guarantee a life without trouble or tragedy. These are the common lot of all of us.

Is there then no reward for living a life of rectitude and uprightness? There is, indeed. We are rewarded not *for* our good deeds but *by* our good deeds. The reward for doing good is becoming a better human being. The greatest compensation for any good deed is simply to have done it. It is inherent in the act itself. Moses Maimonides, the twelfth-century Jewish philosopher, gave us the right reason for doing the right deed: "It is not enough to serve God in the hope of future reward. A man must do right and avoid wrong because he is a man and owes it to his manhood to seek perfection."

His words help us to avoid "the greatest reason." They encourage us to do the right deed for the right reason.

Determining Our Human Dimensions

One of the most disappointing moments of my childhood resulted from the Torah portion entitled Pinhas.

I was about nine years old when my Bible class in the Yeshiva reached that passage where God tells Moses to climb Mount Avarim from which he will glimpse the Promised Land, but he will not be permitted to enter it. He will then die on this side of the Jordan River (Numbers 27:12).

How cruel was the feeling of frustration I felt for Moses. How richly he deserved the privilege of being at the head of his people in their triumphant entry into the land toward which he had led them for 40 hard years.

It was he who led them out of Egypt and through the hostile desert. Again and again when the heat, the hunger, the thirst made them want to turn back, it was Moses who urged them onward, ever onward. When at long last the land appears within view, Moses is summarily told he cannot enter it. That was too crushing a climax to a great drama of courage and perseverance.

With maturity, however, the child's disappointment was softened by the realization that in the untimely death of Moses, the Bible was conveying an inescapable truth. The great always die too soon; for it is in the essence of greatness that it sets up for itself goals which are too lofty to be achieved in a single lifespan.

Every Moses leaves his final Jordan uncrossed and must rest content with only a glimpse of his Promised Land.

Those who strive to eradicate poverty and hunger, those who struggle to wipe out the dread diseases that afflict us in body and spirit, those who dedicate their lives to the elimination of prejudice and intolerance, those who are sincerely engaged in promoting justice among men and harmony among nations – these good people have each chosen a Promised Land to which they will ultimately be denied entry.

But these are the glowing souls who shed their radiance upon the rest of us, and by their faithfulness to the vision that haunts their sleep they are responsible for most of the progress of the human family.

The capacity to strive for a Promised Land is a profound source of both our human frustration and our human glory. In the process of reaching for noble ideals our lives become ennobled. High aims produce high character. We cannot scale any heights on a rope that is attached only to our waist. We must reach beyond ourselves if we are to rise above ourselves.

A good way of determining our human dimensions is by measuring the size of our Promised Land. We are each as big as the goals to which we dedicate our lives.

"Everybody's Doing It"

In Eugene Ionesco's play *Rhinoceros,* a human being actually turns into a rhinoceros. Indeed, before the play is over all but one of the characters have undergone the same transformation.

The key sentence in the play is spoken by the heroine, who witnessed a man turn into an animal. "Just before he became a beast," she reports, "his last human words were 'We must move with the times.'"

The playwright has sounded a warning our generation needs very much to hear. One of the most serious threats to our humanity stems from our misguided desire to "move with the times," to be what everybody else is, to do what everyone else is doing.

To permit what everybody else is doing to determine what we should be doing may find us doing what nobody should be doing. That is a sure way to become one of the herd, to surrender our human uniqueness, and to risk becoming a rhinoceros.

A verse from Exodus raises the same warning flag: "You shall not follow a multitude to do evil" (Exodus 23:2).

No matter how many people steal, stealing remains wrong. No matter how many people are corrupt, corruption remains wrong. No matter how many people betray public trust, that action remains wrong. The fact that any misdeed becomes popular does not make it permissible. The problem of evil is not solved by multiplication.

Moving with the times does not mean surrendering timeless truths or abandoning the accumulated decencies of the centuries.

Moreover, whenever any unworthy action is justified on the ground that "everybody's doing it," we ought to pause and reflect that, as a matter of fact, not everybody's doing it.

There are a host of people day in and day out living by the enduring values, abiding by the time-honored traditions, measuring up to the cherished standards of truth and goodness and integrity. They are the solid little pegs that keep this world of ours together. And they are more numerous than the newspaper headlines would lead us to believe. Crime gets all the attention, goodness goes unreported.

There is nothing sensational about honesty or loyalty or fidelity because, if the truth be told, they are really what most people believe in and practice.

The old adage counsels us: "When in Rome do as the Romans do." The Bible would add – provided that what the Romans are doing ought to be done. Otherwise, "You shall not follow a multitude to do evil."

The Art of Listening

In his autobiography, Shmaryahu Levin, the famous Zionist, recalled an incident from his childhood. It was before the High Holy Days and the Shammash of the community was trying in vain to teach him to blow the shofar. Young Shmaryahu practiced diligently but with frustratingly little success. One day as he was blowing and blowing with only a smothered squeak to show for his efforts, one of the peasants came to his home to visit his father. He picked up the shofar, put it to his lips and blew a powerful blast. Little Shmaryahu ran back to his teacher and asked *"Stych*? How come? Here I, a Jew, practice and strain and produce barely a whimper. This gentile peasant without any preparation, produces so mighty a sound."

The Shammash put his arm consolingly around the little boy and said, "My son, the trick is not to blow the shofar. The trick is to listen to it."

Earlier in the service, before the dramatic sounding of the shofar, the tradtional b'rachah was recited by the Baal T'kiyah: "Praise to You, O Lord, our God, King of the Universe, who has sanctified us by Your commandments and commanded us to listen to the sound of the shofar."

Strange b'rachah, when we stop to think of it. Since the b'rachah is recited by the one who sounds the shofar, shouldn't it read, "Who has commanded us to *blow* the shofar"?

It appears that the central ritual of Rosh Hashanah deliberately focuses attention on the crucial importance of *listening*.

This observation reminds us that the oldest and probably the most widely known prayer in our liturgy, the prayer with which we open and close the day – the Sh'ma – also focuses on the importance of listening. Sh'ma – Listen, O Israel.

Both the b'rachah and the Sh'ma are vivid reminders that one of the basic arts we have to develop in life is the fine art of listening.

This isn't the most popular skill in our time. Turn to the classified section of the newspaper almost any day and you are likely to read of schools offering to teach us how to speak. There are evening classes and afternoon classes at every level, promising to make us into more effective speakers. In a few easy lessons we can hold audiences in the palms of our hands. We can become the life of the cocktail party. Prizes are usually awarded to the graduate who has shown excellence in eloquence. But where are the offers to make us better listeners? Believe me, the shortage of listeners is much greater than the shortage of speakers!

Not very long ago, when a prominent television personality voluntarily withdrew from his coveted position in front of the cameras, the explanation he gave was, "I have become increasingly aware lately that for the past ten years I have been on the air doing a great deal of talking. I want to start looking, thinking and listening to people."

The fact is that we are so constructed that we should devote more time to listening than to speaking. The divine architect endowed us with two ears but only one mouth. For too many of us the mouth is an overworked organ and the ears are in a state of semi-retirement.

The story is told of the bartender who was breaking in his young replacement for the summer vacation. At the bar the young man was beaming with friendliness and just overflowing with a stream of witty patter. Unhappily, he wasn't making much of an impression on his customers. Finally, the veteran called the young man aside and gave him the distillation of years of experience. "Listen, kid, listen, don't talk. These guys want to talk. If they wanted to listen they'd go home."

John O'Hara has written a short story called "The Man Who Had to Talk to Somebody." The hero is a certain Williams who just craved to talk about his problems in the presence of some one who would show interest and sympathy. And so Williams would invite a new acquaintance or fellow worker at the office to join him at lunch or dinner, hoping that ultimately he might find someone who would listen to him as he poured out his heart.

Williams is not an unusual character. He is each one of us. We desperately need someone with whom to share our burdens, our fears and loneliness, our yearnings and our frustrations, our guilts and our hostilities. We need someone to release us from the isolation cell into which we are so frequently maneuvered because no one cares enough to liberate us with a sympathetic ear. In short, we are all in search of the man who has developed the fine art of listening.

One who has practiced and mastered the art of listening, listens creatively. He may have to intrude from time to time to save us from wallowing in self-pity, to burst the balloon of one of our favorite illusions, to encourage us to part with a soothing prejudice. Good listening will not endorse all of our infantile wishes, our pet peeves, our excessive guilts. And a good listener will also hear what is not being said, the sentiments which are frequently concealed by the words. Long ago, Marcus Aurelius, one of the greatest of Roman emperors and philosophers, wrote in his Meditations: "Accustom thyself to attend carefully to what is said by another, and as much as it is possible, be in the speaker's mind."

Martin Buber has left us a particularly dramatic illustration of the decisive role the art of listening can play. One morning, he had a visit from some young man whom he did not know, who had come to consult with him about some problem. In recalling the interview Buber wrote: "I certainly did not fail to let the meeting be friendly. I did not treat him any more remissly than all his contemporaries who were in the habit of seeking me out. . . . I conversed attentively and openly with him – only I failed to guess the questions he did not put."

Later Buber learned that the young man had committed suicide, and the philosopher was guilt-stricken over his failure to sense the awesome earnestness of the young man who had come to him. Buber had only partially listened, or perhaps more accurately, had listened only with his ears. He had not involved himself sufficiently in the situation of the young man and, therefore, had not fully grasped the fateful character of his predicament. He had failed to hear the unspoken cries for help because he had not listened with his whole being.

And how about those children to whom we so infrequently listen? As parents, it is so much more tempting to bark an order rather than to discuss a situation. Our vanity prompts us to interpret a disagreement as a personal affront. And too often we don't try hard enough "to be in the speaker's mind."

The art of listening is one of the most crucial skills that each of us has to develop if we are to play our role effectively in the unfolding drama of a healthy family.

The blessing recited before the blowing of the shofar doesn't merely ask us to listen; it asks us to listen to a particular sound, the sound of the shofar. The Sh'ma, likewise, doesn't ask us simply to listen. It asks us to listen to a particular truth. In other words, we are being asked by our tradition to expose ourselves to specific sounds which can shape us and mold us and guide us.

The sounding of the shofar evokes many themes. To some of us it is a call to penitence. To some of us it is a kind of spiritual alarm clock to arouse us out of our apathy and our lethargy and our indifference. Again, the shofar is a reminder of the revelation at Sinai and the commitment that we Jews have to live as children of the covenant. The shofar is also a reminder of Abraham's readiness to offer up his most precious possession on the altar of his beliefs, and thus it urges us to remember that without the sacrifices of the generations past we would not be here today. Without our sacrifices today our grandchildren will not be here tomorrow. But whatever the shofar says to us, the point is that our tradition believes that the things we listen to can make a difference in the way we live and in the way we behave.

Sounds shape and sustain our souls, and life becomes infinitely poorer and drearier for the Jew from whose life the basic Jewish sounds have been banished.

As Jews we need to hear the call of our brethren in Israel who depend on us for a secure future, and the cries of our brethren in the Soviet Union who depend on us for any kind of Jewish future. But as Jews, we will hear these voices only if we have cultivated the fine art of listening.

Let's Hear It for Shiphrah and Puah!

Two of my favorite women in the Hebrew Bible are Shiphrah and Puah. Never heard of them? You can hardly be blamed. They are mentioned by name only once, and the reference to them is so brief that you could easily miss it. Who were they?

They were Hebrew midwives. When the paranoid Egyptian king decides to destroy the people of Israel, he gives Shiphrah and Puah a blunt order. When you deliver a Hebrew child "if it is a boy kill him; if it is a girl let her live" (Exodus 1:16).

Here was a command crisp and clear from the highest authority in the land who had absolute life and death power over every subject. What did Shiphrah and Puah do? The very next verse gives us the answer: "The midwives feared God and they did not do as the king of Egypt told them; they let the boys live."

Two humble defenseless women dared to defy a direct royal command in obedience to a higher law. They were not afraid of the Pharaoh because they "feared God."

These two heroines deserve to be rescued from obscurity not only for their sake, but also for ours. We in our time have had more than our fill of those who tried to justify the cruelest of crimes by claiming they were obedient to authority.

Adolf Eichmann's chief defense for his active complicity in the ghastly murder of 6 million Jews was that he was "under orders." He was just a little cog in a huge machine. His was not to question why.

In our own past, the Watergate scandal uncovered some of this same mentality that demands unquestioned obedience to the leader. One indicted co-conspirator said in a memo to the White House staff: "I would walk over my grandmother if necessary to assure the president's re-election."

Another very high White House aide explained what was expected of the president's subordinates in these words: "When he says 'Jump,' they only ask 'How high?' "

And a third tried to justify his breaking the law by asking rhetorically: "What do you say when the president calls?"

Shiphrah and Puah would say no to the president as they said no to the Pharaoh.

And if a wicked government gave an obscene order to murder innocent men, women and children they would claim that they were already under orders from a Higher Authority to preserve life.

So let's hear it for Shiphrah and Puah. Better still, let's keep before us always those heroic words: "The midwives feared God, and they did not do as the king of Egypt told them."

Yom Kippur Asks Us to Become Whole

Synagogues are more crowded on Yom Kippur than on any other day of the year. At sundown, the Day of Atonement begins. It is a day of fasting, prayer and self-evaluation.

A prominent feature of the spiritual landscape of this day is the confessional – the recitation of the sins that we have committed that fill us with remorse, and for which we ask a merciful God to forgive us. One of those sins is worth pondering.

"The sin we have sinned before You with the confession of our mouths." We have confessed great truths with our mouths but we have not translated them into deeds. This is the sin of lip service, words that become not a stimulus to actions but a substitute for them. It also happens to be one of our most prevalent sins.

A survey revealed that 95 percent of the American people believe in God. It would seem that God never had it so good as in America today.

But in this same survey there was another question: "Would you say your religious beliefs have any effect on your practice in business or politics?" To this question a majority answered "no." Their religious beliefs had no impact on their daily conduct. For too many of us, religion has become respectable but irrelevant.

This points up one of the deep-rooted maladies of our time that is closely related to our widespread anxieties and emotional ailments. We are split spiritual personalities.

We swear allegiance to one set of principles and live by another.

We extol self-control and practice self-indulgence.

We proclaim brotherhood and harbor prejudice.

We laud character but strive to climb to the top at any cost.

We erect houses of worship but our shrines are our places of business and recreation.

We are suffering from a distressing cleavage between the truths we affirm and the values we live by. Our souls are the battlegrounds for civil wars and we are trying to live serene lives in houses divided against themselves.

It was Harold Laski who warned that "the surest way to bring about the destruction of a civilization is to allow the abyss to widen between the values men praise and the values they permit to operate." We overlook this warning at our peril.

Yom Kippur urges us to narrow the abyss between our professions and our practice, between our words and our deeds. It summons us to restore our battered integrity, to bridge the divide within ourselves. It asks us to become whole.

The Principal Character Is Waiting to Appear

It is told of Thomas Edison that he once stood looking at the ocean and wept as he gazed upon the waves because there was so much throbbing energy going to waste.

A waste far more worthy of our tears is the enormous energy within us that never gets channeled, the love that is never expressed, the kindness that never surfaces, the compassion and tenderness that are never awakened.

Dr. Abraham Maslow, the noted psychologist, has estimated that the average human being achieves only seven percent of his potential.

Would anyone be content with such a slim percentage of success in any field of endeavor? I don't imagine any farmer would be too happy nor would he win any ribbons at the county fair if his wheat fields or his apple orchards yielded only seven percent of their potential. Should we rest content with such a meager human harvest?

Among his literary remains, Nathaniel Hawthorne left some notebooks that contain random ideas he jotted down as they occurred to him. One of the short entries reads as follows: "Suggestion for a story–story in which the principal character simply never appears."

Unhappily, this is the story of too many lives. The principal character simply never appears. The person we might grow into, the human being we might become, doesn't show up.

Our potential greatness lies unrealized, the splendor remains imprisoned, the promise unfulfilled. Our lives develop a static character.

We stop growing morally, spiritually, and intellectually. We do not expand our sympathies. We do not enlarge our interests. We do not further our knowledge. We do not strengthen our self-control. We remain essentially where we were last year, five years ago, twenty years ago.

But when our growth is stunted, we find a sense of discontent gnawing at us. We become "sick with unused self," to use the phrase of one observer of the human condition. We remain haunted by the "principal character" who invades our dreams in the night and mars our serenity by day.

In our heart of hearts, we each know that we were meant to keep growing as long as we keep breathing. If a seed in its dark restless journey under ground is not content until it breaks through the mountain of soil and strains ever higher toward the sunlight, shall we human beings be content to remain "in the original state of nature"?

Whatever our age, it is a time for us to grow–to become more capable of forgiveness, more sensitive to another's pain, more receptive to criticism, more open to a new idea. We must never forget the principal character who is waiting to appear.

Growing Up and Growing Out

Several years ago a comedian who is Jewish was asked in a radio interview how he explains the astronomical sums American Jews contribute annually to their various charities. "Well," he answered, posing as the authority he obviously was not, "first you have to start with 2,000 years of persecution."

Not quite. First you have to start with 3,000 years of indoctrination.

Very early in our history we were taught that the hallmark of a Jew is a profound feeling of concern for the welfare of other Jews. One of the most striking illustrations of this lesson is found in the opening chapters of the Book of Exodus:

"And Moses grew up and he went out to his brothers and saw their burdens" (Exodus 2:11).

It would have been so natural, so understandable and oh so very practical had Moses chosen not to notice his brothers' travail, to claim no kinship with these degraded slaves. How tempting it must have been to cling to the security, the delights, the prerogatives of the royal palace in which his life was so snugly upholstered. But had Moses done so, God would not have noticed him and history would not have remembered him.

The whole course of human events was radically altered because in a decisive moment, an obscure foundling of a condemned people threw off the anonymity and the protection of Pharaoh's palace and "went out to his brothers and saw their burdens."

From that day to our very own, a crucial index of Jewish maturity is the ability to go out to our brothers and be sensitive to their burdens.

Two Chelmite "philosophers," not especially noted for their sophistication, were engaged in a profound discussion: How does one grow, from the feet up or from the head down?

Said the first: "From the feet up, of course. Last year I bought my son a new suit for his Bar Mitzvah, and at that time the pants were just the right length. Now, the pants just reach his ankles. That proves that people grow from the feet up."

"Fool," snapped the second philosopher. "It's obvious that people grow from the head down. If you see a group of soldiers marching, all their feet are on the same level. But if you look at their heads you will see that they are at different heights. That proves that people grow from the head down."

Both Chelmites were wrong. We grow neither from the bottom up nor from the top down. Genuine growth is from the inside out. The truest measure of our growth is the ability to go out to our brothers and become aware of their burdens.

When God measures us, He puts the tape around the heart.

All growth is difficult. Our Sages tell us that no blade of grass grows except for an angel which stands over it and commands: "Grow!"

We are born selfish. To the infant the whole world exists for one supreme purpose—to minister to his needs. Growing up is the slow, painful process of learning that we are here not to be ministered to, but to minister; not to be served, but to serve; not to be fed but to feed; not to be imprisoned within ourselves, but to go out to our brothers.

But we are afraid to venture out. Seeing brothers gives them a claim over us. It is easier not to notice them, to acknowledge no kinship with them.

An eight-year-old unintentionally gave expression to this philosophy of evasion. During a Consecration Service, a rabbi addressed a youngster who bore the name of one of Jacob's sons, and the rabbi expressed the hope that the young fellow "would live a life of dedication to your brothers of the House of Israel." Without batting an eyelash, the youngster replied at the top of his voice: "I ain't got no brothers."

We can only hope that when that young fellow grows up, he will discover that he does indeed "got" brothers, that he is intimately related to them by a thousand bonds of kinship, fate, and loyalty, and that to the extent that he goes out to them, will he fulfill his fundamental duty as a Jew and his fundamental need as a human being.

The act of giving is simultaneously an act of receiving. The benefactor is also the beneficiary. To give is to become enriched.

As we feed, we are fed. As we give, we receive. As we lift, we are raised. As we go out of ourselves into something bigger than ourselves, we become bigger in the process and we provide the most nourishing sustenance our craving hearts demand.

"Help your brother's boat across the river and lo, your own has reached the shore."

Double Surgery

Would you like to hear about my operation? I had one in 1978 – my first since I was eight days old – and if you'd rather not hear about it read no further.

If you're still with me, I'd like to share with you some thoughts that ran through my mind during my hospitalization. I was admitted on July 2, operated on the following day and began my recovery on July 4th.

There was something very suggestive about being in the hospital on Independence Day. I've always thought of myself as a rather independent person.

But that image, I confess, was blown higher than a 4th of July firecracker just as soon as I was admitted to the hospital. Suddenly a whole battalion of trained workers went into action, and as each contributed his or her skill to my welfare, I became so humbly aware that my independence was a fragile myth. Independent? Never did I feel more dependent in all my life.

There was the lovely girl at the admissions desk with a cheerful: "We've been expecting you." A second girl checked out all the preliminary lab work to make sure I was well enough to undergo surgery. A third guided me to the room that was waiting for me.

The room was spotless, the bed neatly made, the hospital gown and robe in a clean state of readiness. A lunch tray soon appeared and the food was fully in accord with my requirements of kosher diet which I had made known in advance.

The afternoon saw a parade of ministering angels to my bedside. A cardiologist, an anesthesiologist, a resident physician – each with his own special knowledge and reassurance. Personalized pre-operative attention was administered by a team of nurses. My temperature and blood-pressure were checked regularly throughout the day and night.

Early the following morning two nurses prepared me for surgery, and I was wheeled into the operating room. Now I was most dependent upon the skilled hands and the trained minds of the surgeon and his team.

The days of recovery involved dozens more in my welfare. When finally I checked out of the hospital, I left behind more than a troublesome gland. Without being aware of it, the doctor had performed double surgery. He also cut out my illusion of independence.

A good and wise God has so created us that we desperately need one another and we lean upon one another – every single one of us.

An ancient sage put it this way: "God divided man into men, that they might help each other."

The Big Role of Little Things

The last page I read to her before tucking her in for the night had the old favorite that begins with the lines: "For want of a nail, the shoe was lost. For want of a shoe, the horse was lost . . ." and so on. The loss of the horse led to the loss of the rider, the battle, and, finally, the kingdom itself. All for want of a nail.

After she had fallen asleep, I wondered whether her five-year-old mind had grasped the profound meaning of the simple poem. Its message is meant for people of all ages: Pay large attention to the little things.

A tragic illustration of the crucial importance of little things was furnished some time ago by the crash of a jet airliner shortly after take-off. All ninety-five persons aboard were killed. An exhaustive study of the disaster concluded that it might have been caused by the loss in the rudder-control system of a little bolt, less than an inch long. For want of a bolt, so many lives were lost.

Little things have not only been responsible for huge losses, they have also triggered great discoveries. A spider web over a garden path led to the suspension bridge. A teakettle singing on the stove was the inspiration for the steam engine. A falling apple suggested the law of gravity. A lantern swinging in a tower was responsible for the pendulum.

On both sides of the historical ledger, great consequences have come from little things.

In our personal lives, too, little things play a far greater role than we usually realize. Little things give us pain, and little things give us pleasure. A cruel word can cast a dreary cloud over the brightest of days; a word of appreciation can send our spirits soaring. A small act of kindness can often make a big difference in the delicate machinery of the human spirit.

When the English writer Oscar Wilde was being led handcuffed from prison to the Court of Bankruptcy, a friend waited for him to pass through the dreary, drafty corridor. As the prisoner passed, his friend tipped his hat to him. Of this gesture Wilde wrote later, "The memory of this little, lovely, silent act of love has unsealed for me all the wells of pity."

Few of us are ever asked to do great things, but we are always given the opportunity to do little things in a great way. Some of the most heroic people I have known have been anonymous little people who inspired me by the spectacular way they performed ordinary, unspectacular deeds.

I have known parents who have cared for a handicapped child day after day, week after week, year after year, compensating for nature's frail endowments with double portions of inexhaustible love. I have known young widows who have managed for long years to be both mother and father to their children. I have known humble people who have a boundless capacity for bringing cheer into lonely lives, who are drawn by some special instinct to human need, who are always scrubbing the little corner assigned to them to make it brighter and cleaner.

Perhaps Rabbi Leo Baeck summed up our theme best: "Piety . . . respects the little – the little man, the little task, the little duty. Through the little, religion meets the greatness that lies behind."

The Darkness in the Heart

A ten-year-old *yeshivah* student studied for the first time about the plagues that were visited upon the ancient Egyptians.

The ninth plague, he learned, was darkness, a darkness so "thick" that "they saw not one another" (Exodus 10:33).

He asked his rebbe: "What kind of plague was that? After all, they could have lit their lamps and been able to see despite the darkness. Isn't that what they did every night when it got dark?"

The rebbe's smile indicated that he was not displeased by the question. Patting the boy on his head, he said: "The darkness from which the Egyptians suffered was a special kind of darkness. It was not a darkness that affected the eyes; it was a darkness that affected the heart. Physically, they were able to see, but they didn't feel for each other; they didn't care for one another. This is what the Torah means when it says, 'They saw not one another.' They were blind to each other's needs. Each person saw only himself. And that is a terrible plague."

Perhaps the rebbe's answer cannot be harmonized with the literal meaning of the Torah text. But this much is certain. He taught the boy a lesson that goes to the very essence of Judaism.

Much as Judaism is concerned with the relationship between the human being and God, *"beyn adam la-makom,"* it is no less concerned with the relationship between one human being and another, *"beyn adam la-haveyro."*

Judaism expects of us that we shall "see" each person as a human being who has needs, feelings, fears, hungers, hopes just as we do; who is a child of God just as we are; who is fully entitled to be treated with the dignity, justice, and compassion we claim for ourselves.

This message is desperately needed in our time. A popular cartoonist depicted multitudes of ant-sized people at the base of a huge pyramid. The pyramid consisted of four words:

I

ME

MINE

MYSELF

The caption on the cartoon read: "Speaking of American Cults," and it provides a striking illustration of the contemporary plague of darkness – "they saw not one another."

The '70s were labeled the "Me Decade." Did we, in the '80s, outgrow the narcissistic preoccupation with the self?

A study indicated that those over fifty are also joining the "Me Generation." One of America's leading advertising agencies surveyed three separate groups of people – men and women between the ages of 50 and 64, men and women between 65 and 80, and widows between 50 and 64.

Common to all these groups was a feeling that they could indulge themselves fully within the limitations of their income. People who had previously put the needs of their parents, spouses, and children above their own are now putting their own needs first. Many were now cashing in their life insurance policies and putting their extra funds into travel, eating out, and other personal pleasures. Moreover, the survey found that there was a diminished emphasis on leaving an estate to their children, and a greater tendency to spend their own funds now on themselves.

To a certain extent this new development may have some healthy aspects. But carried to extremes, the immersion in the self can have some unfavorable consequences.

A great deal depends upon our ability to "see one another." Our own emotional well-being depends on it. Dr. David Goodman, an authority on mental health, has written, "Mental illness is the price you pay for being absorbed in yourself. Mental health is your reward for devoting yourself to your duties and to the welfare of others."

A rabbi making his way through the corridors of the Albert Einstein Medical Center met a friend who was carrying a heart-breaking burden of family problems, including serious illness and divorce. When he asked her what she was doing in the hospital, she proudly announced that she is a volunteer.

"With all your troubles," he asked, "where do you get the strength to help others?"

"Rabbi," she answered, "this work saves me. If I didn't come here twice a week, I don't think I'd be able to carry on at all."

As he left her, he thought of the answer Dr. Karl Menninger gave when he was asked what to advise a person who felt a nervous breakdown coming on. "I would say to that person: 'Lock up your house, go across the railway tracks, find someone in need and invest yourself in helping that person.' "

The poet put this same basic truth about us in rhyme:

> "Man, like the graceful vine, supported lives;
> The strength he gains is from the embrace he gives."

The Torah tells us that, during the plague of darkness in Egypt, "all the people Israel had light in all their dwellings." This is the basic challenge that confronts each of us—to keep aglow that light of understanding and caring which enables us to truly see each other. For it is only when we see the humanity in another that we can preserve it within ourselves.

Thanks for What's Not Lost

Some time ago the nineteen-year-old son of the president of Cyprus was kidnapped by terrorists who threatened to behead him unless his father agreed to release several of their jailed comrades. In a remarkable display of fortitude, the father refused to submit to the kidnappers' demands, and after four tension-filled days, the young man was released unharmed.

When he returned to his family, his mother jubilantly exclaimed, "This is the happiest day of my life!"

Good people everywhere, and especially parents, can understand the mother's unbounded joy. Her son had been snatched from the jaws of death! She had come so close to losing him!

However, as we think about the mother's jubilant reaction, a question rises in our minds. What did the mother have after her son was returned that she did not have five days earlier, before he was kidnapped? In what way was she richer? Why was she so much happier than before? We know the answer, of course. What she now had was a profoundly deepened sense of appreciation for a blessing she almost lost. Only when the life of her son was severely threatened did she realize how vastly she cherished that life.

Every one of us is like that mother: It often takes a serious threat to our blessings to make us aware of them. And, sadly, sometimes we do not value them until they are gone beyond retrieving.

Channing Pollock, in his essay "The Secret of Being Rich," made this pertinent observation: "I should not be the only one to laugh if I stopped in the street to voice gratitude for the air we breathe. But if they could hear me, there would be no merriment from the men who died in sunken submarines or damaged mines or in the Black Hole of Calcutta."

The fact is, of course, that if we were asked to draw up a list of our assets, we would probably never think of mentioning such things as our vision, our limbs, our sanity, our ability to eat and to speak. Everyone has that, we say. Well, on second thought, almost everyone.

But would we be willing to exchange any of these blessings for all those things we want so badly that they fill us with discontent and rob us of a sense of gratefulness?

A worthwhile Thanksgiving Day exercise might consist of sitting down with two sheets of paper. On one we might list all the things we crave and are yearning to acquire. On the other sheet we would enumerate all those things we have and could lose. To our surprise, we would find the first list quickly exhausted while the second would appear endless. We would probably soon tear up the first list, feeling a little ashamed and largely thankful.

We might then understand better the meaning of the prayer:

Thou has given so much to me. Give me one thing more –
a grateful heart.

The Great Act of Faith

One of the most poignant and most painful emotional outbursts in our entire Bible comes from the depths of Rachel's aching heart.

She has seen her sister Leah, her rival for the love of their husband Jacob, give birth to four sons in rapid succession, while she herself has remained childless. Consumed by envy and jealousy, Rachel cries out to Jacob, "Give me children or I shall die!" Jacob responds as much in sorrow as in anger, "Am I in the place of God who has denied you a child?"

This is an important question that each of us might ask ourselves periodically, because we frequently forget our creatureliness and succumb to the temptation to play God. So often we sit in judgment on other human beings about whom we have only the most superficial knowledge, and about whose circumstances we frequently know nothing at all. Our Sages counseled us not to judge another human being until we find ourselves in that person's predicament, until we understand his fears and his frustrations, his hopes and his hungers, his broken dreams and unattained goals. All these are known only to God who, as the Bible reminds us, "sees into the heart." And yet we are so quick to find fault, to denigrate, to condemn. Before we rush to judgment, a good question to slow us down would be, "Am I in the place of God?"

This same question could also be very nourishing for our humility. One long-suffering wife confided to a good friend, "My husband has changed his faith. He no longer believes he is God." So often we strike a pose of infallibility, handing down pronouncements and opinions as though they were carved at Sinai in stone together with the original tablets. We pretend to know all there is to know about everything, while we suppress the haunting suspicion that we may indeed be mistaken and the certainty that what we don't know exceeds by far the little we do know.

One successful businessman put on his office wall in bold letters the sobering words, "I may be wrong." That may have been the reason for his success; his willingness to learn from others, his ability to keep his mind open to a new idea, a different approach. His motto was a free translation of Jacob's rhetorical question, "Am I in the place of God?"

Jacob's question is also good for our sanity. When we recognize our human limitations we stop demanding perfection of ourselves. We are not 100 percent parents, we are not 100 percent mates, we are not 100 percent children. And we ought to stop tormenting ourselves, as we so frequently do, for falling short of perfection in one or all of the myriad relationships in which we are involved. Often we must make painful choices between our mates and our parents, our parents and our children, and we cannot possibly satisfy all.

When we acknowledge the built-in limitations of the human condition we also avoid the destructive tendency to blame ourselves when children do not turn out exactly as we had hoped. Deluded by a sense of omnipotence, we succumb to the illusion that when kids go wrong, it is all our fault. We have done it to them. We forget the many other factors that go into the the making and the shaping of a child – the genes of generations past, the environment, the TV, the friends on the street, the teachers in the classroom, the characters the child encounters in books. These are only some of the multitude of forces at work, and while no parent has the right to abdicate responsibility, neither has the parent the right to arrogate unto himself the feeling of invincibility.

Emerson said there is a crack in everything that God has made. Perfection is beyond human reach. Jacob captured this truth in his question, "Am I in the place of God?"

In a letter to William James, Justice Holmes wrote, "The great act of faith is when a man decides he is not God." When we realize that we are not God, we have a better chance of becoming human.

Forgiving Those We Have Injured

Everybody praises forgiveness, but few practice it. The English poet Alexander Pope wrote, "To err is human: to forgive, divine." But a revised modern version declares, "To err is human; to forgive, unusual."

The Bible records a noble instance of forgiveness when Joseph is reconciled with his brothers. But even there, that forgiveness does not come easily.

Joseph torments his brothers in many cruel ways before he finally reveals his true identity. He then reassures them, "Now, be not grieved nor angry with yourselves, that you sold me hither; for God sent me ahead of you to preserve life. . . . It was not you that sent me here, but God" (Genesis 45:5, 8).

Yes, Joseph does ultimately forgive his brothers. But why does he find it so hard to do so?

Well, we say, because his brothers hurt him. If Reuben had not interceded, they would have killed him. As it was, they stripped him of his beloved coat of many colors, threw him into the pit, and then sold him as a slave. It's not easy to forgive such abuse. But perhaps there was another reason for Joseph's long delay in forgiving his brothers. He may have had trouble forgiving them not because they had wronged him, but because he had wronged them!

Strange as this may sound, it is true that we frequently develop very strong feelings against people whom we have hurt. Long ago, the Roman historian Tacitus wrote, "It is a principle of human nature to hate those whom you have injured." And Joseph Jacobs, a contemporary historian, declared, "The highest and most difficult of all moral lessons is to forgive those we have injured."

In Joseph's case, it was plain that his own inflammatory actions had provoked his brothers' harsh reactions. He had gossiped about them, carried tales about them back to their father, had dreams about lording it over them, and was insensitive enough to tell those dreams to his brothers. And all the while, he strutted around in his coat of many colors—the tantalizing reminder that he was their father's favorite.

Perhaps it was when Joseph finally faced up to his painful truth that he was able to gather enough strength to admit to himself that he had indeed been the offender; then he was able to make peace with his brothers.

Joseph might help us to find our own way to forgiveness. He would urge us to face ourselves honestly and truthfully. We may then be able to forgive those we have injured.

A Drop in a Bucket

Judaism reminds us that there is no common man. Each one of us is uncommon. There has been nothing like us ever, nor will there ever be. There is no such thing as an average man, except on the graphs and the charts of the statisticians.

"Every single man is a new thing in the world and is called upon to fulfill his particularity in the world." Thus taught the *Hasidic Rebbe,* Yechiel Michael of Zlotchov.

In each of us, all the past centuries coalesce. In each of us, all the future centuries have their beginnings. In each of us, there are found very special endowments. "It is a pleasant fact," said Henry Thoreau, "that you will know no man long, however low in the social scale, however poor, miserable, intemperate and worthless he may appear to be, a mere burden to society, but you will find, at last, that there is something which he understands and can do better than any other."

In the eyes of our Creator we are not statistics. We are each the object of God's care and compassion. We are each counted. We are each remembered. We are each one – one unique man, one special woman, one precious little child.

And we each have extraordinary capacities and all kinds of latent force. We each have the power to transform our lives. We can each make a decisive difference in the world.

One of the most debilitating questions is the one which is so frequently asked rhetorically, with a despairing shrug of the shoulders. What can one person do? What can I do to affect the moral fiber of a community? Go fight City Hall! What can I do about raising the level of jungle ethics that prevails in the business world? You have to play their game. What can I do about the symptoms of the deterioration of Judaism in America? There are great factors at work beyond my control. I am just a drop in the bucket.

Well, one man who has made a decisive difference in the spiritual texture and moral tone of our time, Albert Schweitzer, has something very different to say about the human "drop in the bucket." "We see no power in a drop of water; but let it get into a crack in the rock and be turned to ice and it splits the rock; turned into steam, it drives the pistons of the most powerful engines."

We each possess enormous potential, power, and energy within ourselves. If we utilize that power we can indeed effect decisive changes within ourselves. We can leave the world a little better and a little cleaner than we found it.

On Running Away from Ourselves

There is a running boom in this country, not only on the tracks and city streets but also in the bookstores.

One book on running has enjoyed a long run on the national best-seller list. At least thirty other books on running have been published. Running enthusiasts even contend that running can provide a spiritual "high."

After a 26-mile, 385-yard marathon in New York's Central Park, a newspaper ran an enthusiastic lead editorial entitled "Inside, Every One of Us Is a Distance Runner."

That title sent my thoughts running on a somewhat different track. It reminded me that running is an ancient enterprise, as old as the human race (no pun intended). I am thinking not of the kind of running that makes us more fit to face life, but of the kind of running that is an effort to evade life, to escape from its burdens, to get away from it all.

The most celebrated runner in the Bible is Jonah, the central character in the tale of Jonah and the whale , which I consider a whale of a tale, to be taken seriously but not literally.

God sends Jonah to preach a message of repentance to the inhabitants of Nineveh, the capital of Israel's bitter foe, Syria. Jonah doesn't like the idea at all. Why should he care about these Gentiles, and Gentile enemies yet! So what does Jonah do? "And Jonah arose to run to Tarshish, away from God" (Jonah 1:3).

Jonah begins the longest race of all, running away from God. Instead of setting out for Nineveh, he takes a slow boat to Tarshish. This kind of marathon did not begin with Jonah and did not end with him. Inside, every one of us is a little like Jonah. We each have our own Ninevehs from which we want to run.

We want to run from unpleasant duties, from nagging responsibilities, from life's complexities and confusions. We want to run from harsh realities, from our fears and anxieties, from an accusing conscience. We want to run from the boredom and bewilderment of existence.

And there are many ships we board as we head for our own little Tarshish. Some get turned on and some get turned off. Some drop out and some cop out. Some develop asthma and some get headaches. Some get lost in petty pleasures and some in the pursuit of fun.

But if there is one lesson that Jonah teaches us, it is that there is no running away; wherever we go, we take ourselves along. God finds Jonah even in the belly of the whale. The only way to "get away" from ourselves is to effect a change within ourselves. What we need is not a change of scene, but a change of soul.

It is only when Jonah finally goes to Nineveh, when he accepts and discharges his responsibility, when he stands up to life, that he saves both Nineveh and himself. He has stopped running.

Dag Hammarskjöld, the great secretary general of the United Nations, once put the truth simply: "Life demands from you only the strength you possess. Only one feat is possible – not to have run away."

Which Shall We Choose to Remember?

A keen student of human behavior, George Halifax, has correctly said: "Could we know what men are most apt to remember, we might know what they are most apt to do."

A vivid illustration of this truth is found in the story of Joseph. Joseph is facing a memory problem in one of the most dramatic moments in his eventful life. The moment occurs when Joseph, who had been sold by his brothers into slavery, now finds these brothers before him. But now he has become the regent of Egypt, and his brothers, driven by famine, appear before him for food. Joseph has them at his mercy. He can do with them as he wills. But what will he do? His problem is fundamentally one of memory. What should he remember?

He can remember how they maltreated him, cast him into the pit where he might have been left to perish had not an Ishmaelite caravan fortuitously appeared, how they coldly traded him away as if he were no more than a piece of sheepskin or a measure of corn. Or he can remember how he, the young Joseph, had provoked them, how he had brought tales of malice about them back to his father, how he had taunted them with his dreams of his destined domination over them. He can either remember the wrong he suffered or the wrong he inflicted. He can either exact vengeance or make amends. Which experience shall he remember?

This problem is not easily solved. Instinctively, Joseph appears ready to exact vengeance. In a variety of subtle ways he torments his brothers, worries them and hurls accusations against them. All this, however, is but the prelude which leads up to the climax – the moment when Joseph reveals himself to his brothers. When that moment arrives Joseph emerges in heroic stature. He has chosen to forget his brothers' misconduct and to make amends for his own.

When he notices the fear that registers on their faces he tells them: "Be not angry with yourselves that you sold me here, for God sent me before you to be a preserver of life. It was not you but God who sent me here." He then goes on to assure them that he will make arrangements for them and their families to live in Egypt where he will provide for them all. In this way does Joseph solve his personal memory problem.

Each of us at one time or another has to draw up a memory balance sheet. What shall we try to remember and what shall we try to forget?

We must try to forget those things which if remembered would bring out our unworthy traits. We must try to remember those things which if forgotten would suppress our nobler instincts.

Some among us have permitted ties of family and friendship to be broken. There was an unpleasant scene, a heated exchange of words, an explosive moment. We chose to remember that moment while we forgot all the unnumbered pleasant moments of family loyalty, warmth, and friendship. Would it not be much wiser now if we forgot the hurt and remembered only the love?

All of us have suffered wrongs and inflicted them. Too often we recall the instances when we were the victims; we forget those where we were the offenders. Were it not wiser to reverse our memory system – consign the wrong suffered to oblivion and repair, where time yet permits, the wrong inflicted?

All too often we remember with bitterness the unfulfilled promises made to us but we calmly forget the pledge we made and did not honor, the resolve we made and did not keep, the word we gave and did not fulfill. Were it not better that we forgot the first and remembered the second?

None among us has not been both benefactor and beneficiary. We have benefited others to be sure, but in more instances than we normally care to remember we have also reaped the harvest of another's kindness, another's generosity, another's sacrifice. If we enjoy the blessings of health, freedom, democracy, Judaism, it is because others have paid for these, our possessions, with their lives and their blood. Shall the little kindnesses we have shown make us haughty when there is so much that we have inherited which should make us profoundly grateful and humble?

Every day we see about us evidence of human pettiness, greed, self-centeredness. But if we observe carefully we also see human nobility, generosity, self-surrender and genuine religious conviction and action. The cynic remembers only man's faults – that is why he remains a cynic. The wise man remembers his brother's virtues. Which shall we choose to remember?

In making our choice let us remember that we shall be what we remember. Our memories will mold our action, and what others will remember of us will be determined by what we choose to remember.

Doing the Human Thing

On June 4, 1978, sixteen rabbinical students were ordained as Reform rabbis. But the dramatic highlight of the ordination services involved none of the many rabbis on the program. The spotlight and the hearts of all in attendance were captured by a non-Jew – 78-year-old Victor Kugler.

Why all the fuss about Victor Kugler?

Kugler was brought to the services in New York City from Toronto, where he now lives, so that he might be presented with a very special prize for "encouraging the values and ideals which derive from religious teachings."

During the Nazi occupation of Holland, Kugler hid the family of Anne Frank for 25 months in an effort to save them from death.

Anne Frank, we will remember, was the young Jewish girl who, between the ages of 13 and 15, kept a remarkable diary in which she displayed extraordinary literary ability and psychological insight. That diary she wrote while in hiding in the "secret annex."

The annex consisted of four small rooms and an attic, which were sealed from view by a bookcase in Otto Frank's spice importing office in Amsterdam. Kugler manned a desk, took care of the books, and tried to keep up the appearances of business as usual in Otto Frank's shop.

At great personal risk, Kugler smuggled bits of food to the eight members of the Frank family during the long perilous 25 months. Kugler and those he hid lived in constant fear of discovery and death.

That discovery came in July 1944, when the Gestapo raided the secret annex on a tip from someone who was paid about twelve dollars for betraying the hideaway.

Kugler was taken to a concentration camp but, fortunately, was able to escape. Not so fortunate were the members of the Frank family. Of the eight inhabitants of the hideaway, seven were to die in concentration camps. Anne herself died in Bergen Belsen. Only her father, Otto, and her diary survived.

Referring to his efforts on behalf of the Frank family, Kugler said modestly that he did the "human thing." "I did nothing special; I could not leave my best friends to the Nazis."

It is saddening to reflect that doing the "human thing" has become so special in our time that it earns prizes and ovations. In an era when there has been so much evidence of "man's inhumanity to man," the "human thing" was like a tiny flickering candle in a vast ocean of blackness. But it is precisely these little candles, the brave and good Kuglers, who give us hope for the future.

Perhaps it was Mr. Kugler himself who kept alive in young Anne Frank the faith which shone through these words which appeared in her diary.

"It's really a wonder that I haven't dropped all my ideals, because they seem so absurd and impossible to carry out. Yet I keep them, because in spite of everything I still believe that people are really good at heart. I see the world gradually being turned into a wilderness. I hear the approaching thunder, I can feel the suffering of millions, and yet, if I look up into the heavens, I think that it will all come out right one of these days; that this cruelty will end, and that peace and tranquillity will return again. In the meantime, I must hold on to my ideals for perhaps the day will come when I shall be able to carry them out."

Anne never lived to carry out her ideals. Saintly Victor Kugler challenges us by his own example to translate her faith into fulfillment.

The Book of the Living

Some time ago I read a slim, sensitive volume entitled: *Rise Up and Walk*, by one Turnley Walker. In it he describes his dreadful encounter with polio which struck him down in his middle thirties. He sketches the delirium of pain and fear, the sense of guilt over creating massive expenses while helpless to provide income for his wife and children, the initial loss of faith in ever writing the book he was just about to begin. He succeeds in conveying the feeling of disaster of a young man who suddenly realizes that he no longer has control over his pain-racked limbs. His bed is a "pit of helplessness," – walking, "a forgotten miracle." Slowly and marvelously his motion is restored to him and the book is abundant proof that he has been left with no emotional or mental scars.

Now, in the book, Mr. Walker describes not only his personal reactions but also those of his two fellow sufferers on either side similarly afflicted. The 37-year-old lawyer on one side sobbing in bed and whispering "God I'm scared"; the successful manufacturer on the other side also grappling with fear, defeatism, despair.

After I finished reading the book a curious, though irrelevant, thought came to me. It took the form of a question. "How," I asked myself, "would the lawyer and the manufacturer have behaved if they had known that Walker was going to record their behavior in a book? What if they had realized that their every reaction and outcry and exclamation and conversation were being written down for all the world to read? Would they have been more courageous, more trusting, more hopeful?"

As these questions punctuated my thinking, I suddenly realized that they were prompted by a comment of our sages which I had read some time previous. It was related to the biblical story of Joseph and his brothers. We recall that when the brothers saw the proud, tale-bearing Joseph approaching them in the fields, they plotted at once to kill him. But Reuben, the oldest, wanted to save Joseph. And so Reuben counsels his brothers not to kill him but rather to cast him into the pit. Reuben had planned to return after his brothers' departure, to rescue Joseph and to bring him home. We know of course that when Reuben later returns to the pit, he discovers to his great dismay that Joseph is gone. It is upon this incident that our rabbis comment: "If Reuben realized that the Torah was recording his every deed he would have picked Joseph up bodily and he would have carried him home to his father." He would not have resorted to subterfuges or schemes. He would have said to his brothers: "Be men, be human. After all he is only a spoiled child. That's not how brother treats brother. And if not for his sake, then think of father. How dare we even entertain such a thought? I'm taking Joseph home now—and don't anybody try to stop me!"

Yes, Reuben, that's how you might have spoken. That's the speech you might have delivered if you had only realized that your deeds were being written down for all generations to read. You would not have resorted to chance. You would have shown a manhood worthy of the occasion. You would have been more outspoken, more courageous. If you had only known. . . .

This then was the origin of the questions which came to me after finishing Mr. Walker's book. What if the lawyer and the manufacturer realized that their deeds were being written up for all to read?

From here let me now carry this question closer home. What if we realized, every one of us, that someone around us was writing a book about us—recording our every action in our places of business, in our offices, in our homes, in our places of amusement and recreation?

What if we knew that someone was noting, for all to read, our relationship to our subordinates, our loyalty to our mates, our faithfulness to truth, our response to charitable appeals, our obedience to justice? How would we behave? What if we suddenly realized that the curtain of secrecy and privacy had been ripped away, and instead, the full glare of the public spotlight was turned relentlessly upon us and exposing us constantly to view?

I suppose most of us will say: Fortunately that possibility is only the product of the rabbi's morbid imagination. That's a frightening thought which happily is unrelated to reality.

On Rosh Hashanah let us face the challenging truth that what I have been describing is not an imaginative fantasy but a striking fact. Whether we like it or not, whether we are aware of it or not, everything that we do is written down indelibly in the record. And I mean this not only in the theological sense in which Rabbi Akiba taught and Judaism believed: that our actions are part of the Divine record. I mean more specifically that everything we do is written down in the human record—becomes a vital part of somebody's book of life.

During the High Holy Days we repeat often the prayer that we may be inscribed *"B'sefer Hachayim*—In the book of life." The word *"Hachayim"* is usually rendered "life." But it also means "the living." *"Sefer Hachayim,"* would then mean, "the book of the living." If we understand it in this sense, then we grasp the truth which I have tried to underscore. Whether we like it or not, we are being written up in a book, in many books. Our actions are shaping human biographies, are being imprinted on living parchment, are being woven into the plots and dramas of human destiny.

Most of us enjoy the great privilege and the greater responsibility of parenthood. How often do we pause to realize that we are daily making indelible entries into our children's book of life? Do we fully appreciate how responsive our children are to our influences and how enduring these influences prove to be?

Luther Burbank, the famous scientist and botanist, pointed out that metals are the hardest things to change. They require tremendous force to mold them. To change gold you must use a heavy hammer. Gold will resist acids and oxidation. To change iron you have to use tremendous heat and outside influences of every type. A plant will respond to the most delicate outside forces. But the most sensitive thing of all is a child. A child will respond to a thousand outside forces which neither a plant nor a metal will feel. Therefore, it is we whose deeds are being inscribed boldly between the covers of our children's book of life. This truth is attested to by every autobiography.

Chaim Nachman Bialik was considered until his death in 1934 the Hebrew poet laureate. In one of his very touching poems he tries to trace to its origin the sigh, the *krechtz,* which is so frequently heard in his poems. And he tells us how in his childhood, his widowed mother would slave in the market place by day and toil with her domestic chores at home late into the night. Long after she thought all her children were asleep, she would be sewing and baking. Little Chaim in his bed overheard her unanswered protests to the Almighty and could hear her tears rolling into the dough that she was kneading for tomorrow's bread. When she served her family the warm bread on the following morning, Bialik says, he ate it and with it there entered into his bones his mother's tears and her sighs. Unbeknown to her, of course, she was making decisive imprints on little Chaim's scroll of life that no subsequent experience could eradicate.

If we ourselves paused briefly to trace back the significant passages in our personal autobiographies to their source, would we not find that much of the authorship was done by our parents. And if a trained analyst would apply his magnifying glass to our book of life he would find even more than we recognize. The most vital passages in our book of life would be traced back to our first and most persistent heroes – our parents.

Charles Francis Potter in his book, *The Preacher and I,* makes this interesting comment: "A eulogy is customary which is a sort of laudatory biography. But I am always aware, when listening to the remarks of the mourners and looking into their thoughtful faces, that the true life story of the deceased, including his mistakes, as well as his good deeds, is engraved deep in the memory of his friends and that he wrote it there himself."

If we move a bit further with this thought we realize that it is not only in the books of the lives of those dearest to us that we make vital entries. The pen of our deeds often leaves its lasting sketches on the volumes of casual acquaintances or even total strangers. Open up your own book of life and read. Did the teacher who awakened within you a love for literature realize how significant a passage she was writing? Did the hero who conquered his severe handicap appreciate how much courage he gave you to surmount your own? Did the anonymous Jews who purchased Jewish survival with their lives realize how deeply their deeds etched themselves onto the impressionable slate of your soul?

In his book *The Bond Between Us,* Dr. Loomis relates a significant personal experience. Shortly after he settled in California his wife died of pneumonia. Within the next few days, three doctors came individually to console him. Each of them gave him a blank check to fill in any amount he needed and to return the sum whenever he became affluent enough to do so. In recalling the incident, Dr. Loomis writes: "This act in a way prompted every decent thing I have done in all the years since."

This, then, is a basic truth of human experience. Whether we like it or not, we are being inscribed *B'sefer Hachayim* – in the book of the living. In the biographies of our loved ones and fellow-men, in the ledger of the general community, in the chronicles of Judaism – we are constantly making entries. What kind of entries am I making? – this might well be the question with which we ought to begin and end every God-given day.

Let us consider some specific areas of our lives against the background of this truth. At the White House Conference on Child Study there were listed nineteen requirements, the first of which reads: "For every child, spiritual and moral training to help him stand firm under the pressure of life." Are we providing our children with a training which is equal to and stronger than the pressure of life today? Have we succeeded in creating a spiritual climate in the home through the practice of *Tzedakah,* the observance of Jewish ritual, the reading of uplifting books, the playing of ennobling music, and above all by treating one another with kindness and warm regard? Someone once said, "My religion is my mother." Are we, through our personal behavior, helping to make religion real to our children? Are we living the truths upon which we want them to build their lives? What kind of entries are we making in our children's Book of Life?

As Americans we must also ask ourselves a series of important questions. The ledger of Democracy is the sum total of the lines contributed by each of its citizens – whether they be occupants of high political office or humble workers in a factory or on a farm. Each of us makes a contribution to the volume of America. What kind of passages are we writing?

Are we practicing the slogans of brotherhood and tolerance

which we urge upon the Protestant majority in our own dealings with the Black minority?

We are all quick to recite the freedoms which, as Americans, we enjoy. But are we as prone to accept the responsibilities these freedoms involve? Are we using freedom of conscience to conscientiously seek the truth so that we may do it? Are we using our freedom of speech to speak out fearlessly in behalf of justice when it is violated? Are we using our freedom of thought in election years to think straight and hard about the fundamental issues so that our ballot may be cast with intelligence? Are we using our freedom of worship to strengthen the will to worship in ourselves and in those about us? Are we sufficiently dedicated to "free enterprise," to give up willingly a portion of our enterprise to secure freedom at home and abroad?

Do we appreciate the fact that the word "bless" and the word "bleed" come from the same root, and thereby remind us that our American blessings were dearly purchased? Do we act as though we realized that we can not preserve our Bill of Rights unless we are prepared to pay our bill of duties? What kind of entries are we making in America's Book of Life?

Lastly, let us consider our contribution to Judaism. Here, too, we must realize that the ultimate story will be the sum total of the individual paragraphs we each insert.

There was a time when we indulged ourselves in the comforting illusions that we could afford to let our rabbis worry about preserving and observing Judaism while the laymen went their merry ways. Today we know better. Today we realize that in order for the narrative of Judaism in America to be inspiring and significant, each Jew must write a meaningful passage. The story cannot be "ghost" written.

Well, what kind of passages are we each writing? Is Judaism to us like a woman in the ballad "a sometime thing?" Do we take it with us into our offices, our places of business, into the market-place, and make known our Jewishness through honest dealings and integrity? Are we using the vast leisure at our command, more than employed men have ever known, to inform ourselves about the unequalled heritage of Judaism, to enrich the communal institutions with our voluntary efforts?

Are we using the vast resources of the richest Jewish community in our history to strengthen our Seminaries and schools of Jewish learning and to support the third Jewish commonwealth in Israel through the purchase of bonds?

Are we availing ourselves fully of the opportunities for spiritual growth and weekly recreation which our Synagogue and Shabbat offer?

What kind of entries are we making in the Jewish Book of Life?

The American poet-philosopher, George Santayana, once wrote that "we commit the blotted manuscript of our lives more willingly to the flames when we find the immortal text half engrossed in a fairer copy." On Rosh Hashanah let us resolve to live with the constant awareness that our every deed is being inscribed on human parchment. We may never write a line which is printed, but we are all the authors of vital passages in living volumes. Let us strive to make "fairer copy." Let us so live that whatever text we inscribe in the *Sefer Hachayim*, the Book of the living, shall be *"L'maancha Elohim Chayim* – For Your sake, O God of Life." Amen.

Malicious Gossip – Moral Leprosy

A young physician in a small New England community was called in the middle of the night to an outlying farm where an elderly woman had suffered a heart attack. En route to the woman, the doctor drove his car into a tree and was seriously injured. Before another doctor could be summoned, the woman died.

The road on which the doctor's mishap occurred was a straight one, and the night had been clear. Soon someone suggested: "The doctor must have been drunk." Within hours that chance remark swept the community as an uncontested truth. The doctor's drunkenness had cost the poor old woman her life.

The local minister was one of the few people who refused to accept the gossip as fact and decided to investigate. He learned that the doctor had been working without sleep for more than 24 hours. The accident was the result of sheer exhaustion. Moreover, the county medical authorities determined that even had the doctor arrived on time, he could not have saved the woman's life.

Thus the doctor was officially cleared of any blame, but it took two years for his practice to recover. The gossip had proved quite damaging.

Sensitive to the exorbitant price paid by the victims of gossip, Judaism was sharp and severe in its condemnation of this social sin. The rabbinic teachers took the Hebrew word for "leper," and by dividing it into two words read it to mean "he who speaks evil of another." Thus they considered slander in the moral realm what leprosy was in the physical realm—a loathsome disease.

Gossip, the sages said, harms three people: the one who speaks it, the one of whom it is spoken, and the listener. Once spoken, the malicious words cannot be recalled. They are like the feathers of a bag that has burst open on a windy night. There is no way to retrieve them.

One of God's most precious gifts to us is the power of speech. It separates us from the beasts and from the world of nature. It should be used with kindness, care and compassion.

Henry Van Dyke has given us two excellent guideposts. "Never believe anything bad about anybody unless you positively know that it is true. Never tell even that unless you feel that it is absolutely necessary and that God is listening while you tell it."

The Art of Loving—Ourselves

When Rabbi Akiba was asked to single out what he considered the fundamental principle of the Torah, he pointed to the glowing verse in Leviticus which has become known as the Golden Rule:"You shall love your neighbor as your self." We like that answer, don't we? It leaves us feeling warm all over. In a world where men are usually at each other's throats, it is reassuring to hear the call to love each other unconditionally. Under the spell of this enchanting doctrine, my neighbor seems to have first call upon my affection, my compassion, my generosity.

If the truth must be told, Rabbi Akiba was not quite prepared to go that far. His reservations are reflected in a discussion of a hypothetical situation of which we read in the Sifra, the oldest Rabbinic commentary on Leviticus. A and B are making their way through the desert. A has a limited quantity of water while B has none. The amount of water is sufficient to enable one of them to reach civilization. If they share the water, neither will survive. What is the morally correct answer to this fateful dilemma?

A colleague of Rabbi Akiba, Ben Petura by name, declared that the right course is for A to share his water with B even though this action seals a double doom. Rabbi Akiba ruled otherwise. It seemed to him a wanton waste of one life to act in a way which makes it necessary for two to die where one could survive, and perhaps run for help for the other. But who shall drink – A who owns the water, or B whom he is obliged to love as himself? Rabbi Akiba permits A to drink his own water because "your life takes precedence over the life of your fellowman."

Rabbi Akiba, it appears, noted carefully that the Golden Rule commanded man to love his neighbor *as himself*. If indeed the Torah had wished to obligate man unconditionally to surrender his life for his neighbor, it should have said: "You shall love your neighbor *more than* your self." Under the circumstances then, I have a prior obligation to love myself.

From a spiritual point of view, Rabbi Akiba's position seems invulnerable. For ultimately why am I duty bound to love my neighbor? Is it not because he, like myself, is a child of God, the embodiment of the divine essence, a unique, unduplicable creature? I must love in him that which I love in myself. Conversely, I must love in myself that which I love in him. I must remember that I, no less than he, am a refraction of divinity. I must love that divine essence wherever I encounter it, and since I meet it first in myself, my obligation to love starts at that point.

What Rabbi Akiba was saying to us in effect was this. Self-love is a legitimate principle by which to order our lives. It is not something for which we need to apologize or of which we should be ashamed. Indeed, the *biblical* verse which most eloquently urges us to love one another, assumes our right to love ourselves. It even uses that love as a standard by which we are to measure our love for our neighbor. Nor was Rabbi Akiba's an isolated opinion in the tradition. Gentle Hillel seems to be saying no less in his well-known rhetorical question: "If I am not for myself, who will be for me?" Another echo of this same thought is found in the Talmudic principle *"Adam karov li'atzmo*–a man is his own next of kin." If I am to feel a sense of kinship with my neighbor who is close to me, can I feel any lesser kinship to my closest neighbor–myself?

Erich Fromm, in his brief and valuable study *The Art of Loving,* makes an acute distinction between selfishness and self-love. He shows that they are not at all synonymous. On the contrary, selfishness and self-love are actually opposites. The selfish person who is interested exclusively in himself, who seems bent on taking pleasure and incapable of giving any, who judges all people and all things by their usefulness to him–such a person does not really love himself too much. He loves himself too little! Indeed he is incapable of loving and actually hates himself. He stands in the way of his own pleasures. He seems to be caring too much for himself, but he is only masking his underlying failure to care for his real self. The selfish person who cannot love others, cannot love himself either.

The cruelty we inflict upon others is matched only by the cruelty we inflict upon ourselves. We can and do punish ourselves in a variety of terrible ways. If we do not love ourselves properly, we are inflexibly unforgiving to ourselves. Old transgressions, real or imagined, are kept constantly fresh and bristling, and we exact perpetual atonement from ourselves by harsh self-condemnation. In the absence of a wholesome love for ourselves, we make grossly inflated demands of ourselves, demands which by their very nature we cannot satisfy. Thus they contain within themselves their inevitable frustrations with which they plague and torment us.

So much of the sickness in the world comes from this sickness of soul. Too often, we do not have a healthy love for ourselves. We grossly exaggerate our inadequacies and thus fail to live with courage and daring. We underestimate our powers and permit them to go untapped and uncultivated. The worthy ambitions we never attain are insignificant alongside the ones morbid self-deprecation keeps us from striving for.

The bruises the world can inflict upon us are no greater than those we are prone to inflict upon ourselves. In extreme instances of self-hate, man resorts to alcoholism, dope addiction, physical self-mutilation and even suicide. Suicide also takes more subtle forms. Sometimes it is only partial as when a man kills off his creative instincts or perverts his talents. Our suicide can also be drawn out, a sort of chronic condition, with a little piece of ourselves being killed off at a time. "Which of us," asks Balzac, "hasn't killed himself two or three times before he is thirty?" If we are not kindly disposed to ourselves, we offend those who wish to show us kindness, repel the love that is tendered, the embrace that is freely offered. Our self-contempt breeds poisons in others no less than in ourselves.

The importance of loving ourselves acquires heightened emphasis from the simple reflection that we cannot escape ourselves. When the presence of others proves too much a drain upon our resources or good-will, we can find relief by withdrawal or separation. If that is not immediately possible, we find solace in the knowledge that it can be effected after a while. But what comfort is available when we cannot tolerate our *constant* companions – ourselves? Anyone who has engaged in the futile endeavor to leave himself behind is likely to exclaim, as Emerson once did: "I went to Naples and behold, Emerson was there." One of life's unavoidable coercions is the obligation to spend our entire lives with ourselves. We are our own inescapable neighbors. It is therefore an act of elementary wisdom to develop kindly feelings for that neighbor. You shall love your neighbor who is yourself.

To remain incapable of loving is not merely to offend against our fellow man. It is to sin most grievously against ourselves. In the commandment to love one another we find more than a basic principle for the moral society. It is a deeply-rooted need for a healthy individual. This was what Hillel taught in the second part of the maxim we referred to earlier. After affirming his primary duty to love himself, "If I am not for myself, who will be for me?", he hastened to add: "But when I am *only* for myself, what am I?" How large a package does a man make wrapped up in himself? To love my fellow man is, in the last analysis, not an act of altruism. It is the highest kind of self-love. You shall love your neighbor if you truly love yourself.

For that is how God made us. We live as we love. We are not meant to be separate and apart. We are meant to belong to one another, to reach out across the darkness, to huddle together in the cold, to hold hands in the slippery places, to skip together in the sunshine. Love blunts the sharp edge of sorrow, provides a handle for our burdens, adds richness to music, depth to beauty.

Touch Me with Noble Anger

In the late 1970s, during the days of long lines at the gas pump, one motorist saw another get into line in front of him. Some hot words were exchanged, and the fellow who was in line first got so angry he whipped out a gun and killed the other fellow.

Some teenagers at a London birthday party were celebrating rather noisily through the night. One of the disturbed neighbors got so angry he threw a firebomb into the house. Result: nine killed and thirty injured.

Some time ago a fire killed twenty-six people at Stouffer's Inn in Harrison. New York. The fire was believed to have been started by a disgruntled employee who got angry because he'd been told that he was going to be dismissed.

We read these stories and we are quick to moralize what a terrible and destructive emotion anger is. ANGER, we are reminded, is only one letter removed from DANGER. And we can sympathize fully with the little fellow whose angry outburst brought him swift punishment. "Dear God," he was later heard praying, "please take away my temper, and while you're at it, take away my father's temper too."

Our society frowns upon any display of anger. It is considered a nasty breach of social etiquette. It is viewed as evidence of a lack of self-control. And as the expression *getting mad* indicates, to be angry is often taken as a sign of madness. The Roman poet Horace defined anger as "temporary lunacy."

Despite all this, there is in fact nothing wrong with anger. It is not "bad" or "sinful"; it is as normal and as healthy as grief, love, joy, fear, sadness. Anger is a basic part of our human equipment, found in earliest infancy, as a response, for example, to frustration or rejection.

Anger that is denied an outlet is like a festering sore which can poison the body and the mind. It is the stuff of which ulcers are made. It can cause blood pressure to rise, depression to set in.

Anger that is bottled up can lead to guilt, anxiety, dangerous driving. In its ultimate form, it turns in upon oneself and can even lead to suicide. When an angry person says, "Boy, am I burned up," he may be giving an excellent description of the ravages being wrought within him by suppressed anger.

If our prisons are full of people who expressed their anger in unacceptable ways, our psychiatric hospitals are full of people who have not been able to express their anger at all.

We have to overcome our fear of expressing the anger we feel. As the late Dr. Michael J. Halberstam counseled, we have to "let ourselves really get mad." Moreover, we should express our anger "loud and clear, at the real target, complete with shouting and table-pounding if the feeling is strong enough – but please, no pounding on people."

We can go further and observe that anger, constructively channeled, can be a mighty force for good. The wheels of progress were frequently moved by the steam of anger. Moses left the security of the Pharaoh's palace and threw in his lot with his miserable brothers and sisters because he was profoundly angered by injustice and oppression. Lincoln's fierce opposition to slavery was born out of anger; when he stood one day at a slave auction and saw a screaming woman being wrenched away from her husband and child, he vowed in his indignation: "That's wrong, and if I ever get a chance to hit it, I'll hit it hard."

Long ago a Hebrew sage taught that "he who conquers his anger is more to be admired than he who conquers a city." To conquer anger does not mean to try to suppress it, to be ashamed of it, to deny its legitimacy. To conquer anger means to express it at the appropriate time, in an appropriate manner.

Aristotle anticipated modern psychology when he wrote: "Anybody can become angry – that is easy; but to be angry with the right person, and to the right degree, and at the right time and for the right purpose and in the right way – that is not within everybody's power and is not easy."

Perhaps then the prayer of the little fellow is not our prayer after all. We should not ask God to take away our temper. Instead, we should ask in Shakespeare's words: "Touch me with noble anger."

Uncritical Lovers – Unloving Critics

The biblical character Balaam is better remembered for his talking donkey than for any of the words he himself uttered. But we may be surprised to learn that some of the most extravagant and beautiful tributes to the Israelites in our entire Bible were spoken by Balaam.

Balaam, we will recall, was believed to possess a special power. As Balak, the king of Moab, said to him: "I know that whomever you bless is blessed and whomever you curse is cursed." And since Balak dreaded the alleged military might of the approaching Israelites, he engaged Balaam to put the curse on them. Much to Balak's dismay, however, he who came to curse remained to bless.

His praise borders on the rhapsodic. "None has beheld iniquity in Jacob, neither has one seen perverseness in Israel; the Lord his God is with him. . . ." And in a burst of admiration which has become the first words we utter when we enter the synagogue, Balaam exclaims: "How beautiful are your tents, O Jacob, your dwellings, O Israel!"

Now the strange thing about Balaam is the fate he suffered at the hands of the Jewish authorities in post-Biblical times. He is called *Bilam ha-rasha*, "Balaam the wicked." Why such a harsh verdict? Is this the way to treat a friend?

A Hasidic *Rebbe* gave a suggestive explanation for the unfavorable light in which the tradition regarded Balaam. His intention was not to help the Israelites but to hurt them. By lauding them so profusely he wanted to persuade them that they had already attained perfection and therefore did not need to strive to improve themselves.

Had they taken him seriously and accepted his inflated estimate of themselves they would have deteriorated and disappeared as did the other peoples the Bible mentions.

What saved the Israelites from such a fate were the stern rebukes and the strong criticisms of the prophets of Israel. Because the prophets loved their people, they sought to spur them on to ever greater achievement, and they therefore never grew weary of castigating them for their moral failures and shortcomings.

The *Rebbe's* insight was echoed by Winston Churchill who once wrote in another context: "Censure is often useful, praise often deceitful."

But how many of us are philosophical enough to accept censure and criticism? The Book of Proverbs assures us: "Rebuke a wise man and he will bless you"; but how many of us bless our critics? Criticism is a blow to our ego, an assault upon our self-image. Words of criticism hurt; often they hurt longer than a physical blow. How true the

Yiddish adage: "A slap passes, a word remains." We can even understand the outraged complaint of Chicago's former mayor, Richard Daley: "The press has vilified me, they have crucified me; yes, they have even criticized me!"

Hard as it is to accept criticism, it is so necessary and so beneficial. Taken seriously it can prove a great stimulus to growth. A genuine friend is not one who rehearses all our virtues. We already know them quite well, thank you. A good true friend is one who cares enough about us to call attention in a gentle way to our faults. That's a friendship worth cultivating.

What is true of us as individuals is also true of a country. A reliable measure of our loyalty is our willingness to criticize the land we love. We thrill to the patriotic fervor of Capt. Stephen Decatur who exclaimed: "My country, may she always be in the right, but my country, right or wrong!" However, we suspect that a more helpful patriotism was voiced by the American statesman Carl Schurz: "My country, may she always be in the right. If right, to be kept right, if wrong to be set right."

America, John Gardener once observed, is caught in a crossfire between its uncritical lovers and its unloving critics. The same might be said of Israel. There are those who love Israel so totally and so fervently that in their eyes Israel can do no wrong. And there are those who oppose Israel so completely that in their eyes Israel can do no right.

We heard a great deal from these unloving critics during the Lebanese incursion. So intemperate was their attack, so violent their language, so distorted their perspective, that Norman Podhoretz could amply document a charge of anti-Semitism against them.

What America needs, what Israel needs, what each of us needs, are neither uncritical lovers nor unloving critics. The uncritical lovers overlook faults. The unloving critics are blind to virtues. What we truly need are loving critics. Because they criticize out of love they bring growth and blessing. They also prove themselves worthy descendants of the prophets in whose footsteps they follow.

The Obsolete Commandment

Two young men were leaving a service during which they had heard a sermon on the Ten Commandments. After a few moments of silence one of them muttered: "Well, at least I never made any graven images."

The second commandment does seem to be so universally observed that it has been called "the obsolete commandment." Who worships graven images today, anyway?

When we read in the *Sidrah* that our ancestors fashioned a golden calf and worshipped it, it all sounds so very primitive. We're way beyond that, aren't we? Josephus was so embarrassed by the golden calf episode that he omitted it altogether from his Greek narrative of Jewish "Antiquities." Why tell the "goyim" about this spiritual relapse our ancestors suffered only forty days after they stood at Mount Sinai?

On second thought, however, perhaps the worship of the golden calf is not merely an incident that happened long ago; it may even be a metaphor depicting our own situation.

A magazine cartoon showed two cigar-smoking, well-dressed men relaxing in huge upholstered chairs. One confides to the other: "It was terrible! I dreamed the dollar was no longer worth worshipping!"

"Contemporary life," wrote Will Herberg, "is idolatry ridden to an appalling degree." Perhaps the second commandment isn't obsolete after all.

Somebody has identified a new disease in our country. It is called "Materio-Sclerosis," an insatiable hunger for the acquisition of things, more things, more expensive things.

On any given Sunday morning our pulpits and airwaves carry messages denouncing communism as "godless materialism" or "atheistic materialism." How about our own brand of materialism?

The Communists admit they are materialistic but we deny it. We imprint on all our currency (in very small letters) "In God We Trust." But do we trust in God as much as we trust in that money? Did Dr. George A. Butterick exaggerate when he said that in our society success consists of "a fairly nasty mixture of cash and gadgets?"

The officiating clergyman at the funeral of Harold Wallace Ross, the editor and founder of *The New Yorker,* said of him: "He hated all tyrannies, not least the insidious tyranny of things." In this land of the free many of us have succumbed to the tyranny of things. We suffer from materio-sclerosis. In the inner shrine of our personal sanctuaries, there stands a calf of gold.

All this is not to say that we are supposed to renounce all striving for wealth and take to the hills. Judaism never considered poverty a virtue. As one of Sholom Aleichem's characters says: "Poverty is no crime but it is no great honor either."

Just as Judaism did not consider poverty a virtue, it did not consider wealth a sin. It did not say with the New Testament that "It is easier for a camel to pass through the eye of a needle than it is for a rich man to enter into the kingdom of Heaven."

What Judaism did do was to alert us to the perils inherent in possessions, the tyranny which lurks in things, the danger of becoming afflicted with materio-sclerosis and worshipping the golden calf.

What are some of the symptoms of this idolatry? We make a graven image of gold when we sacrifice our health for it, when we surrender our moral integrity for it, when we neglect our families for it, when we betray our principles for it.

We worship the golden calf when we forget that some of the most precious things in life cannot be bought with gold. Genuine love, true friendship, a clear conscience, strength of character, peace of mind, serenity of spirit, self-respect – these are not listed on any exchange.

Henrik Ibsen spoke directly on this theme when he wrote: "Money can buy the husk of things but not the kernel. It brings you food but not appetite, medicine but not health, acquaintances but not friends, servants but not faithfulness, days of joy but not peace or happiness."

Before we leave our theme we ought to note that the Torah tells us that our ancestors used their treasures not only to fashion a golden calf but also to build a sanctuary in the desert. This prompted a rabbinic comment: "With jewels they sinned and with jewels they were restored to God's favor."

Gold need not become an object of worship. Used with wisdom and compassion it can help bring an awareness of God's presence even in a wilderness.

Are We Outliving Ourselves?

In J. P. Marquand's novel, *Point of No Return,* there is a sharply pointed comment made about the principal character. It is said of him, "He knew all the little answers but he missed the large questions." He knew the little answers – how to keep advancing himself on his job, how to make life comfortable – but he missed the big questions: What is the purpose of life? How can it be made meaningful? What does it all add up to?

So much of our daily living is devoted to the little answers. What shall I wear today? What movie shall we see tonight? What shall I prepare for dinner? These are typical of our ordinary pedestrian concerns. But what of the truly larger questions that go to the very core of the human enterprise?

I would like to direct our attention to a question suggested by one of the saddest lines a man ever wrote about himself. The writer was the great 19th century poet, Lord Byron, whose poetic genius was in sharp contrast to his woefully dissolute character. His untamed passions precipitated his untimely death at the age of thirty-six, but even before then he summed up his personal tragedy in a self-indictment which was remarkable both for its insight and its frankness. "I have outlived myself," he wrote, "by many a year."

At first blush this sounds like a fantastic statement, but it was frightfully true. Byron was perceptive enough to realize that he had lived on after the best in him had died.

We human beings, who are capable of living on after we have died, are also liable to die while we are still alive. This, I take it, is the true meaning of the oft-quoted rabbinic paradox: "The righteous, even after death, are alive. The wicked, even while they live, are dead." This affliction, however, is not limited only to the wicked. Listen to one of the most kindly and dedicated spirits of our time, Dr. Albert Schweitzer: "The tragedy of life is not . . . in the fact of death itself. The tragedy of life is what dies inside a man while he lives."

Let us ask ourselves the big question: Are we outliving ourselves?

To help us in our probing let us break down our big question into three more specific ones which, I believe, touch on those sensitive areas of life which are most perishable.

Let us ask in the first place: Have we outlived our ideals and our dreams?

Dr. Albert Schweitzer, whom we quoted a moment ago, has

penetratingly described the sad process by which we shake off the lovely buds which flower on our youthful tree of life. One of the glorious characteristics of youth is its capacity for bold dreams, its ability to believe in the good and the true and the beautiful. But as we grow older we tend to imitate the weary and the cynical adults, and we shed the high resolves and noble dreams which set us aflame in our tender years. Dr. Schweitzer describes the process:

"We believed once in the victory of truth; but we do not now. We believed in goodness; we do not now. We were zealous for justice, but we are not so now. We trusted in the power of kindness, peaceableness; we do not now. We were capable of enthusiasm, but we are not so now. To get through the shoals and storms of life more easily we have lightened our craft, throwing overboard what we thought could be spared. But it was really our stock of food and drink of which we deprived ourselves; our craft is now easier to manage but we ourselves are in a decline."

It would be most instructive for all of us and very humbling for many of us, if we compared our goals today with the ideals we cherished ten or twenty years ago. How many lives have suffered a progressive deterioration of motive, a gradual contraction of purpose and shrinking of the horizons?

How many of us went forth in our chosen vocations dedicated to justice and then decided to play it safe?

How many of us swore in our youthful hearts that we would try to heal the hurt of humanity only to find ourselves preoccupied exclusively with our own comforts and luxuries?

How many of us stood on the threshold of parenthood and vowed that we would execute faithfully the sacred responsibility it confers, only to become absentee parents who give our children everything except what they need most, ourselves?

How many of us promised ourselves that when we had more time, when life's economic demands would become less insistent, we would take seriously our obligations as Jews? We would read, we would attend adult classes, we would lend a hand in communal endeavors, we would take our children to the finest place a parent can take a child–to synagogue services. Then we came upon more leisure than Jews have ever had, we became more comfortable than a Jewish community has ever been, and we decided to invest our added time and resources exclusively in amusement, recreation and self-delight.

There is a melancholy anecdote concerning two little girls in Nazi Germany. Each thought herself to be a pure Aryan. When they became more intimately acquainted, one confided that she had a Jewish grandmother. "That's strange," said the second one, "I have a Jewish grandmother too."

The first thought for a moment and said: "I know what it is. That's what happens to people as they become older. They turn into Jews."

Well, many promised ourselves in our younger years that as we grew older we would turn into better Jews. But do the advancing years find us growing closer or drifting further away?

How many of us have become so preoccupied with immediates that we have lost sight of ultimates, so that George Eliot's description of Silas Marner might well apply to us too: "His life had reduced itself to the mere functions of weaving and hoarding without a contemplation of an end towards which these functions tended. So year after year Silas Marner had lived in this solitude, his guineas rising in the iron pot, and his life narrowing and hardening itself more and more into a mere pulsation of desire and satisfaction, which had no relation to any other being."

Here then is a big question indeed for each of us: Have we outlived our dreams and our ideals?

Dr. Schweitzer advises us: "The great secret of success is to go through life as a man who never gets used up. Grow into your ideals so that life can never rob you of them." Yes, that is the secret of successful living, not in the sense that the popular slogans and catch phrases of our commercial society envision it, but as it is seen by people who hold life sacred and look upon man as a creature of infinite potentialities. For what after all is our uniquely human endowment? Our will to live? Scarcely! The horse also wants to live. Our preeminence over the beast is that we want to live a maximum life. We can become possessed by a dream, enslaved by an ideal, and we can go through life without getting used up.

When we return the Torah to the Ark we pray, chadesh yamaynu k'kedem – "Renew our days as of old." Against the background of what we have been saying this becomes one of our most urgent needs. We need to renew the high resolves and deep yearnings of old if we are not to outlive our own grandest aspirations. And the message of our tradition is that this prayer can be answered. The lesson of the lives of the great souls of Jewish history is that this prayer has been answered.

"Ah, great it is to believe the dream
As we stand in youth by the starry stream,
But a greater thing is to fight life through
And to say at the end, the dream is true."

Let us proceed now to our second question which I would put as follows: Have we outlived our appreciation for the commonplace blessings of life?

The importance of holding on to our youthful sense of wonder and enthusiasm at the sheer glory of living is so obvious that I hesitated to deal with it. But the longer I go on observing life, the more convinced I become that the true function of the pulpit is not so much to elucidate the obscure as it is to emphasize the obvious.

A bold fact of our daily lives is that they are too often untouched by an appreciation for the countless blessings close at hand precisely because they are so close at hand. Much of the prevailing tension in our personal lives issues from our inability to find satisfaction in our already abundant possessions. Much of our chasing after excitement and thrills is rooted in our failure to find contentment in the more placid joys of life. Much of the wearying monotony and insipid taste of our daily routine stems from our failure to behold in each day a never-ending succession of God's unfolding kindnesses. And if we have outlived this gratefulness for life's bounty, have we not left behind life's most tasty ingredient? For is not the City of Contentment, as someone said, located in the State of Mind?

Do you recall what Emily says in Thornton Wilder's drama *Our Town*? You remember that after her death Emily is permitted to relive a day of her childhood. When she does so, she realizes how badly she failed to appreciate the beauty and the significance of life. "It goes so fast. We don't have time to look at one another. . . . I didn't realize. . . . So all that was going on and we never noticed. . . . One more look- . . . .Good-by. . . . Good-by Grover's Corners. . . . Mama and Papa. . . . Good-by to clocks ticking . . . and Mama's sunflowers. . . . And food and coffee. And new ironed dresses and hot baths . . . and sleep and waking up. Oh, Earth, you're too wonderful for anybody to realize you. Do any human beings ever realize life while they live it? – Every, every minute."

Some of us must travel half way around the globe before we discover the beauty of our homes and the blessing of the familiar faces. Others must become physically stricken before we know the glory of walking and feeding ourselves. Still others must be threatened with the loss of loved ones before we appreciate their sustaining influence in our lives. And almost all of us must see the threatening fist of the conqueror before we wake up to the privileges of freedom and equality which are the American heritage.

But Judaism has a simpler prescription for keeping alive a sense of gratefulness. That is the way of prayer. To most of us, prayer is synonymous with petition. We are moved to pray only when we want something very badly – the recovery of a loved one, a year of life and sustenance for our families, escape from immanent danger. If we examine our prayer-book carefully, however, we will find that so much of it is a catalogue of life's blessings whose daily recitation is designed to impress upon us the inexhaustible wealth with which a merciful God has endowed us.

The Jew who has prayed thoughtfully in the morning has been reminded, among other things, of the joy of waking up, the boon of being free, the blessing of sight, the privilege of being a moral creature, the miracle of the human body, the benediction of being under the benevolent care of God who clothes us, guides us, gives us strength when we are weary and "who has provided for all my needs." This mood of gratefulness runs through our prayerbook and in the heart of the Jew who uses it, it puts a magnet which, as it sweeps through the hours, finds in every one of them particles of mercy and blessing.

For the last, I have left the most important question of all: Have we outlived our belief in God?

The newspaper reported an amusing and instructive coincidence some time ago. In a small town in Minnesota three ministers posted the titles of their Sunday morning sermons on their respective bulletin boards. And as one walked through the town, these are the titles he read in order:

> Where is He?
> He is Here.
> God Changes His Address.

As this item caught my eye, it occurred to me that this is the sad sequence that modern man has followed in his religious development. As a child he was full of questions about God. What is God like? Why can't I see God? If I close my room, can God still get in? Where is He?

The questioning stage gave way to certainty. The growing child was most receptive to a belief in God, when it was sympathetically presented. He then felt with assurance: "He Is Here."

But somehow as he grew older, his certainty left him and if God did in fact exist, He was no longer too close, for God had changed his address.

Now this seems like a strange thing to talk about to Jews who have come to synagogue on Kol Nidre to pray. Surely if anyone believes in God, he would be the synagogue Jew. And I suppose if we were to ask for a show of hands now, God would get a rather substantial vote.

But I often wonder just how vital and significant this belief in God is to us. Does it really make a difference in our lives or is it similar, say, to our belief that the world is round? Interesting, of some consequence to map makers, pilots, and ship captains, but of no real relevance to our daily doings.

Do we believe in the God of Micah who makes demands of us in our places of business, in our dealings with our fellow man: "What does the Lord your God require of you, to do justice, to love mercy, to walk humbly with thy God?"

Do we believe in a God who is not remote, but who as the Psalmist says: "Is near to all who call upon Him, to all who call upon Him in truth?"

Do we believe in God even when He has prospered us so that we say "For it is from Your hand that we have all?"

If we have outlived that kind of dynamic belief in God, if as far as we are concerned God has changed His address, has not something of greatest importance gone out of our lives?

One of the leading religious spokesmen of our time has put it this way: "Whoever discards religious faith should appoint a day of mourning for his soul, and put on sack-cloth and ashes. He must take from his life the greatest thought that man the thinker ever had, the finest faith that man the worker ever leaned on, the surest help that man the sinner ever found, the strongest reliance that man the sufferer ever trusted in; the loftiest vision that man the lover ever saw, the only hope that man the mortal ever had."

An atheist has been defined as one "without invisible means of support." If life is to stand under the tremendous pressures that weigh down upon it, if it is to be filled with a sense of worthwhileness and beauty, we need invisible means of support. We must recapture the conviction that God has not changed His address.

Give Me the Facts

A famous television detective would begin his investigation by saying: "Give me the facts. Just give me the facts." He would then take those bare facts and reconstruct the crime that had been committed.

Despite our celebrated sleuth's skillful use of the facts, the fact is that facts alone are not enough on which to build a philosophy of life. What is decisive is what we do with the facts of life, how we interpret them, what meaning we see in them.

A dramatic biblical illustration of this truth is found in the celebrated espionage mission Moses launched in the wilderness. He sent a dozen men, one each from the twelve tribes of Israel, to infiltrate the land of Canaan and study the possibility of subduing it. The twelve performed their sensitive mission and returned with their reports. They all surveyed the same land, observed the same people, evaluated the same conditions, and came back with two diametrically opposite conclusions. Ten said that there was no way they could conquer the land. Two said they could indeed accomplish this objective. So here we have it. The same set of facts, but oh, what different conclusions!

The fundamental truth about us is that we see facts not as they are but as we are. Experience is not what happens to us but how we perceive and react to what happens to us. The same facts will produce totally different reactions in different people.

A shoe company, we are told, sent two salesmen to explore the market potential for their product in Africa. After several weeks of investigation, one salesman wired back: "Nobody wears shoes. Consumer demand is zero. The situation is hopeless."

The other salesman wired back an entirely different message: "Nobody wears shoes. Demand limitless. No competition. The situation is fantastic." Same facts—different interpretations.

A much more serious and fateful illustration of this truth was provided by the reactions of various people to the Nazi nightmare. When postwar Germans were asked why they did not help their Jewish fellow citizens, many of them answered, "What could we do?" When the Danish people who risked their lives to save their Jewish countrymen were asked why they helped them, they answered. "What else could we do?" Same facts – different interpretations.

You see, we human beings not only react, we also respond, and the measure of a human being is to be found in the nature of that response. Any clergyman can cite from his personal experience so many illustrations of people whom sorrow made bitter. He can also cite as many or more illustrations of people whom sorrow made better.

There are people who emerge from an encounter with grief richer human beings, taller in stature, more compassionate, more sensitive, more appreciative of the gift of life. They can then say with the poet William Wordsworth: "A deep distress hath humanized my soul."

The same fire that melts the butter hardens the egg. The same wind that extinguishes a match will fan a flame into a stronger blaze. Man does not live by facts alone.

An aggressive atheist in a mood to advertise his point of view painted these words on a roadside billboard: "God is nowhere." A seven-year-old girl riding in the family car passed the billboard. She was thrilled and excited, for she read these words: "God is now here."

The Art of Giving Thanks

The obligation to cultivate a lively sense of appreciation for the manifold blessings a gracious God heaps upon us daily, runs like a golden thread throughout the fabric of our religious faith. The Jew who adheres faithfully to his spiritual obligations is enjoined to recite no less than one hundred blessings from the time he awakes in the morning to the time he retires at night. So highly did our sages prize the mood of thanksgiving that one of them declared: "In the time to come, all the offerings will be abolished except the thank-offering; all the prayers will be abolished except the prayers of thanksgiving." Thus the art of giving thanks enjoyed a special pre-eminence over all the other religious disciplines. Our tradition would seem to agree with Cicero that gratitude is not only the greatest of virtues but the mother of them all.

At first blush, it appears easy and natural to cultivate the art of giving thanks. It is no more than a question of good manners, a widely used social amenity transposed into the domain of religion. One of the first phrases we teach the mumbling child is "thank you," to impress upon him a sense of gratitude for the favors he enjoys. What could be more natural then, than to pause occasionally to drop God a brief "thank you" for His kindness which endures forever? And yet as we view human nature at work, we cannot fail to be impressed with the difficulty so many of us have in developing the art of giving thanks.

A well-known legend underscores this unhappy truth. Two angels were each given a basket and sent to earth to gather up the prayers that were offered there. One was to collect only man's petitions. The other was to gather up his prayers of gratitude. When they returned, the angel bearing the requests was carrying a basket filled to overflowing. The other angel was deeply depressed for his basket was all but empty.

The angels might very well have performed their mission among us in this land of vastly disproportionate good fortune. Our gripes and grumblings are louder than our expressions of gratitude. We complain more often than we experience contentment. Our awareness of what we lack is more persistent than our acknowledgment of what we possess. Our clamoring is constant while our appreciation comes at widely separated moments.

How then can we cultivate the fine but difficult art of giving thanks regularly?

Needed first is a sense of humility, the kind of humility which overwhelms Jacob when he is returning to meet his brother Esau. Jacob is bringing with him great wealth which he has acquired during his twenty years with Laban. As he surveys his vast possessions he recalls how little was his when last he stood in this very place as a fugitive from Esau's wrath. And in his prayers he exclaims: "I am unworthy of all the kindnesses which You have shown to Your servant, for it was only with a wanderer's staff that I once crossed this Jordan and now I have flourished into two mighty camps." Jacob is embarrassed by his riches because they serve to remind him of his own unworthiness. He better than anyone else, knows that his extravagant blessings far outweigh his modest desserts.

Jacob's reaction is far from typical. One of the built-in hazards of being human is the overpowering temptation to greet success in a mood of self-congratulation. The weeds of pride flourish most conspicuously in the soil of prosperity. The Bible speaks of the pride which goes before a fall. It would be no less in order to call attention to the pride which comes after a rise. When life becomes comfortable and upholstered, when our undertakings prosper and our possessions multiply, we are so prone to proclaim ourselves self-made men. What further demonstration do we need of our resourcefulness, our wisdom, our ingenuity, our cleverness?

Moses was not only a giant in the realm of morality but apparently he was also a keen student of human behavior. How well he understood the need to sound the repeated words of caution against the all too prevalent tendency to regard our blessings as proof of our ability or our virtue: "Beware lest you forget the Lord your God . . . Lest when you have eaten and are satisfied you say in your heart: 'My power and the might of my hand have gotten me this wealth.' " Apparently, Little Jack Horner was not the only one to become persuaded that he was really a very good boy simply because he had managed to pull a few plums out of life's pie. It never occurred to him to reserve a kind thought or word for the one who had baked the pie or the One who made the plums to grow.

It is supremely significant that the ancient Biblical festival of thanksgiving, the festival of Sukkot, which served as a model for the pilgrims, was born not in mighty prosperous Rome, nor in secure, amply endowed Greece. Thanksgiving had its origin in weak, insecure and tiny Judea. The poet was undoubtedly correct in speaking of "the glory that was Greece and the grandeur that was Rome." But while Greece enjoyed glory and Rome was resplendent in grandeur, it was lowly Judea that had gratitude.

Nor should we forget the bleak background against which the pilgrims marked their first Thanksgiving. Of the 102 passengers who landed at Plymouth Rock, 51 died within the first six months. Their graves had to be kept level with the ground in order to save them from desecration, and to keep from the Indians the knowledge of the frightful toll of casualties. Not a single family had been spared by death.

The survivors lived on the fringe of starvation in a hostile, unchartered world. They never knew what it was to have enough or to be secure. They stood alone against the forces of nature and man. These were the people who gathered to give thanks to Almighty God for His blessings and to express their humble dependence upon His mercies for their continuing life.

We need to approach our greater blessings in a similar mood. Like Jacob we too should confess: "*Katontee*–I am unworthy." Have we indeed created ourselves? Is it our genius that fashioned that most intricate of all miracles–the complex and wonderful mechanism we know as the human body? Have we set the stars in their courses, or commanded the sun to rise and set? Has our wisdom made the seed, or taught it how to yield the golden grain and the luscious fruit? Have we taught the birds to sing or the waves to dance? Did we create the air that surrounds us, or the breathing apparatus which sustains us? Has our blood purchased the freedom we enjoy? Have our bodies manned the ramparts of our faith? Have our minds discovered the cures that heal us, the vaccines that immunize our children, the skills that have extended our life span? Is it because of our excessive virtue that we live in a country which has only 6% of the world's land surface, 7% of the world's population and produces 50% of the world's goods? Are we more deserving than the hundreds of millions of fellow humans around the world who are hungry, cold and illiterate? Has our abundance of nobility spared us the fate that overtook six million of our brethren in Europe, or the devastation that was visited upon that unhappy continent in two world wars? I who can speak this message, and you who can hear it, have we been more upright and more compassionate than those who cannot speak and those who cannot hear?

Can we make even so fragmentary a list of our blessings without becoming submerged by an overpowering sense of humility, a moving and profound sense of gratitude?

If pride is one enemy of gratitude, callousness is another. The more often and the more regularly we receive any blessing, the less likely are we to be mindful of it, much less to feel under any obligation for it. That which is constantly granted is taken for granted.

Helen Keller expressed a similar sentiment from the vantage point of her personal tribulation. "I have often thought," she wrote, "that it would be a blessing if each human being were stricken blind and deaf for a few days at some time during his early adult life. Darkness would make him more appreciative of sight; silence would teach him the joys of sound."

After we read these words, there is a gnawing insistence to the poet's question:

> "Why is it we must come to know
> Belatedly from other's woe
> The gratitude we always owe?"

The answer is largely callousness. If we are to cultivate the fine art of giving thanks, we must keep a keen edge on our sense of awareness of the myriad blessings which are ours. A hundred blessings a day.

In addition to our pride and our callousness, there is still a third enemy of gratitude, closely related to the second but sufficiently distinct to be identified by itself. We might call it false perspective. If callousness makes us insensitive to the things we have, false perspective prompts us to focus unduly on the things we lack.

To keep our perspective clear, we might do well to follow the advice of Robert Southey. In one of his letters he tells us of a Spaniard who "always put on his spectacles when he was about to eat strawberries so that they might look bigger and more tempting. In just the same way," adds Southey, "I make the most of my enjoyments."

If only we could learn to magnify our blessings instead of exaggerating our troubles! Most of the time we are putting on our spectacles when we look at the things we lack. How large they loom. How we permit them to rankle. How often we permit the fly in the ointment to grow so huge that we see only the fly and forget that we also possess the ointment.

Grandma's eyesight wasn't as good as it used to be but there was nothing wrong with her perspective. When asked about her health she answered softly: "I have two teeth left, and thank God they are directly opposite one another." Her spectacles were properly focused.

Viewing our blessings in proper perspective means something else too—something which goes to the very heart of the art of giving thanks. A true perspective on our possessions serves to remind us that they are given to us in trust, to use not only for our own pleasures and gratification, but also in the service of others. Gratitude at its highest goes beyond counting blessings. It involves sharing blessings. It leads not only to a sense of thankful dependence upon God, but also to an awareness of our duty to our fellow man. It talks not only of indebtedness to be acknowledged, but also of debts to be discharged. It takes us beyond saying thanks to giving thanks.

On our festivals the Torah commands us to be joyous. The Hebrew word spelling out this injunction is *"Visa-machta*–you shall rejoice."* By a slight revocalization of the word, our sages make it read *"Visee-machta*–you shall cause to rejoice."* They then go on to remind us that we must use our festive days as occasions to bring joy into the lives of "the stranger, the orphan and the widow." We are not truly grateful until we make it possible for others to experience gratitude too. True thanksgiving prompts us first to look up and then to reach out.

This, after all, is what we really mean when we say "much obliged." We mean that we are much obligated, we have incurred a debt which we are duty bound to repay. What is involved is not generosity but common honesty.

The truth is that every blessing we enjoy has been sacrificially paid for by others. We are indebted far beyond our embarrassed means to make adequate recompense. It is no accident that the word "bless" and the word "bleed" come from the same root. Every important blessing we enjoy–our freedom, our health, our heritage, our security–is dipped in the blood of generations of benefactors. There is nothing we can give which we did not first receive. Such obligations can never be fully liquidated. But neither are we exempt from making some sustained effort at repayment.

If we are truly thankful for our freedom we must be vitally concerned with the plight of those who still wear chains. If we are grateful for our share of God's abundance, we must share that abundance with the ill-fed, the ill-clad, the ill-housed. If we are genuinely appreciative of our own good health, the plight of the handicapped becomes a legitimate claim upon our financial resources. If we are sincere when we exclaim of our spiritual legacy, "happy are we, how goodly is our inheritance," then it becomes incumbent upon us to strengthen the institutions dedicated to disseminating a knowledge of Judaism. The art of giving thanks means ultimately no appreciation without reciprocation.

Every day is Thanksgiving Day on the calendar of the religious

Jew. To our one hundred daily blessings we might add one prayer of petition:

> "You have given so much to me.
> Give me one thing more – a grateful heart."
>
> Amen

IV

WHEN LIFE IS DIFFICULT

*God never closes a door in our lives without opening
another. Whenever one area of life is sealed off
another comes into view.*

Use and Misuse

A critic once wrote of a volume under review: "The cruelest thing you could do to this book is to read it a second time." One of the hallmarks of our Bible that makes it a classic is its capacity to yield new meanings and fresh insights every time we read it.

A case in point is the *Sidrah, Vayakhel*. Truth to tell, it is hardly a candidate for anyone's favorite Torah portion. It consists largely of a listing of the materials that went into the construction of the tabernacle in the wilderness, and the dimensions of each of its important appurtenances. Those of us who do not have any conspicuous architectural skills or curiosity, will probably skim over most of these chapters in a hurry.

But a rabbinic comment on this *Sidrah* calls attention to a truth worth pondering. Our Sages pointed out that in the previous Torah portion we read that our ancestors used their jewels to fashion a gold calf around which they danced as they chanted the idolatrous heresy: "This is your God, O Israel, who brought you out of the land of Egypt" (Exodus 32:4). In *this* Torah portion we read that these same ancestors used their jewels to build a tabernacle to the glory of the one God.

This use of the same materials for such vastly divergent purposes prompted our Sages to comment: "With earrings they sinned and with earrings they were restored to God's favor."

In this brief comment the rabbis emphasized the ambivalent

character of our possessions. They can be used for the meanest or the noblest purposes. They are in themselves morally neutral. Whether they are good or bad depends upon us, on how we use them.

This simple truth has wider ramifications. It applies to other crucial areas of our lives. Science, which has done so much to prolong human life and improve its quality, was used by the Nazis to build more efficient gas chambers and to conduct the most brutal experiments without anesthesia on men and women. The automobile which rushes a physician on a mission of mercy, carries a drunken driver on a mission of murder.

An article on lasers in one of our national magazines points out that next to the computer, they are the most versatile invention of the twentieth century. Lasers are still in the nursery stage, but the infant is growing fast. Lasers are already cutting concrete and steel and are being used to perform delicate eye surgery. Lasers may turn out to be an unprecedented boon by generating a new and inexhaustible source of energy, or they may further imperil our fragile planet by leading to ever more destructive and devastating weaponry.

The road to hell is paved with good inventions.

What is true of our possessions, of science, and indeed of all the instruments we use, is also true of most of our human endowments and emotions.

A *Hasid* once asked his *Rebbe* why the Almighty created the quality of human skepticism. After all, he said, everything that the Holy One, blessed be He, made, He fashioned for some benevolent purpose. But what possible benefit can skepticism bring? It only leads people to doubt the existence of the Almighty Himself.

To which the *Rebbe* replied: "My son, skepticism does indeed serve on occasion a most noble purpose. When a poor man comes to you for help do not send him away with the assurance that God will help him. At this time you must be a skeptic and doubt that God will help him. You must help him yourself."

Is anger good or bad? Again, it depends. To be sure anger is only one letter removed from danger. It wrecks homes, destroys friendships and frequently leads to impulsive violence. But on the other hand, as Tevya would say, the prophets were God's angry men. Oppression made them angry, injustice made them angry, human cruelty and dishonesty made them angry. And if they are still revered today, it is due in no small measure to their marvelous capacity to get angry at the right time, to the right degree, for the right reasons.

What is true of our instruments and our human endowments is also true of our circumstances. They too are neutral. Whether they bless us or break us depends on how we confront them, how we use them.

Edmund Ward in *The Main Chance* advises: "Drink champagne for defeats as well as victories. It tastes the same, and you need it more." I'll drink to that! But for a different reason. We should drink champagne to defeats because no defeat is final and no defeat cannot be used to teach us an important lesson.

William Bolitho has illumined this truth for us: "The most important thing in life," he wrote, "is not simply to capitalize on your gains. Any fool can do that. The important thing is to profit from your losses. That requires intelligence and it marks the difference between a man of sense and a fool."

In 1849 Nathaniel Hawthorne was dismissed from his government job in the customhouse. He came home a beaten man.

His wife listened to him as he poured out his heart, threw a few logs on the fire, set pen, ink and paper on the table, put her arms around him and said: "Now you will be able to write your novel." He did. That's how *The Scarlet Letter* came to be written.

In 1845, Heinrich Graetz, a newly ordained rabbi, applied for an important synagogue pulpit in Upper Silesia. During his trial sermon he developed pulpit palpitations, lost his train of thought and stammered through an incoherent sermon. He did not get the pulpit. His disappointment was crushing. Happily for us, he went on to discover his great literary and scholarship powers, and he became the eminent historian whose six volumes of Jewish history remain classics in their field.

A friend who was showing some slides of his pilgrimage to Israel projected one picture which baffled him. He paused a while and then confessed: "I'm not sure whether this is a picture of a sunrise or a sunset."

Unwittingly, he made a profound statement about many of life's experiences. So often we think we are going through a "sunset," and night is approaching and the outlook is black. But we later discover to our delight that it wasn't a "sunset" after all. It was really a "sunrise" ushering in a new day with new beginnings, new possibilities and new hope.

L'hayyim – To Life!

The *Sidrah "Hayyei Sarah"* contrasts sharply with its opening theme. The first portion of the Torah reading (Genesis 23) speaks of the death of the first Jewish mother, Sarah, Abraham's weeping and mourning for her, and then her burial. But despite its preoccupation with Sarah's death, the *Sidrah* bears the title *"Hayyei Sarah,"* *"The Life of Sarah."*

Nor is this the only time we find in the Torah a *Sidrah* whose title is in such striking contrast to its contents. The last Torah portion in Genesis begins with a deathbed scene. The Patriarch Jacob is taking final leave of his family. He blesses his grandchildren and his children. "And when Jacob finished charging his sons, he gathered up his feet into the bed, and died, and he was gathered unto his people" (Genesis 48:33).

The Torah then describes Jacob's burial and the period of mourning which both preceded and followed it.

What is the title of this *Sidrah? "Vayehi"–"And He Lived."*

It would appear that in these two titles of Torah portions dealing with death, our tradition wanted to soften the pain of bereavement by focusing on life. When a loved one dies we are overwhelmed by the awareness of what death has taken from us. At such a time our tradition would have us remember also what that life has left with us.

Death can only take from us what might have been. It cannot take from us what has already been. It cannot rob us of our past. The days and years we shared, the common adventures and joys, the "little, nameless acts of kindness and of love"–all these are part of the ineradicable record. Death has no dominion over them.

We who have lost loved ones know with unwavering certainty that for us our loved ones always remain living presences. Hans Zinsser went even further when he wrote: "At times the dead are closer to us than the living, and the wisdom and affection of the past stretch blessing hands over our lives, projecting a guardian care out of the shadows and helping us over hard places. For there are certain kinds of love that few but the very wise understand until they have become memories."

As we study human reactions to sorrow, we are struck by the frequency with which people who were so grievously impoverished by a death could yet find strength to express gratitude for that life.

Listen to the Chicago born Hebrew poet Reuben Grossman whose son Noam studied at the Hebrew University, became an officer in the Haganah and was killed in Israel's War of Independence. After his son's death, the poet changed his name to Avinoam which in Hebrew means "father of Noam." At the end of the *Shivah,* the father wrote a poem entitled: "Therefore, We Thank You God."

In it he lists all the things in Noam's life for which he feels "thanks pouring from the wound of our heart." Among them are:

> "For pleasant years,
> For one and twenty years
> Wherein You honoured us with him and lent him us,
> For his steps walking humbly by our side on the little isle of
>   life:
> Years sown with the peace of his being,
> When like a gliding swan he made his way erect with grace;
> Years shining with smiles
> Which like sunrays he spread around him,
> With good-hearted whispers, pardons by concession and
>   understanding,
> Years shining with the light of his two eyes,
> Where dreams yearned, mingled with the sorrow of fate,
> Having a pure look and upright before God and man.
> For this little gift,
> For twenty-one full years of life You gave him and us,
> We thank you. . . ."

Another bereaved father who found the strength to express gratitude amidst his grief was the celebrated American newspaper editor William Allen White. In reply to a friend who wrote him a condolence letter upon the death of his daughter Mary, White wrote a most moving and poignant letter of appreciation which he concluded with these words:

"Mrs. White and I are standing on our feet, realizing that the loss is heavy and the blow is hard, but not beating our hands against the bars and asking why. On our books Mary is a net gain . She was worth so much more than she cost, and she left so much more behind than she took away that we are flooded with joyous memories and cannot question either the goodness of God or the general decency of man."

When our tradition put the stamp of life on chapters dealing with death it also pointed perhaps to the powerful truth that ultimately it is not death but life that has the last word. The soul is imperishable and "the grave is not its goal." The souls of our loved ones, like our own, came from the great Source of Life and flow back into the eternal stream after our earthly pilgrimage is ended.

The pain of parting is mitigated by our faith in a divine providence which permits no life to be utterly destroyed. We are sustained by "the Soul's invincible surmise." This was the faith burst forth out of Emerson after the death of his young son: "What is excellent, as God lives, is permanent."

Perhaps all of Jewish wisdom in this matter is captured in the common practice we have all seen. Upon returning from the cemetery after a burial, we take a little whiskey and before we drink it we raise the glass and say: *"L'hayyim"* – to life!

Covering Our Sackcloths

It was a period of profound crisis for Samaria, the capital of the northern kingdom of ancient Israel. The King of Aram and his armies had besieged the city and its inhabitants were being starved to death. So intense had the hunger become, that mothers began to devour their young. When this news reached the King of Israel, the Bible tells us, "he rent his clothes . . . and the people looked and behold he had sackcloth within upon his flesh."

What a shock that sight must have been to the people! Each citizen knew of his personal troubles and tragedies. But how amazed they all must have been to see that beneath his royal robe, even the king was wearing a sackcloth – the symbol of personal sorrow and misfortune.

A deep truth speaks out to us from this incident – one that we ought to keep steadily before us especially in time of trouble. "Why did this happen to me?" people frequently ask the rabbi amidst sorrow, as though they alone were singled out by a malicious destiny as a target for its bitter shafts. We rarely stop to realize that even kings wear sackcloths.

The better I get to know people, the more impressed do I become with this one fact. Rare indeed is the individual without a sackcloth. Some of us wear the sackcloth of a deep frustration – a career to which we aspired but did not attain, a heart we sought but failed to win. Some of us wear the sackcloth of a haunting sense of inadequacy, or a deeply bruised conscience or an aching void left by the passing of a loved one. Blasted hopes, unrealized dreams, anguish and grief – is any life unfamiliar with them? Is not the sackcloth the common garment of all men?

There is a second significance to the biblical incident. The king wore his sackcloth *underneath*. He did not make of it his outer garment. He did not display it too prominently either to others or to himself. Here was an act of wisdom we would do well to emulate.

Fathers and mothers have sustained grievous losses during the past few years. Ours has been the tragic generation of which our stages spoke – the generation where parents bury children. Doubly tragic are those afflicted parents who have not learned to cover their sackcloths, who have made of it their outer garment.

In this matter, the rituals of Judaism concerning mourning contain an excellent prescription for emotional recovery from misfortune. Judaism prescribes a terminus to mourning. Just as it is a law that the *Kaddish* must be said for eleven months, so is it a law that the *Kaddish* may not be recited longer than eleven months. The *Shiva* period may likewise not be prolonged beyond seven days. After *Shiva*, the mourners must leave their sorrow-laden homes and go out into the healing sunshine of human society. After the prescribed period of mourning, the sackcloth must become an undergarment.

Some time ago, the widow of Colin Kelly was remarried. To some, her remarriage appeared as an act of disloyalty to the memory of her husband. In defense of what she had done, she said quite simply: "Of course you can never forget the past and the past will always color the present. But I do not think that you should let the past affect the present so much that there can be no future." This is an attitude which can usefully be applied to every sackcloth that life imposes. We must never let the past affect the present so much that there can be no future. If life is to be lived at all, we must learn to cover our sackcloths But with what shall we cover them?

The first thing we can use to cover our sackcloths, it seems to me, is the Robe of Understanding. We tend to regard trouble as an intruder and interloper who has no place in life's scheme of things. In the words of a popular song, we often think that the world was made only for fun and frolic. Nothing makes the wearing of life's sackcloths more difficult to endure than the fact that we are not prepared for them.

If we would learn to wear life's sackcloths properly we must cover them with the Robe of Understanding. We must realize that, as the Bible puts it, "Man is born to trouble." Trouble far from being a gate-crasher in life's arena actually has a reserved seat there. Human life is attended at its beginning by the piercing cries of the infant and, at its end, by the agonized wailing of the bereaved. In between, there are sadness, heartbreak, disease. For that reason, the great tragedians of literature have not wanted for themes. All they had to do was to observe life carefully and report it faithfully, and the tragedy spelled itself out. "Man is born to trouble."

I know that many will feel that such a gloomy view of life leads to pessimism and despair. Actually, the reverse is true. If we accept realistically life's sombre back-drop then the manifold blessings we enjoy will emerge in bolder relief. The love which nourishes us, the friendship which warms us, the beauty which inspires us, the health which sustains us – all these and the countless other blessings which are ours will be all the more gratefully welcomed.

God grant us the Robe of Understanding to cover our sackcloths.

But the Robe of Understanding, beautiful and becoming as it is, is not enough. For at best it can only teach us the spirit of resignation to our troubles, and it is not enough to merely accept trouble. We must do more. We must learn to use trouble and convert it into a stepping stone to triumph. For that we need the Robe of Wisdom.

In the 48th chapter of the Book of Isaiah, there is a very remarkable verse. The prophet is chastising his people, and among other things he says to them, according to Moffat's translation: "I purged you, but nothing came of it, testing you in the furnace but all in vain." Here the prophet is rebuking his people for having been through the furnace of affliction and having learned nothing from the experience,

"What," he is asking them, "have you to show for all the sufferings you experienced? The tragedy is not that you endured pain; the tragedy is that your pain was wasted, leaving you none the wiser, none the better."

Yes, the prophet expected his people to do more than accept trouble. He expected them to *use* it. The fact is that some of life's most valuable lessons can be and have been learned precisely in the classroom of adversity. We discern most clearly many a basic truth of life when our eyes are dimmed by tears. Robert Browning Hamilton expressed a common human reaction when he wrote:

> "I walked a mile with Pleasure
>   She chattered all the way
> But left me none the wiser
>   For all she had to say.
>
> "I walked a mile with Sorrow
>   And ne'er a word said she
> But oh the things I learned from her
>   When Sorrow walked with me."

We speak very often of *"victims* of circumstance" – people whose souls are crushed beneath the wheels of unfortunate events. We would do well to start thinking of *"victors* of circumstance" – people who use even negative circumstance and distill from it some new insight into life, keener understanding or more beautiful character. We often speak of people who were successful because they knew how to take advantage of good "breaks." We would do well to start thinking that people can be successful if they have the wisdom to capitalize on their bad "breaks." It is possible to be like Wordsworth's "Happy Warrior."

> "Who doomed to go in company with Pain
> And Fear, and Bloodshed, miserable train!
> Turns his necessity to glorious gain."

Or as the Psalmist puts it:

> "They pass through a valley of tears and
> convert it into a life-giving fountain."

God grant us the Robe of Wisdom to cover our sackcloths.

Thirdly, may I suggest that we cover our sackcloths with the Robe of Service. There is a legend of a sorrowing woman who came to a wise man with the heart-rending plea that he return to her the son she had just lost. He told her that he could comply with her request on one condition. She would have to bring to him a mustard seed taken from a home entirely free from sorrow. The woman set out on her quest. Years elapsed and she did not return. One day the wise man chanced upon her, but he hardly recognized her, for now she looked so radiant. He greeted her and then asked her why she never kept their appointment. "Oh" she said in a tone of voice indicating that she had completely forgotten about it, "well this is what happened. In search of the mustard seed, I came into homes so burdened with sorrow and trouble that I just could not walk out. Who better than I could understand how heavy was the burden they bore? Who better than I could offer them the sympathy they needed? So I stayed on in each home as long as I could be of service. And," she added apologetically, "please do not be angry, but I never again thought about our appointment."

Here is a most profound truth to remember when life makes us don a sackcloth. Trouble and sorrow naturally make us think only of ourselves. But after the first impact of the blow has worn off, our emotional recovery depends upon our ability to forget ourselves. And there is no better way of forgetting about ourselves than by thinking of and serving others. Human experience every day confirms the truth of the legend. He who can do no better after sorrow than engage in the futile search for the mustard seed to restore the loss which is in fact irretrievable, is destined to spend years of avoidable heartache. But happy is he who can rise from his mourner's bench and so lose himself in the service of others that he finds himself unknowingly climbing the mountain of healing to which the road of service inevitably leads.

God grant us the Robe of Service to cover our sackcloths.

The last and most significant robe with which we might cover our sackcloths is the Robe of Faith–faith in the immortality of the souls of our beloved.

The Yizkor prayer which is recited four times every year makes a bold affirmation about the human soul. It declares that death has no dominion over it. "May God remember the soul of my mother. . . ." "May God remember the soul of my son. . . ." The soul survives to be remembered. It does not perish with the death of the body. This same faith is echoed in the *El Mole* Rahamim prayer where we speak of the soul as being bound up in "the bond of life everlasting." Thus Judaism, like all great religions, teaches that "Death is not a period which brings the sentence of life to a full stop. It is only a comma that punctuates it to loftier existence." Here is the most comforting of all robes to cover the sackcloth of bereavement.

To be sure, like all daring affirmations of Judaism, the belief in immortality cannot be scientifically demonstrated. It is, as the philosopher Santayana correctly called it, "the Soul's invincible surmise." But if it is a "surmise" it is one of mankind's most persistent surmises. From ancient man in his primitive beliefs down through the long corridors of time stretching into the present most sophisticated faiths, men have always held the human soul indestructible. Nor has this belief been limited to religious thinkers alone. Philosophers, poets, physicians, scientists, all answer "present" when the roll is called among the believers that death is not the end. How the soul *survives* is, of course, a mystery. It is no less a mystery, however, than how the soul *arrives*. It originates with the Source of all Life and flows back to its origin.

When death robs us of a loved one, the pain of parting can be assuaged through our faith that the essence of our beloved lives on not only in our hearts and in our memories but more especially with the Author of life Himself. It is this faith which burst forth out of Emerson after the passing of his little son. "What is excellent," he wrote in his "Threnody," "as God lives, is permanent."

God grant us the Robe of Faith to cover our sackcloths.

The story of a king introduced our problem. The story of another monarch will sum up our solution. Alexander the Great, it is told, once commissioned an artist to paint his portrait. He gave him only two conditions. It was to be an exact likeness, unfalsified. Moreover, it was to be handsome and attractive. The artist had no easy task, for over his right eye, Alexander had a prominent battle scar. The artist was thus confronted with a painful dilemma. To omit the scar would be a violation of the first condition. To include it would be a violation of the second. Finally, the artist came up with the solution. He painted Alexander in a pensive mood, his face supported by his right hand with his forefinger covering the scar.

We cannot eliminate life's scars upon our souls, for we should not be true to life. Nor can we permit them to be prominently viewed, for they would then make life ugly and unlivable.

We must learn to cover the scars upon our souls, the sackcloths upon our flesh. With the Robe of Understanding which teaches us to accept trouble as part of the price we pay for being human; with the Robe of Wisdom which helps us use trouble, and convert it into triumph; with the Robe of Service which enables us to recover our own strength while at the same time bringing strength to others; with the Robe of Faith which whispers comforting assurance that the soul is mightier than death; with these robes, let us cover our sackcloths and thus make the portrait of our lives beautiful and inspiring to behold.

Where Is God When Tragedy Strikes?

QUESTION: In the newspaper account of the funeral service for a twenty-year-old murder victim, the officiating rabbi is quoted as offering the following prayer: "Eternal God, our Creator, who makes and takes, You have given, now You have taken away. May she rest in peace." Is the prayer that the rabbi offered a standard Jewish prayer, or was he expressing his own sentiments? Do you agree with those sentiments?

ANSWER: The prayer that the rabbi offered was not a standard Jewish prayer. It is, however, based on the well-known verse which Job uttered in the face of his multiple tragedies. "The Lord has given, and the Lord has taken away; blessed be the name of the Lord" (Job 1:21). This verse is included in the traditional Jewish funeral service and I am sure that many rabbis read it.

The officiating rabbi whom you quote paraphrased the words of Job in the prayer he offered at a desperately difficult time for the family and for the rabbi.

I empathize deeply with his effort to console a devastated family, but I confess that I am uncomfortable with his choice of words. They seem to imply that it was God who has "taken away" the twenty-year-old innocent victim, that the murderer God's of the young woman was God's doing or God's will. I find that idea totally unacceptable.

Our belief in God affirms the sacredness of life and the sanctity of every human being, created in His image. The Author of life urges us to care for life, to treasure it, to preserve it. Therefore, it is inconceivable that God would send a madman to destroy a promising young life and thereby, incidentally, inflict on her parents in this instance the unspeakable horror of burying a child.

I cannot conceive of the murderer as God's messenger. On the contrary, everything this murderer has done is in flagrant violation of God's will.

God has endowed each of us with the freedom to choose how we shall live. We may either do His will or flaunt it. He says to us: "Behold, I have put before you life and death, blessing and curse. Choose life – if you and your offspring would live – by loving the Lord, your God, heeding His commands and holding fast to Him" (Deuteronomy 30:19-20).

Though He pleads with us to choose life, we can choose not to choose life. When we spurn life and choose death, when we pervert justice and do injustice, when we resort to violence, corruption, greed, selfishness, oppression – when we do any of these things, the responsibility rests with us. It is squarely our own and not God's. "The fault, dear Brutus, is not in our stars, but in ourselves, that we are underlings."

Where is God in this terrible tragedy?

God is in the compassion we feel for the bereaved parents.

God is in the sympathy and in the support that kind friends extend to the survivors.

God is in our resolve to apprehend the murderer and to prevent further shedding of innocent blood.

God is in the strength that the victim's loved ones will somehow find as they make their way through the valley of the shadow.

God is in the healing that will come to them ever so slowly but ever so surely.

God is in the power of the human spirit to rise above sorrow and to transmute suffering into song, adversity into artistry, and pain into poetry.

We come from God and we return to Him, and with the Source of life no soul is ever lost. God is also in the great gift of remembrance. As the poet said, God gave us memory so that we might have roses in December.

The High Cost of Loving

When I was young, there was a popular song that soothingly assured us that "the best things in life are free." I have since experienced enough to learn that some of the best things in life are prohibitively expensive. Often they appear to be freely given but carry an invisible price tag. Love is one of those things.

Those of us who have lost loved ones have learned in our sorrow that we pay an enormous price for love when it ceases to flow. We pay in the coin of grief, longing, yearning, missing. It hurts so much, doesn't it?

The bitter truth is that every love story has an unhappy ending, and the greater the love the greater the unhappiness when it ends.

Whenever we love someone, we give a hostage to fortune. Whenever we permit someone to become very dear to us, we become vulnerable to disappointment and heartbreak.

What, then, is our choice? Never permit ourselves to love anyone? Never permit anyone to matter to us? To deny ourselves the greatest of all God-given joys?

If loving is expensive, being unloved and unloving costs even more. I believe that even in our grief we can still agree with the sentiment of a contemporary writer: "To love and be loved is to feel the sun from both sides."

And one more consideration can be mentioned. If some fairy angel came to us in our deepest sorrow and offered to remove all our pain and all our longing, but with them the angel would also remove all our memories of the years and the adventures we shared, would we agree to the bargain? Or would we consider those memories so precious, so infinitely dear, that we would hug them close to our hearts and refuse to purchase instant relief by surrendering them?

An ancient Greek legend gives a clue to the choice we would probably make. It tells of a woman who came down to the River Styx where Charon, the gentle ferryman, stood ready to take her to the region of the departed spirits. Charon reminded her that it was her privilege to drink of the waters of Lethe, and that if she did so she would completely forget all that she was leaving behind.

Eagerly she said, "I will forget how I have suffered." To which Charon responded, "But remember, you will also forget how you have rejoiced." Then the woman said, "I will forget my failures." The old ferryman added, "And also your victories." Again the woman said, "I will forget how I have been hurt." "You will also forget," countered Charon, "how you have been loved."

The woman then paused to think the whole matter over, and the story concludes by telling us that she did not drink the waters of Lethe, preferring to hold on to the memory even of her suffering and her sorrow rather than surrender the remembrance of life's joys and loves.

An old Yiddish proverb consoles us in our suffering by reminding us: "Not to have had pain is not to have been human." The pain passes, the memories remain; loved ones leave us, but having had loved ones endures. And we are so much richer and so much enlarged for having paid the high cost of loving.

Companions for Our Loneliness

At Yizkor time our thoughts turn almost inevitably to one of the dreariest companions of grief – loneliness. When we lose someone dear we feel an aching sense of emptiness, an unrequited yearning for that which can never be again. I think that one of the saddest words in the vocabulary of anguish is loneliness. It is also one of the most oppressive sentiments to which grief exposes us. But loneliness is occasioned not only by grief. It happens to be one of the fundamental problems of being human. Indeed, ours has been called the Age of Loneliness.

Some time ago there appeared a book by David Reisman called *The Lonely Crowd*. It was a serious sociological study which could not be read on the run, and yet it enjoyed a remarkable popularity. One publisher suggested that people bought the book because of its title. They thought they could find in it some relief for the loneliness which gnaws at the heart of modern man and woman.

That title is very suggestive. We are members of a lonely crowd. It is possible to live among multitudes and yet feel desperately alone. Henry Thoreau defined city life as millions of people being lonesome together. Lucy Freeman, the newspaper woman who recorded her own struggle for emotional and mental health in a revealing book called *The Fight Against Fears,* describes a sentiment which many will recognize: "By society's standards I was successful, but I was miserable. I had never known more people – nor been lonelier."

A dear friend, whom I visited several weeks after the death of her husband, was deeply appreciative of the attentions shown to her by well intentioned visitors. But then she added, "I can be with dozens of people and yet feel so terribly alone."

Loneliness, it would seem then, is not necessarily relieved by being among people. On the contrary, so often our loneliness is only accentuated when we are among people but cannot feel a part of them.

As we think about this problem for just a moment, we begin to realize that loneliness is one of life's inescapable burdens. It is one of the central and inevitable facts of life. When we are gripped by a sense of loneliness we sometimes think we are unique in feeling this sensation. The truth is, however, that to live is to be lonely.

Long ago our Bible spoke of that isolation, that apartness, that singleness which the individual feels not only in moments of sorrow but in moments of rejoicing as well. The author of Proverbs put his finger on the core of our problem when he said: "The heart knows its own bitterness and no stranger shares its joy." We come into the house of the mourner but not into his heart. We dance at the *simcha* of a friend but we cannot hear the special strains of music which his soul plays within. Whether we like it or not, the Creator has sentenced each of us at birth to some inevitable measure of solitary confinement. We are alone. We are alone in groping, uncertain youth. We are alone in withdrawn old age. We are alone in moments of crisis. We are alone when we are in pain. We are alone when a loved one is taken from us. We are alone when a child leaves us. We are alone in moments of moral decision. We are alone under our burden of guilt. We are alone on life's ultimate journey.

What shall we do with our sense of loneliness? What can we do to mitigate it, to reduce it, and to soften it? Are there companions for our loneliness?

I should like first to make the paradoxical suggestion that one way of handling our loneliness is not to be alone less but to be alone more. We need to cultivate the art of being by ourselves more and with other people less. The Rabbi of Sassov said that a human being who does not have an hour for himself each day is not a human being. What he was urging us is not to be lonely but to be alone, to develop the ability to enjoy solitude or, if you will, our own company. Loneliness hurts. Solitude helps.

For many of us this is a very difficult thing to do. In this age of togetherness we have made it a fetish to be doing things with other people. So many of us are like the man who was the subject of one of Nathaniel Hawthorne's short stories. This man vanished into thin air whenever other people who had been in the same room with him left it. What Hawthorne was saying was that this man existed only when he was surrounded by other people. Left alone, he disappeared. This is true of many of us. We seem to have no independent existence. We seem to be allergic to ourselves. We are almost afraid of ourselves, afraid of confronting ourselves as we are. A contemporary has defined hell as the time people must spend by themselves with their television sets out of order.

To cultivate the art of solitude means to learn to get to know ourselves and to enjoy being with ourselves. Surely there must come a day for each of us when we will have to be by ourselves. It would seem to be the most elemental kind of wisdom to prepare ourselves for that day. What a pity to find ourselves at such a time living with a stranger.

But there are additional reasons why we must cultivate the art of solitude. When we are alone we discover our own inner strength. We deepen our spirit. We are enabled to reflect, to evaluate, to examine, to weigh, to contemplate, to meditate, to be renewed—words that are disappearing from our vocabulary because they describe actions which are disappearing from our lives.

It is no accident that some of the great discoveries of the spirit were made in solitude. Moses, alone in the wilderness, discovers God. Moses, alone on Sinai, brings down to mankind the imperishable words. Newton, alone under a tree, discovers the law of gravity. In solitude man is most a man. No creativity is possible without it. The artist, the writer, the poet, the philosopher, the scientist, each pursues the muse in solitude. He courts her when they are alone. She comes to him when there is no one to intrude on their privacy.

What is true of the creative spirit is true of each of us. We must use some times to be alone, to see what our own souls wear. Indeed, without solitude we are in peril of losing our souls, of losing the essence, the uniqueness, that unduplicated identity which is the special possession of each of us. To be able to be alone without feeling lonely is one of life's greatest achievements. When we acquire it we gain a priceless possession. "Let us keep our silent sanctuaries," counsels a contemporary French writer, "for in them the eternal perspectives are preserved." Our first companion, then, is each one's own self which if properly cultivated can do much to mitigate loneliness.

There is a second companion that we need for our loneliness. What God has said of Adam is true of each of us. "It is not good for man to be alone." Periodic solitude is an indispensable ingredient for nourishing the inner life, but it cannot be the complete diet. In addition to cultivating an appreciation for ourselves, we must cultivate an appreciation for other people. This, indeed, is the prescription which God Himself wrote for His lonely man. When God decides that it is not good for Adam to be alone, He says immediately, "I shall make for him a helpmate." Adam, like all of us, needs someone to love, someone to care about, someone to elicit from him his generosity, his concern, his affection.

The most isolating form of loneliness is not to be apart from people; it is to be apathetic to them, to be indifferent to them, to feel unrelated to them. It is not enough to be in contact with people. We must feel concerned about them. "Hell," said Dostoyevski, "is the suffering of being unable to love." When we are self-centered, when our selfishness builds tall walls around us to insulate us from other people's troubles and triumphs, when we become enmeshed in what Shelley once called "the dark idolatry of self," we suffer from the severest of all forms of loneliness. We are unrelated, unattached. We need to break out of the prison of our aloneness, out of our self-imposed solitary confinement. We must transcend our separateness. We must become related to other people through love.

One of the great gifts that God has given us is this capacity to love, to care about others. Love is the key that unlocks the prison doors. And we are loved in direct proportion to our ability to love. We receive as we give.

In the Book of Ecclesiastes, the warning is sounded, "Woe to him that is alone, for when he falls he has not another to pick him up." Of course that is true. To be alone means to have no one to relieve your own sadness, to soothe your hurt, to soften your anguish. But that is only half of the truth. The other half is that if there is no one about whose hurt you care, if there is no one whom you want to lift up when he falls, if there is no one whose pain adds to your sadness and whose achievements deepen your own joy, then you are alone. You see, we can turn that statement in Ecclesiastes around and have it read: "Woe to him who has no one whom he cares to pick up when he falls, for he is alone." If we do not enjoy the blessings of love we suffer the burdens of loneliness.

"What makes loneliness an anguish," wrote Dag Hammerskjöld in *Markings,* "is not that I have no one to share my burden, but this: I have only my own burden to bear."

To look at the world through the eyes of love is to become related to all mankind, and thus to become insulated against the ravages of loneliness.

As Jews there is a special companionship that is ours. In addition to *"Ahavat Habriyot,* the love of our fellow man," we are also committed to *"Ahavat Yisrael,* the love of our people." Our people have a special claim upon our affection. They are related to us by intimate and mystic cords which touch us in a unique manner. Their fate is our fate. In their destiny we are directly involved. Without in any way diminishing or compromising our love for all people, we love our own people with a warm and overflowing love. In return, here, too, we are again anchored and shielded against loneliness. How can we be lonely when we consider ourselves part of the household of Israel?

The Jew who is joined by his deeds, by his observance, by his gifts and by his hopes to the living body of a living people, has thereby done at least as much for himself as he has done for his people. When Hillel counseled us: "Separate not yourself from the community," he was speaking not only out of a concern for the community, but also because he cared about the individual. This love, *Ahavat Yisrael,* is one of the time honored Jewish companionships to protect us against loneliness. "All our ancestors are in us," exclaims Richard Beer-Hoffman. "Who can feel himself alone?"

For last I have left the most decisive answer to the problem of loneliness suggested by the title of one of Dr. Abraham Heschel's books, *Man Is Not Alone.* This is the answer of our faith. Man is not alone because there is God.

There are many indictments that can be directed against atheism. It looks upon the universe as an accident and man as a fluke. It leaves man without a purpose for which to live, without a blueprint by which to live. It strips his life of ultimate significance and plays Russian roulette with his dreams for a redeemed world. But above all, atheism stands condemned because it consigns man to unrelieved, abject, inconsolable loneliness. Someone once suggested facetiously that on the tombstone of an atheist there be inscribed the epitaph:"All dressed up and no place to go." But that is not the whole of it. The penalty for atheism is not only that we have no destination after life on earth, but also that we have no companionship during life on earth. Man is totally, utterly alone.

There are abundant rewards that faith in God confers. The universe becomes the purposeful creation of a Divine Intelligence. Man becomes "crowned with glory and honor" by Him who made man "but little lower than the angels." Man's life is sacred. His highest hopes for a world of brotherhood, justice and peace are underwritten by Him who put those yearnings into his heart. But above all, faith in God offers man the most soothing balm for the ache of loneliness – the sustaining, never-failing, ever-present companionship of Him who is near to all who call upon Him in truth.

A colleague tells that when his pious grandmother became advanced in years, she was usually attended by one of her children. Whenever he called her, one of them would answer the phone. One day she answered! Startled, he asked: "Bubba, are you alone?" She replied: "Dear child, I'm never alone."

Bubba had the most reliable companionship to insulate her against loneliness.

Without this companionship we remain unattached, separate and alone. We may try to fill the gnawing emptiness with things we can put into our pockets or into the vault. These may provide comforts for our bodies but they are powerless to comfort our unsatisfied spirits. Friends and loved ones are indispensable but there is just so much they can do and no more. The words of Dr. Heschel underline a poignant truth. "We are alone even with our friends. The smattering of understanding which a human being has to offer is not enough to satisfy our need of sympathy. Human eyes can see the foam, but not the seething at the bottom. In the hour of greatest agony we are alone. It is such a sense of solitude which prompts the heart to seek the companionship of God." When we feel that companionship, we have discovered the ultimate answer to our loneliness.

This companionship sustains us in every circumstance. In the sharp loneliness of pain we hear the whispered reassurance: "I the Lord am your Healer." In the bitter loneliness of bereavement we feel with the Psalmist: "Though my father and my mother leave me, the Lord gathers me in." In the chilly loneliness of fear we tap reservoirs of courage which well up out of the ancient words: "The Lord is for me. I will not fear. What can man do unto me?" In the sublime loneliness of rapture we feel with Isaiah: "Holy, holy, holy is the Lord of hosts. The whole earth is filled with His glory." And when the shadows lengthen and the sun begins to sink in the western sky, and we feel the aching loneliness of leave-taking from all we have known, and treasured and hugged close to the heart, we can go serene in the faith "in Him who can go with me, yet remain with you and be everywhere for good."

As we venture forth into the New Year, let us resolve to make it a year of growing companionships – companionship with ourselves through solitude, companionship with our fellow man through love, companionship with our people through loyalty and companionship with God through faith. Then shall we know the joy of life's unending journey, for though we shall often be alone, we need never again be lonely.

Who Is Handicapped?

During the hot days of July 1981, nine handicapped adventurers captured the headlines and won our hearts. Five of them were blind, two were deaf, one was an epileptic, and the last had an artificial leg. These intrepid nine conquered snow-capped Mount Rainier, which towers 14,410 feet in forbidding, defiant majesty. When word reached us from Washington State that they had successfully completed their climb to the frozen summit and had safely negotiated the treacherous descent, we all stood taller.

The breathtaking accomplishment of these people was a dramatic demonstration of the power of the human will to triumph over massive obstacles. It was also a much-needed reassurance to all who are handicapped. And when I say, "all who are handicapped," I really mean to include all of us as well, since in one way or another, each of us is handicapped.

On the very day the mountain climbers completed their heart-pumping triumph, a forty-year-old man had come to see me in my study. In appearance, he is tall, handsome, vigorous, well groomed. Except for the disturbed look in his light blue eyes, he might be a matinee idol. All his organs and limbs are intact. But he is an extremely unhappy man.

He has survived a divorce and then the death of his second wife some years later. He is still mourning her terribly. His efforts to enter into new relationships with women have proven disappointing. He is so down on himself that some days it takes all his strength just to get out of bed. His work on the job is perfunctory and far below par. He is in real danger of losing that job. Question: Is this man handicapped?

One of the most moving scenes in the play *Butterflies Are Free* shows a young girl about to desert her blind lover. She justifies her flight by shouting at him, "Because you're blind, you're crippled." To this taunt the young man replies out of his darkness, "No, I'm not crippled. I'm sightless but not crippled. You are crippled because you can't commit yourself to anyone."

Not all handicaps are physical and not all handicaps are visible, but to be human is to be handicapped, to be flawed. "There is a crack," wrote Emerson, "in everything God made."

Some of us are handicapped by a disturbing sense of inferiority and inadequacy. Some of us carry childhood scars inflicted by constant criticism and bitter rejection.

Some of us feel unworthy of being loved: others cannot give love. Some of us are burdened by guilt; others are filled with rage. Some of us are consumed by envy; others are driven by greed.

Some of us have forfeited our self-respect; others never acquired it. Some of us are battered by fear; others are buffeted by frustration and failure. Some of us are imprisoned by selfishness; others are enslaved by alcohol or pills. Some of us suffer heartaches because of our children; others are tormented by our parents. Some of us carry within us the gray ash of burned-out dreams; others are haunted by fractured hopes and unfulfilled promises. Some of us are convinced of our own worthlessness; others are persuaded of life's meaninglessness.

According to an old Italian story, in Naples there was a man who could not shake off a feeling of deep depression, so he went to a doctor for help. After a thorough examination, the physician said to the patient, "There is really nothing physically wrong with you. May I suggest that you go to the theater tonight to see the great comedian Carlini. He brings laughter to large crowds at every performance. He will surely drive away your sadness."

At these words, the patient burst into tears. "But, Doctor," he sobbed, "I am Carlini!"

To know that being handicapped is the common lot of each and every one of us may make our own handicaps a little easier to accept. We have not been singled out by a malicious fate for special abuse. We are simply paying the price of being human.

And before we become too envious of the other fellow who seems to have it all, we might pause to reflect that he too carries his own shabby secrets and dark sorrows, his own heavy, invisible handicaps.

Of course, we must take care to ensure that we do not use our handicaps as an alibi to justify failure. All human progress and achievements were accomplished not in the absence of handicaps but in the face of them. "I thank God for my handicaps," wrote Helen Keller, "for through them I have found myself, my work, my God."

One of the blind mountain climbers explained the success of the adventure quite simply: "We had a lot of help from each other on the trip." Our own perilous journey through life is an adventure filled with obstacles, risks, and pitfalls that each of us must negotiate burdened as we are by an assortment of handicaps. We can, however, succeed. But we need a lot of help from one another on the trip.

The Kaddish

The *Kaddish* exercises a powerful grip. It is recited every morning and evening by bereaved Jews in every land, by the learned and the unlettered, by teen-agers and graybeards, by the richest and the humblest. The sense of obligation to recite the Kaddish is the strongest motivating factor behind the organization and perpetuation of the daily prayer service in hundreds of congregations.

Jews who know few other prayers know the Kaddish. Jews who keep few other traditions are faithful in reciting it for eleven months after the death of a parent, and every succeeding year on the Yahrzeit, the anniversary of the death in the Jewish calendar.

The Kaddish is the prayer which bears most eloquent testimony to filial reverence and respect. In Yiddish a man affectionately refers to his son as his *Kaddish'l,* his little Kaddishsayer. This is a son's posthumous gift to his father, a refuge against oblivion.

In several modern prayer books, the Kaddish is the only prayer found in transliteration. Worshippers in liberal congregations may recite any other prayer in translation, but never the Kaddish, which is always recited in its original Aramaic, the vernacular of the people. Even the Reform prayer book, which has eliminated much of the Hebrew of the traditional *siddur,* has preserved the Kaddish in Aramaic and added a paragraph to it.

The enduring appeal of the Kaddish in the face of the most forbidding circumstances was attested to in a melancholy way by Heinrich Heine. He was among those post-Emancipation Jews who sought to obtain through baptism the fuller freedom and larger opportunities denied to members of his faith. The hoped-for benefits of this act of desertion never quite materialized. In the end, he felt excluded from both camps. Significant was Heine's way of expressing this bitter truth:

> No Mass will be sung,
> No Kaddish will be said;
> Nothing said and nothing sung
> On the anniversaries of my death.

The unspoken Kaddish, the unmarked Yahrzeit–these epitomized for Heine better than anything else his ultimate alienation from his people.

It is easier to describe the magnetic hold of the Kaddish than to explain it. Though it is "the mourner's prayer" it contains not a single reference to death, resurrection or immortality. The anguish of sorrow or the pain of parting are not even touched upon. The thoughts uppermost in the mourner's mind and the feelings in his heart find no expression in the Kaddish. (For this reason the Reform prayer book added a paragraph which explicitly refers to the departed.) The traditional Kaddish is instead a hymn of praise to God.

Glorified and hallowed be His great name in the world which He
has created according to His will. May He establish His kingdom
during your lives and the life of all Israel. Let us say: Amen.

Let His great name be blessed to all eternity.

Hallowed and extolled, lauded and exalted, honored and
revered, adored and worshipped, be the name of the Holy One,
blessed be He; though He be beyond all blessings, hymns and
praises which are uttered in the world. Let us say: Amen.

May abundant peace and life descend from heaven upon us
and upon all Israel. Let us say: Amen.

May He who ordains the harmony in the universe bring
peace to us and to all Israel. Let us say: Amen.

One of our oldest prayers, the Kaddish was not originally designed as a prayer for mourners. Some of its passages were part of the
Temple services. Its two basic themes – the sanctification of God's
Name and the hope for the coming of His kingdom – are echoed in the
best-known Christian prayer:

> Our Father who art in Heaven
> Hallowed be Thy name.
> Thy kingdom come;
> Thy will be done. . . .

Some of the phrases and ideas of the Kaddish are suggested by
Biblical phrases. Others were added with the passage of time.

In its present form (attained twelve centuries ago, in the Gaonic
period), the Kaddish was recited at the conclusion of a lecture in the
House of Study. In the view of our sages, one of the most effective
ways of bringing God's kingdom nearer was through the study of
Torah and the good deeds to which such study leads. The teacher
would therefore follow his discourse by reciting the Kaddish, the
sublime expression of that hope.

The link between the Kaddish and the House of Study is reflected
in the *Kaddish d'Rabbanan,* "The Scholar's Kaddish," recited after the
reading of a passage from the Mishnah or the Talmud. This is the basic
Kaddish with a special prayer inserted on behalf of "the teachers and
their disciples and all who engage in the study of Torah."

Later, the Kaddish passed from the House of Study into the House of Prayer. In the synagogue it was and is recited at the conclusion of a distinct section of the service (the half Kaddish) and also at the conclusion of the entire service (the whole Kaddish).

Still later, the custom arose for disciples to recite a special Kaddish at the end of the seven-day mourning period for a learned Torah scholar. This Kaddish followed the religious discourses delivered in his honor. Subsequently, the democratic impulse extended this honor to every Jew.

This then was the route traveled by the Kaddish – from the House of Study to the House of Prayer to the house of mourning.

The only *explicit* mention of the dead is found in the special Kaddish recited at the graveside immediately after burial. It contains this added section:

> Magnified and hallowed be His great name in the world that is to be created anew when He will revive the dead and raise them up into life eternal and when He will rebuild the city of Jerusalem and establish His Temple in the midst thereof and uproot all false worship from the earth and restore the worship of the true God.

The earliest reference to the Kaddish as a mourner's prayer is found in a thirteenth-century prayer book (*Mahzor Vitry*). There is, however, an earlier legend connecting the recitation of the Kaddish with an orphan. Rabbi Akiba once met a ghost carrying a burdensome load of wood for the fires in hell to which he had been condemned for having exploited the poor during his life as a tax collector. He had only one hope for release from his torments. If his infant son could be taught to recite the Kaddish in public so that the congregation could respond with "May God's great name be praised for ever," he would be spared further sufferings. Rabbi Akiba found the child and taught him to recite the Kaddish and thus effect his father's release from Gehenna (or hell).

This legend establishes a connection between the Kaddish and the orphan. It also introduces a thought that was to dominate many writings in the Middle Ages – that the Kaddish has the power to release the dead from suffering. So strong was this belief that it survived the determined opposition of many leading rabbis and was largely responsible for the practice of engaging someone to say the Kaddish for a man who left no sons.

Traditional authorities differ on whether a daughter may recite the Kaddish where there is no son. Most modern Jews would agree with the position taken on this matter by Henrietta Szold. To her the Kaddish was essentially an expression of identification, a means of linking herself with her family and with her people, past and future. She had seven sisters and no brothers. When her mother died, a friend of the family offered to say the Kaddish for her. Henrietta graciously refused. She explained:

> The Kaddish means to me that the survivor publicly and mark-edly manifests his wish and intention to assume the relation to the Jewish community which his parent had, so that the chain of tradition remains unbroken from generation to generation, each adding its own link. You can do that for the generations of your family. I must do that for the generations of my family.

But what of the intrinsic meaning of the Kaddish itself? Though not originally designed to be recited by the mourner, does it have nothing to say to him or her?

The Kaddish makes several vital affirmations addressed to the mourner's emotional and psychic needs. The very name of the prayer Kaddish means *sanctification*. From beginning to end it sanctifies the name of God, thus attesting human submission to, and acceptance of, His will. It proclaims that in spite of our loss we are among those who add our praise to the glorification of God's name. Our belief in God is strong enough to overcome bereavement.

Sorrow often places a severe strain upon our faith in God and in the goodness of life. "How can I believe in God if He permits such things to happen?" The structure of our faith totters in the winds of misfortune. The Kaddish is intended to steady and restore our perspective. We have returned what was lent to us and what we have enjoyed. In this spirit a father who had lost his daughter wrote: "On our books she is a net gain. She was worth so much more than she cost and she left so much more behind than she took away that we are flooded with joyous memories and cannot question either the goodness of God or the decency of man."

The Kaddish proclaims further that this is a "world which He has created according to His will." Even though sorrow may temporarily dull our vision or threaten to rob life of meaning, we affirm that there is a plan and a purpose to life.

The Kaddish also offers the reassurance that God can supply one of the mourner's most desperate needs – the need for inner peace and serenity. "May He who makes peace in His heights, bring peace unto us . . ."

Modern studies of the dynamics of grief indicate that in every situation there is present an element of guilt. No human relationship is so perfect that the survivor cannot berate himself for things done and said and for things left undone and unsaid. The mourner needs peace from an accusing conscience. The mourner needs the peace which comes from the faith that He who has created imperfect creatures makes allowance for their imperfections.

The mourner also needs release from the anxiety over his own death that the death of a loved one often engenders. He needs relief from the fears which thrive in the soil of sorrow. He needs surcease from the resentments and rebellions that follow in the wake of separation. The hope that such peace can come to him may help dispel the heavy overcast of grief and anxiety.

Finally, the Kaddish offers the mourner a challenge to contribute his energies to the making of a better world. Emotionally and psychologically the Kaddish is a link with the past. But the Kaddish itself looks forward not backward. "May He establish His kingdom." This cannot remain a passive hope. It must involve the mourner actively in the creation of a better world. The Kaddish sounds a call to action on behalf of that kingdom for whose advent we pray.

By requiring that the Kaddish be recited with a quorum of worshippers, Judaism renders the mourner a profound service. A *minyan* almost invariably includes other mourners and thus brings home the realization that we alone have not been singled out.

The burning question: "Why did God do this to me?" loses much of its sting when others also rise to recite the Kaddish. We are not lonely travelers in the valley of the shadow. We thus see death for what it is – not a malevolent act of a vindictive God, but part of the incomprehensible mystery of human existence in which light and dark, joy and sadness, birth and death are interwoven and inseparable.

The Three-Walled Sukkah

A rabbinic comment on the Book of Job seems to be speaking to us most intimately at the *Yizkor* hour on Shemini Atzeret.

Job was a good man who suffered compound calamities. A Midrash tells us that "When Job complained about his misfortunes, the Holy One, blessed be He, showed him a Sukkah of three walls."

What was the Almighty trying to teach Job through this strange symbol? What would a three-walled Sukkah say to a man in the depths of despair and anguish?

We can only guess at what the author of this Midrash had in mind. Each of us can read different meanings into the enigmatic metaphor.

Let us suggest a few things it might say.

One message may be that the three-walled Sukkah is God's way of reminding Job that every person's Sukkah has one wall missing. Sure, everyone would like to have a four-walled Sukkah – a happy marriage, gifted children, a successful career, good health, and a long life. In actual life, however, no one has a four-walled Sukkah. Sorrow, failure, loss of health, disappointment – in varying degrees – these are our common human lot. There is a democracy in suffering – no one is exempt. You Job are not alone in your travails. Three-walled Sukkahs are the rule, not the exception.

A second message is conveyed by the strange symbolism. Rabbinic law tells us that "a three-walled Sukkah is kosher for use" (on the holiday). Despite the missing wall, the Sukkah continues to stand. Somehow life goes on. Life, it has been observed, is full of heartbreak but it is also full of overcoming it.

In the first flush of sorrow we say, "Oh, I can never get over this, I cannot survive such a blow." But somehow we do survive and we do go on. In life, a piece of a wall falls away now, another piece at another time, but the Sukkah remains standing.

Which rabbi or counselor has not heard people cry out when the wound is raw, "How do I go on?" The only honest answer is, "I don't know how to go on but I do know that others have gone on and you are probably as wise, as brave, and as strong as they."

But if life is to go on, if we are to survive the collapse of a wall of our Sukkah, we must learn to look at the three walls that are standing rather than at the one which has fallen. Some of us having sustained a grievous loss either of a loved one or a fortune cannot erase the loss from our minds. We keep talking about it, bemoaning it, weeping over it.

Harold Russell, the handless veteran of World War II, told us his story in a book ironically titled *Victory In My Hands*. One sentence in that book deserves to be held before every Job: "It's not what you have lost, but what you have left that counts."

So, God was saying to Job, stop thinking only of the pains you suffer, you also have pleasures to enjoy. Stop counting and recounting your losses, and begin counting your blessings. Sure you have lost a wall of your Sukkah, but there are three walls remaining. Make the most of those three walls. You will be held accountable for what you do with those remaining walls.

And remember, Job, that you belong to a people which has mastered the art of surviving in a three-walled Sukkah. Your people survived the loss of a land, dispersion, persecution and bigotries of varying intensity and severity. Despite these multiple deprivations, your people retained their humanity, their compassion, their dedication to justice, and they have extravagantly enriched an undeserving mankind in a measure grotesquely disproportionate to their meager numbers. We have shown the world how to live in a three-walled Sukkah.

And one last thing Job. Because a wall of your own Sukkah has collapsed, you have an unobstructed view of your neighbor's Sukkah. Look carefully and you will see he, too, is missing a wall in his Sukkah.

Perhaps this is why we come together to say Yizkor. As we look upon others remembering and memorializing, we are so vividly reminded that we all are knit together in the common brotherhood of pain and vulnerability. Another's pain does not lessen our own, but it may help to move us from self-pity to the healing which comes from trying to bind up the wounds of another.

In the blessing for the food which we recite after the meal on this festival we insert these words: "May the All-Merciful raise up for us the collapsed Sukkah of David." We look forward to the day when all Sukkot will be full and intact. Until that blessed day arrives we must make do each of us with a three-walled Sukkah and make that Sukkah as beautiful as we can.

Fear Not Death

The emotion grief is actually a composite of many different feelings. Added to the pain of parting, there may be loneliness, remorse or even a harrowing sense of guilt. Not infrequently grief also contains a burdensome ingredient of fear – the fear of death.

However one looks upon death, it is certainly a venture into the unknown, and we usually experience deep anxiety in the presence of the unfamiliar. Little wonder then that the thought of death has so often evoked dread. William Randolph Hearst had so powerful a fear of death that the very mention of the word in his presence was strictly prohibited. Even in his newspapers, the subject had to be handled with utmost delicacy.

Yet it is possible to face death without dread. Many have so faced it. When the father of Robert Browning lay on his deathbed, his cheerfulness so surprised his physician that he asked the patient's daughter in a low voice: "Does the old gentleman know he is dying?" The patient overheard the question and answered: "Death is no enemy in my eyes."

In Jewish history there have been tens of thousands of men and women who in times of persecution deliberately chose death rather than live with dishonor. These acts of *Kiddush Hashem,* "sanctification of the Name of God," are a powerful tribute to the loyalty and the heroism of the martyrs. In a sense, they also reveal the equanimity with which these pious souls faced death.

Perhaps the most famous of Jewish martyrs in Talmudic times was Rabbi Akiba. As he was being put to death by the Romans for the capital offense of teaching Judaism, he said to his weeping disciples: "All my life I was disturbed over the verse 'And you shall love the Lord your God with all your heart, with all your soul and with all your might.' The phrase 'with all your soul' has been interpreted to mean that we must serve God even at the peril of our soul. And I was agitated over my inability to fulfil this verse. At last the opportunity has presented itself to me to love God 'with all my soul.' Now I am at peace."

Strangely, it is not the exceptional person who faces death serenely. While so many live with a fear of death, they actually seem to die in a spirit of calm acceptance. Such at least, is the overwhelming testimony of those who see people die.

Dr. Frank Adair is only one of many prominent physicians who bear witness to the courage and calm that ninety-nine percent of dying patients exhibit. Dr. Adair said: "The haunting fear which the average person carries all through life is dissipated by the approach of death."

If we can succeed in accepting the inexorable fact of our own death with equanimity, perhaps it will mitigate our sorrow over the death of our loved one. We can even learn to regard death not as an enemy but as a friend, who at the appointed hour leads us like Longfellow's little child at bedtime "half willing half reluctant to be led."

Sancho Panza in *Don Quixote* spends a desperate night clinging to a window ledge, afraid of falling. When day breaks, he discovers that all the while his feet had been only an inch from the ground.

Our fear of death may be as groundless as Sancho's fear of falling. Death may be but the threshhold over which we pass from time to eternity, from the realm of the perishable to the realm of the indestructible. And if we come to terms with death, who would dare to set a limit on what we could extract from life?

It is a real hour of triumph when we can banish the fear of death from our hearts and honestly say with the poet Sarah Williams:

> "Though my soul may set in darkness, it will rise in perfect
>   light,
> I have loved the stars too fondly to be fearful of the night."

The Things We Learn from Sorrow

The moment of bereavement is the most dreaded of all moments. So deeply do we fear separation from those we love that we try desperately to prevent the very thought of it from stealing into our consciousness. When in unguarded moments it succeeds in breaking through, we hasten to expel the unwelcome intruder. It is therefore not altogether strange that sorrow finds us emotionally unprepared and perhaps even rebellious and resentful.

If we are wise, however, we will accept sorrow courageously now that it has forced its way into our lives. Despite its forbidding countenance, sorrow possesses great potential power to expand our lives, to enlarge our vision and to deepen our understanding. It has played a beautiful and transforming role in the lives of countless bereaved who could say in a mood of melancholy gratefulness with Wordsworth: "A deep distress hath humanized my soul."

Through the portals of sorrow we can enter into the suffering of others. Our human compassion is kindled. Our sympathies are awakened. Grief can also help purge us of pettiness and selfishness. It can elicit from us powers of fortitude and patience which, but for it, might have never been quickened into life. Sorrow can thus bring us closer to our fellow humans and help introduce us to ourselves. The recorded experience and testimony of poet, psalmist and philosopher all tend to confirm overwhelmingly the observation of Jean Paul: "There is a purity which only suffering can impart; the stream of life becomes snow-white when it dashes against the rocks."

The abundance of elegaic poetry and music in world culture points up another benevolent service which sorrow frequently renders. Where we do not permit it to embitter us or crush us, it often arouses deep latent powers of creativity by which the human spirit transmutes suffering into song, adversity into artistry, and pain into poetry.

Thus it is quite possible to emulate those of whom the Psalmist wrote: "They pass through a valley of tears and convert it into a life-giving fountain." Our sorrows can serve as "needles with which God sews our souls to eternal truths." If we face sorrow affirmatively and creatively we can use it to enhance life's meaning and beauty for others no less than for ourselves.

This truth seems to be symbolized by a strange tree which grows near Bombay. It is called "The Sorrowful Tree" because it has the remarkable characteristic of blooming only in the night. Just as soon as the sun sets, the flowers come bursting out. May not this also reflect our uniquely human endowment? Like that tree we can also bring forth flowers of surpassing beauty in the dark night of sorrow.

Time – The Gentle Healer

In the hour of bereavement we feel most acutely what Swift called "the sting of perishable things." At the moment of deep hurt it appears indeed that there is no balm for our gaping wounds. We tend to despair of ever regaining our emotional equilibrium.

At such a time we are scarcely amenable to solace. Words of comfort ring hollow in the dark night of sorrow. That is why an ancient sage counseled wisely: "Do not comfort your friend when his deceased is still lying before him." Premature comfort can often be more harmful than no comfort, because it seems to mock the hurt, to make light of our torment.

It is never too soon, however, to accept the reassuring thought that pain, no less than pleasure, is transient. A simple farmer was asked by a visitor from the city during a severe rainstorm whether he thought it would stop raining. He answered drily: "It usually does."

Nature rushes benevolently to our assistance when we have been hurt, whether in body or in spirit. If we do not despair, the healing process does restore us as it has healed other mourners from the beginning of time. To be sure, the scar may very well continue to throb sensitively when we experience emotional bad weather. The sense of loss may always remain with us; but the sharp pain subsides and we discover the way to a healthy readjustment to our new circumstances. The Psalmist wisely spoke of walking "through the valley of the shadow." No road of life can detour around the valley. By the same token, however, the valley is open on both sides. Having entered into it, we need not make it our permanent dwelling place. After we have lingered there for a while, we can walk through it and out. With the Psalmist we can then affirm gratefully out of the depths of our own experience: "Though weeping tarries in the night, joy comes in the morning."

Grief Softened by Gratitude

The dreary clouds of grief which gather in the wake of death cast thick gloom over the lives of the bereaved. An aching void, an overpowering loneliness, a fear of facing the future alone, a gnawing pain over the unlived years – all these combine to throw deep darkness over our days. Yet there are small pin points of light that penetrate the overcast.

Amidst our grief, if we pause to reflect, we can find, as others have, genuine cause for gratitude. This gratitude may not dispel the gloom but it can relieve it.

Even while we mourn the death of a loved one, there is room in our hearts for thankfulness for that life. We have lost what we have had. For those years of love and comradeship there is no adequate compensation. Impoverished as we are by the passing of our beloved, we should be poorer by far if we had never tasted the joy and richness of that union. Sadder than losing a loved one is never having had a loved one to lose. Helen Hayes expressed this thought most pointedly after the death of her highly gifted daughter. "Tragic that it should have ended," she said of Mary's life, "but how much better than if it had never been."

We can be grateful, too, that while death robs us of our loved ones, it cannot take from us the years that passed and their abiding impression. These have entered into our lives and become part of ourselves. With the poet Georgia Harkness we can say of the loved one we mourn:

> To know this life was good –
> It left its mark on me.
> Its work stands fast.

Sober reflection can also lead us to a more sympathetic appreciation of the vital role death plays in the economy of life. Life's significance and zest issue from our awareness of its transiency, its "fragile contingency." The urge to create, the passion to perfect, the will to heal and cure – all the noblest of human enterprises grow in the soil of human mortality. They would vanish if life on earth were an endless, unrelieved process.

To the person of religious faith there remains the profoundest source of gratitude amidst grief – the reassuring conviction that the soul is imperishable and "the grave is not its goal." The souls of our loved ones, like our own, come from the great Source of Life, Himself, and flow back into the eternal stream after the earthly pilgrimage is ended.

Thus the pain of parting is mitigated by faith in a divine providence which permits no life to be utterly destroyed. It was this faith which spoke out of Job in his hour of anguish and has since been repeated by countless bereaved believers: "The Lord has given, The Lord has taken back, praised be the name of the Lord."

Memory – Life's Afterglow

In Maeterlinck's beautiful play *The Blue Bird,* the children Tyltyl and Mytil are about to set out in search of the fabled blue bird of happiness. The Fairy tells them that on their journey they will come to the land of memory where, upon turning the magic diamond in Tyltyl's hat, they will see all their departed loved ones – their grandparents, brothers, and sisters. "But how can we see them when they are dead?" asks Tyltyl in amazement. To which the Fairy answers gently: "How can they be dead, when they live in your memory?"

This power of memory to confer immortality upon those we love has been gratefully acknowledged by mourners of all times. Death cannot rob us of our past. The days and years we shared, the common adventures and hopes, the "little nameless, unremembered acts of kindness and of love" – all these are part of the ineradicable human record. Death has no dominion where memory rules. This thought received eloquent affirmation by Whittier who prayerfully asked: "Grant but memory to us and we can lose nothing by death." Centuries before him a Talmudic sage declared: "The righteous are considered alive even in death."

Strangely, these very memories which ultimately help us to cheat death are likely to be quite painful while the anguish of parting is still fresh.

An acquaintance of mine, whose wife had died after a brief illness, refused to return, after the funeral, to the home they had shared. For some time he also avoided meeting any persons they had known, or visiting any places that would evoke reminiscences of the past. He was thus expressing in a rather extreme way a feeling many mourners experience. "The leaves of memory" do seem "to make a mournful rustling in the dark" when the darkness has just fallen.

Time, however, that most faithful ally of the mourner, serves him loyally here, too. With its benign alchemy it gradually draws the sting out of memory and converts it into a source of comfort and often, if the departed has lived well, inspiration. Those who have witnessed a western sunset know that the most enchanting time of day is often around evening. After the hot summer sun sets, while nature breathlessly waits for the light to be rolled away before the darkness, the sky is suddenly clad in the spectacular brilliance of multicolored light. These indescribably gorgeous colors are the day's afterglow.

Wordsworth said that infants who come into the world come "trailing clouds of glory." It is equally true to observe that many depart from the world trailed by "clouds of glory." Memory perpetuates these and does not let them die. "God gave us memory so that we might have roses in December."

How to Face Sorrow

Sorrow tests us as no other experience. It kicks out from under us the social stilts on which we frequently stand, and rubs off the veneer we habitually wear. It most accurately mirrors us as we truly are, because in the fearful encounter with it we are compelled to draw most heavily upon our own human resources. Kind friends and loved ones can be of real service, but the ultimate verdict, whether sorrow defeats us or we surmount it, is rendered by our own wisdom and courage. When Macbeth asks the doctor whether he can prescribe "some sweet oblivious antidote" to a sorrowing heart, he answers: "Therein the patient must minister to himself."

This is not to say, however, that there are no outside sources of strength and counsel available to us. Quite the reverse is true. Others before us have endured the agony of grief, and from the experience they distilled a measure of wisdom which they have recorded. In more recent times the psychology of grief has been explored more scientifically and the findings, taken together, constitute a genuine strategy for meeting sorrow and subduing it.

In the first place, we ought not to feel ashamed to express the genuine grief we feel. It is for such a time as this that our tear ducts were made. The poet in a romantic mood may speak of "the silent manliness of grief," but it is hardly evidence of manliness to remain silent in grief. Such silence, such repressed emotions, may be most dangerous to the mourner when they erupt at some later day in a more violent and damaging form. Ovid stood on firm psychological grounds when he cautioned "Suppressed grief suffocates." Judaism encourages us to " weep for the dead."

The second principle to guide us in our sorrow is that we must avoid the temptation to overindulge our grief. Grief in moderation is beneficial and healing. Taken in excess, it can destroy our will to live, and rob us of our initiative. If we do not retain a vigilant emotional watch, grief can easily degenerate into self-pity, which Fulton Oursler correctly called "a passport to insanity."

To guard against this psychic pitfall, we resort to a third principle which urges us to accept bravely what we cannot change, to go out of ourselves to transmute sorrow into service, to pass from feeling sorry for ourselves, which paralyzes, to feeling concern for others, which heals.

Here is a most profound truth to remember when grief darkens our lives. Trouble and sorrow naturally make us think only of ourselves. But after the first impact of the blow has worn off, our emotional recovery depends upon our ability to forget ourselves. And there is no better way of forgetting about ourselves than by thinking of and serving others. The road of service leads in time to the green pastures of healing .

Converting Sorrow into Service

A story both sad and inspiring is woven about Leland Stanford University near San Francisco. It is named after the only son of the former governor of California. While on a visit to Italy with his parents, Leland Stanford, Jr., age nine, became ill and died. The grief-stricken parents returned to California and resolved to become the benefactors of other children, to give them the opportunities they could no longer lavish upon their own son. Thus they erected and heavily endowed the university which bears the name of their son. Here boys and girls of every group in America enjoy the opportunity of a university education. This blessing to untold young people was born in the anguish of a personal sorrow which heroic parents converted into a public service.

Doors

Death, the poets tell us, has a thousand doors. Sometimes it closes a door slowly on the creaking hinges of drawn-out illness so that we have time to steel ourselves for the grim inevitability that awaits us. At other times, death springs a trap-door which slams in our faces with terrifying and stunning suddenness. But whether death heralds its arrival or catches us unawares, one thing is certain. It bolts tight a door to a precious life and leaves us with a sense of loneliness, yearning and aching emptiness.

When we stop to consider the matter further, we realize that it is not only death which closes doors on us. Life does that very thing – less dramatically, less conspicuously, perhaps, but no less emphatically.

Shakespeare in his oft quoted passage in *As You Like It,* divides life into seven ages. Man begins as "the infant mewling and puking," and then, he is "the whining school-boy, with his satchel and shining morning face, creeping like snail unwilling to school." Later he is the lover "sighing like a furnace"; then the soldier "seeking the bubble reputation even in the cannon's mouth." In his 5th age he is "the justice in fair round belly with good capon lined." In his 6th age we find him "with spectacles on nose and pouch on side." Shakespeare brings this procession to an inglorious conclusion by ending with "second child-ishness," when we find our hero "sans teeth, sans eyes, sans taste, sans everything."

Now we may not agree with Shakespeare's division of life. Students of human behavior today are more inclined to trace the growth of personality in emotional stages – infancy, childhood, adolescence and maturity. But whatever the categories we use, Shakespeare was eminently sound in telling us that every stage of life is separated from the next by "exits and entrances," by the closing of doors.

The pretty little girl leaving hesitantly for her first day in the nursery school has closed a big door of life behind her. The 9 year old en route to his first overnight camp, waving a reluctant good bye to his parents from the bus as he fights back the tears, has closed a big door of life behind him. The quaking Bar Mitzvah boy standing alone before a congregation chanting prayers and making pledges, has closed a big door of life behind him. The prim little 12 year old, acting like 15 as she glides out with her first movie date, has closed a big door of life behind her. The hopeful young man who has just "popped the question" has, at the same time, closed a big door of life behind him. And when years later he proudly negotiates that three mile walk down the fifty foot aisle with his daughter leaning ever so gracefully on his arm, he knows what every parent knows after the marriage of a child, that he has closed a big door of life behind him.

All of life is a constant succession of closing doors each accompanied by its own internal revolutions and peals of alarm.

This is true not only of our emotional life but also where our physical capacities are concerned. Here, too, the doors sometimes swing shut violently accompanied by a resounding crash. There is an accident or a heart-attack and we awake to find that a whole series of hitherto automatic and almost effortless actions are now out of bounds. Small, "normal" exertions, feeding oneself, shaving oneself, walking a few steps – actions so small and so normal that we were scarcely aware of them, much less, experienced gratitude for being able to perform them, now become infinitely precious because a door has been slammed between us and them.

Most of the time, however, life is closing doors behind us very softly, so softly we scarcely hear the lock snap. And then one day we awake to the realization that we can no longer spend fourteen hours a day at the office, that perhaps we had better start heading for the club-house after the 9th hole, that maybe the Mrs. has the right idea in suggesting a split-level home with fewer steps. We're not quite sure precisely when our physical capacity began to wane, when the distance between holes started to grow longer and the steps in the home steeper. We can't recall turning the knob on the door. Perhaps it was one of those new-fangled electronic doors which operates so sneakily and so noiselessly. But in our heart of hearts there is oppressing certainty that a door of life has been closed quite securely.

Yes, life, no less than death, is a constant series of doors being closed.

Having made these none-too-cheerful observations, I think that we are now ready for our first important truth about this matter. It is this: A vital index of our maturity as men and women is the gracefulness with which we accept the closing of the doors, which death and life alike impose. That such acceptance is often enormously difficult goes without saying. But unless we prove capable of doing precisely that, we forfeit the opportunity to live creative and meaningful lives.

When death closes the door to a life we have loved it is worse than futile to spend the rest of our days in vain efforts to batter down the door, or in asking the unanswerable question, "Why did the door have to swing shut on me?" – or, in pretending that the door was never closed at all.

I am thinking of a very unhappy woman who, for years after her husband's death, has not permitted one item of his clothing to be removed or one piece of furniture in his study to be rearranged. "I want things to be just as they were when Bill was here," is her explanation. She may be soothing herself with the thought that she is being loyal to his memory but that poor woman is betraying her future. Unfortunately, she has not yet come to terms with the reality that the door on her Bill's life has been shut tight.

As human beings, in our quest for maturity, we often have a strong hankering to retrace our steps down life's corridor and to re-open the doors of infancy and childhood. Then, life was protected and sheltered; then, all our needs were catered to, all life centered around us, all decisions were made for us. Small wonder then that when life becomes complicated and perplexing we should want to run back, to unwind the spool of time.

Psychologists call this phenomenon "regression." The married woman who is forever solving her marital problems by packing off for mother's, the harassed head of the family who meets every financial crisis by getting another asthma attack so that the burden of worry is shifted to other shoulders – each of these has failed to accept graciously the inescapable fact that the doors of infancy and childhood have been sealed tight. They can beat on the doors of the nursery and dress in the faded wardrobe of childhood but only at the cost of remaining emotional dwarfs with overgrown bodies. Growing up, if it has any meaning at all, means that we avoid the hazardous and unrewarding effort to pick the locks on the doors that have closed on our yesterdays.

And what shall we say of those who refuse to pay the toll on the bridge of time by pretending that they are still as young as their kind friends tell them they look? What the doctor said of Jim is true of many Americans, I am afraid. When Jim collapsed in his office the examining doctor who had known him well confided to a mutual friend: "Jim sacrificed for his beliefs." "What beliefs did he cherish?" the friend asked. "Jim believed," answered the doctor, "that he could live a 30 year old life with a 55 year old body."

Many of us harbor such suicidal beliefs. Too often, as our powers wane, our ambitions flourish. When we should be diminishing our financial pressures we are building them up; when we should be curtailing our social round we are expanding it; when we should be pumping the brake, our foot finds the accelerator. We pay a heavy penalty indeed when we refuse to accept gracefully the inescapable fact that life has closed some important doors in our physical lives quite securely. We cannot break these doors. We can only break ourselves against them.

Another vital truth is suggested by a brief but beautiful prayer found in the N'eilah service on Yom Kippur. "Open to us a gate at the time when a gate is closed." The author of the prayer was underscoring one of the basic truths of the spiritual life.

God never closes a door in our lives without at the same time opening another. Whenever one area of life is sealed off to us, another comes into view.

I had a vivid illustration of this truth while working on this very theme. I was writing in my study at home and had closed my door. Suddenly a gust of wind blew through the adjoining bedroom and slammed shut the bedroom door which had been open. But the impact of the door that slammed forced open the door to my study. This is what happens in life all the time.

The implications of this truth are profound indeed. They touch upon every aspect of life and death. Our tradition sublimely insists that death itself is the closing of one door and the simultaneous opening of another. "This world," taught our sages, "is only a vestibule before the palace of the world to come." When the door closes on the vestibule, it opens into the palace. There are a host of compelling reasons which nurture our faith in the immortality of the human soul. The reasonableness of the universe demands it for, as the physicist Robert Millikan said: "The Divine Architect of the Universe has not built a stairway that leads to nowhere." Our own souls hunger for it and God has given us no hunger which He does not satisfy. We hunger for food and He provides food. We thirst for drink and He provides water. We hunger for love and He has put love into the world. We hunger for eternal life and I believe He satisfies that craving too. These are only some of the persuasive arguments which convince me of the truth that: "Death is not the master of the house. He is only the porter at the king's lodge, appointed to open the gate and let the King's guests enter into the realm of eternal day."

Yes, God does open to us a door at the time when he closes the door of death.

And how about us the living? What doors open to us when the door of sorrow closes?

The more I observe life, the more impressed do I become with the large number of doors which open to us at such a time.

Do you remember the parable of the Dubno Maggid? He tells of a king who once owned a large, beautiful pure diamond of which he was justly proud for it had no equal anywhere. One day, through a mishap, the diamond sustained a deep scratch. The king called in the most skilled diamond cutters and offered to reimburse them hand-somely if they could remove the imperfection from his treasured jewel. But none could repair the blemish. After some time a gifted lapidary came to the king and promised to make the rare diamond even more beautiful than it had been before the accident. The king was impressed by his confidence and entrusted his precious stone to his care. And the man kept his word. With superb artistry he engraved a lovely rosebud around the imperfection, and he used the scratch to form the stem.

A deep truth speaks to us out of this parable. When sorrow inflicts a bruise upon us, we can use even the scratch to make our lives more radiant and more lovely. Sorrows are often "the needles with which God sews our souls to eternal truths."

Despite its grim appearance, sorrow possesses vast potential power to expand our horizons, to deepen our understanding, to enlarge our visions. It has played a transforming role in the lives of countless bereaved.

Through the door of sorrow we can enter into the suffering of others. Our human compassion is kindled. Our sympathies are awak-ened. It can elicit from us powers of fortitude and patience which, but for it, might never have been quickened into life. Sorrow can also help purge us of pettiness and selfishness. It can, thus, bring us closer to our fellow man and help make us taller people. God does, indeed, open to us a door at the time when He closes the door of sorrow.

As we grow and develop, God is forever opening doors in front of us as He closes doors behind us. Our mistake is that we lose heart, we don't trust Him. We know where we've been but we don't know where we are going. We want things to be just as they were in "the good ole days." To have faith in God, means among other things, to believe that the door He now opens to us leads to a stage of life with its own unique satisfactions and delights, its own rich adventures and challenges. As our physical powers diminish, added time and energy become available for life's less taxing but no less rewarding activities. We have more time to study, to reflect, to listen to music, to cultivate friendships, to help along a cause, to elevate our souls, to get to know ourselves better.

Life would become drab indeed and quite insipid to our taste if the years of our lives were not kissed each with its own charms and capacities, each with its unique colors and shadings. Life's beauty comes precisely from the changing configurations and patterns of the years, from God's great mercy in constantly closing and opening doors for us.

For last I have left two striking illustrations of our theme which deal not with the doors that are softly closed behind us but with the doors that seem to be maliciously slammed in our faces.

The first is a page from recent Jewish history. If ever there was a period of closing doors in Jewish life, it was in the holocaust of Nazi Europe. Indeed it was a horrible succession of N'eilahs for six million of our brethren – fathers, mothers and children. When we think of those dark, dreary, maddening years, we visualize the closing of the doors of crematoria, gas-chambers, railways cars, concentration camps. All exits were sealed off, every escape hatch swung shut. The allegedly civilized world did distressingly little to open the doors of doom. The British, then in control of Palestine, were busy hunting down and turning back the ships that managed to bring a few pitiful remnants of the disaster.

And yet it was precisely at this time, under the impact of the doors being slammed in the faces of our European brothers that the doors to Eretz Yisrael were forced open. Locks that had remained bolted for nineteen centuries were not sprung open, and a new magnificent chapter began in the saga of Israel. God opened for us a gate at the time of the closing of the gate.

The second illustration points up this truth in the life of a single individual.

On May 3, 1941, Peter Putnam not yet 21 and a Junior student at Princeton University, with everything to live with and apparently nothing to live for, made an important decision. He was going to commit suicide. Carefully he wrote out his suicide note and stuffed it into his wallet. From his pocket he drew a gun loaded with three bullets. The hands on his purple leather travelling clock showed twenty past ten. It was the last thing Peter Putnam was ever to see. For it was at that moment that Peter Putnam pulled the trigger of the gun pointed at his brain. Peter Putnam, with the door of hope and zest for living seemingly shut in his face, had taken the only way out.

Peter Putnam did not die but he had succeeded in blinding himself for life. Surely we would imagine if Peter Putnam had felt no reason for living before his suicide attempt, he would feel even less reason for doing so now. Let us listen to him tell the story from this point.

"What surprised and exhilarated me, as I returned to consciousness, was not so much that I was alive, but that I was so terribly glad to be alive. . . . The future, including future blindness, seemed a challenge to which I was now wholly committed, and this challenge transformed my view of the world. Graduation from Princeton, a meaningless formality toward which I had been stumbling with half a heart, now seemed the very symbol of my first step toward this new world. In short I wanted to live as I had never wanted to live before."

In February 1942, accompanied by his seeing eye dog Minnie, Peter was back at Princeton. He helped write and direct the Princeton Triangle show and acted in it. He graduated Magna Cum Laude, and went on to earn his Masters and Doctors degrees. In the meanwhile he found time to get married, to raise a family of three children, to learn how to ski! His second book, *Cast Off the Darkness,* has been published.

Peter Putnam in his darkness saw the door God opened for him after all the doors had been shut tight.

I said earlier that what we pray for is that God should open for us a gate at the time when a gate is being closed. I'd like to emend that somewhat now because, you see, we don't have to ask God to do that for us. God is always doing precisely that. What we should pray for is that we be granted the courage and the patience to find the door He opens at the time when doors close; that we do not despair, that we do not surrender our faith and our hope, that we hold on tenaciously until we find the way to renewed life and renewed zeal.

Death Teaches Life

The existence of death has ever served as a lesson to life. We cannot for long evade the consciousness of our mortality nor fail to draw from it some fundamental attitudes on how our lives shall be conducted.

Death, however, has not taught the same lesson to all people. To some, the presence of death has been a spur to unbridled self-indulgence and the uninhibited pursuit of pleasure. Thus among the Romans, a human skeleton was frequently exhibited among the celebrants at festive parties with the exhortation: "Let us enjoy life while we may." Herodotus tells us that a similar custom prevailed among the Egyptians. At joyous occasions, the image of a dead man carved in wood, or a coffin containing the embalmed remains of some ancestor, would be presented to each guest by a person whose function it was to pronounce distinctly as he did so: "Look upon this and be merry; for such as this, when dead, shalt thou be." The prophet Isaiah sums up the slogan of those to whom life's brevity is a stimulant to unrestrained hedonism in the words: "Let us eat and drink, for tomorrow we die."

This approach to life testifies to a failure of nerve and leads to moral bankruptcy. It is a philosophy of despair which not only fails to bring satisfaction but overlooks the many sources of real joy that life generously affords. Where the sole objective of living is reduced to an endless round of pleasure-seeking, the ultimate verdict must be a cynical refrain of disillusionment: "Futility of futilities, all is futility."

There are others whom death has instructed more wisely. To them life's brevity has been an incentive to live more nobly, more generously, more creatively. They have recognized that while a limit has been set to the length of our days, we alone determine their breadth and their depth. Thus Joshua Loth Liebman counsels: "We must make up for the ... brevity of life by heightening the intensity of life." Frances Gunther urges us to embrace life and those we love "with a little added rapture and a keener awareness of joy." Bertrand Russell, in a somewhat bleaker mood, realizes that we and our comrades alike are subject to "the silent orders of omnipotent Death." He would therefore have us "shed sunshine on their path ... lighten their sorrows by the balm of sympathy ... strengthen failing courage ... instill faith in hours of despair." The Psalmist of an earlier age contemplated life's transiency and prayed: "So teach us to number our days that we obtain a heart of wisdom."

In the hour of bereavement the death of a loved one can teach us to pitch our lives at the highest level. Yes, life is brief, but we determine its quality. Indeed, precisely because of its brevity, we must be very discriminating as to what we put into it. "Life," said Disraeli, "is too short to be little."

Death Is Not the End

Ours is an age in which theological matters do not occupy too prominent a role in our thinking. We are nonchalant about beliefs and
doctrines over which former generations speculated abundantly and in
which they believed passionately. The belief in immortality is one
such doctrine towards which we display conspicuous indifference. Our
emphasis has been largely humanistic, underscoring the importance of
leading worthy lives here and now and letting the hereafter take care of
itself. We normally presume that it makes little difference one way or
another whether the soul survives death or not.

In the time of bereavement, however, it matters profoundly
whether we believe that death is "a period which brings the sentence of
life to a full stop," or whether we believe that "it is only a comma
which punctuates it to loftier significance." It makes an enormous
difference whether we believe that the essence of our loved ones has
been totally erased from the slate of life, or whether it survives with the
Author of Life, Himself. Our personal indifference departs when
sorrow enters. Thus, even so confirmed an agnostic as Robert G.
Ingersoll, speaking at the funeral services for his brother, felt con-
strained to add this comforting assurance: "But in the night of death,
Hope sees a star, and listening, Love can hear the rustle of a wing."

From the ancients with their naïve beliefs down through the long
corridors of time reaching into the present most sophisticated faiths,
people have persistently and in decisive numbers held the human soul
indestructible.

This was the conviction that welled up in the heart of Charlotte
Brontë as she lay dying. "God will not separate us now; we have been
so happy." Our craving for eternity in a world which responds to our
every other fundamental yearning and need points to a God who, in
the words of the Hebrew prayer-book, "implanted within us everlasting life."

Simple parables illustrate great truths. Little David found a bird
nest near his home which contained some speckled eggs. He visited it
for a few days and then had to leave on a trip to the city. Upon his
return he rushed to the nest to look at the eggs. To his deep dismay he
found that the beautiful eggs were no longer there. Indeed, there were
only broken, empty shells. With tears in his eyes he ran to his father
and cried: "Father, they were such beautiful eggs. Now they are all

spoiled and broken." "No, son," his father reassured him, "they are not spoiled. The best part of them has taken wings and flown away."

It Is for Us the Living . . .

In describing the death of David, the Bible says: "And David slept with his fathers." This expression induced a Talmudic sage to ask why the Bible employed the word "slept" rather than "died," which the Bible used elsewhere. The answer he gave to his own question was that since David was survived by a son who cherished the same high ideals and values which were dear to him, David did not really die. He lived on in his progeny. Therefore David "slept."

Rabbi Phineas bar Hama, the sage in question, was not alone in calling attention to the power of the survivors to confer a measure of immortality upon the departed. People have always felt that they perpetuate the pulsating influence of their beloved dead when they identify themselves with their pursuits and reach out for their goals. By extending the impact of the remembered personalities beyond the span of their days, the survivors attest to the deathlessness of their loved ones. In a very real sense, it is the living who determine whether or not the departed live on.

In our own war-filled years, this interdependence of the generations has become more pronounced. Our liberty, our security, our very right to exist have been dearly purchased. On far-flung battlefields, young men have died in unprecedented numbers in the cause of Freedom and Democracy. To them we feel an obligation too sacred to be discharged by mere rituals of remembrance. To them we owe the fulfilment of the vision which lured them on to their premature deaths. To them we owe a world united in peace and brotherhood, a society in which diverse political systems, religious orientations and racial groups live and work together for the common good. To the extent that we strive to achieve these difficult yet attainable goals, do we redeem their deaths from futility and we invest our lives with high purpose.

Whether we mourn the honored dead who fell in the cause of peace or grieve over the loss of someone who stood near to us, we would do well to hear and heed the wise words the poet spoke on behalf of the dead to the living:

"Complete these dear unfinished tasks of mine
And I, perchance, may therein comfort you."

A Letter to a Boy Who Has Lost His Mother

Dear John:

You are about to mark your 13th birthday so soon after the death of your mother, a professional pianist, and your Aunt Winnie has asked me to write to you at this time.

She is Catholic, and so are you, and it is strange that she would ask a rabbi to try to offer you some comfort over your terrible loss. I believe that she turned to me because, as she wrote, your mother "was very much touched" by one of my recent columns, and Aunt Winnie was hoping that in some way I could reach out and touch you.

I cannot always honor the requests made by my readers, but this particular request I could not refuse. You see, John, I too lost my mother when I was a young boy. By a marvelous coincidence, I was, like yourself, the youngest of three brothers, and I, too, had a younger sister. Our situations are so similar that in talking to you I feel almost like I am talking to the frightened and bewildered young boy my mother left behind after he had just passed his 11th birthday.

You probably know, John, that a Jewish boy at 13 celebrates his bar mitzvah. This is the ceremony that marks the crossing of the threshold of maturity and the assumption of greater responsibility. Of course there is no instant growing up, and the line that separates childhood from manhood isn't crossed in a single day. But religiously speaking, a Jewish boy at 13 does take on the obligations of an adult.

I remember, John, that my mother's death was, for me, a kind of premature bar mitzvah. Almost overnight I grew up because I had to. My father left for work early in the morning, and we children had to run the home and our lives largely on our own. There was no one to remind us how to dress, how to eat, when to do our homework. It was grow up or else. I had a cousin who was six weeks younger than I, and we were very close. Within a few months I felt so much older than he. My mom's death made me grow up.

There is another thing that being an orphan did for me, my brothers and sister. Almost miraculously, we stopped fighting with each other. To defend against our chilly fate, we suddenly huddled closer together and gave each other additional warmth and affection. To this day I don't think there is a closer family than ours, even though we are separated by many miles.

And I believe that my mom's death did one other thing for me: it helped me to feel the pain of those who are bereaved, lonely and hurt. Perhaps that is why I became a rabbi and devoted my life to a calling that demands large doses of compassion and kindness. Maybe my youthful grief was also responsible for the first book I published, *A Treasury of Comfort.*

You see, John, there is a law of compensation at work in the world. Often when something very precious is taken from us, other things are given in return. Those things don't take the place of what we have lost, but often they make us better people than we might otherwise have become.

It is now 52 years since I saw my mother alive, and I tell you, John, that there has scarcely been a day during all these years that I haven't seen my mother's beautiful face. She is forever 39. And now I am much older than she. I know how close you were to your mother, and I have every reason to believe that she will be with you always, with her hands of blessing touching your head. In one of her poems, Sara Teasdale wrote: "Places I have known come back to me like music,/ Hush me and heal me when I am very tired."

This is true not only of places, but of people we have known. Again and again, when you are very tired, Mom will come to you like the music she played so brilliantly, to hush you and heal you. At all times may her memory be a source of courage to you, summoning you to reach ever higher so that your life may be an eloquent tribute to the one who gave you life.

May He who gives strength to the weary and wipes away the tears from all faces, grant comfort and healing to you and to your family.

With genuine sympathy,
Rabbi Sidney Greenberg

The Fine Art of Forgetting

The rabbi in Leon Uris' novel about the persecuted Jews in the Warsaw Ghetto, *Mila 18,* makes a penetrating observation. He declares that when a Jew says "I believe," he really means, "I remember." It is quite true that historical memories are the glue which has kept our people together over the centuries.

A Jew is born 4,000 years old. We have a special Sabbath called "*Zakhor,*" remember. All of our festivals are designed to relive ancestral experiences in ages past. "You shall remember that you were a slave in the land of Egypt," is a Biblical exhortation that is repeated again and again.

In our personal lives there are a host of rituals designed as mnemonics to help us remember our loved ones who have died. There is the Kaddish, yahrzeit, Yizkor. We name our children and our grandchildren after them. We put their names on memorials in synagogues, we plant trees, and we give *tzedakah* in their memory.

For all the emphasis we place on the importance of remembering, it is appropriate that we reflect from time to time on the importance of forgetting.

Ingrid Bergman once said that she was fortunate to possess the two assets on which happiness depends–good health and a poor memory. That talented lady gave us a much needed reminder that the ability to forget is no less important than the ability to remember.

We often apologize for forgetting things. In his farewell address, Moses rebukes his people for forgetting a crucial fact: "You forgot the God who brought you forth" (Deuteronomy 32:18).

But important as is the power to remember, no less important is the power to forget. Life, as we know it, would be unbearable if we were not blessed with what one eight-year-old called "a good forgettery."

If we had to live each day burdened with the weight of past griefs and bereavements, if we could not banish from our minds our accumulated failures, fears and frustrations, if the wounds we suffer on life's battlefield were always raw and gaping–then life would be a heavy curse.

Long ago, our Sages taught us this same truth. In a charming legend we are told that after the Almighty finished creating the world, He was about to release it when He suddenly realized that He had omitted an indispensable ingredient without which life could not endure. God had forgotten to include the power to forget. And so He blessed the world with that special gift, and then He was content that it was now fit for human habitation.

Many of us could use that gift. So many families remain splintered and fragmented because of some slight, real or imagined, suffered long years ago which the offended party cannot or will not forget.

Some time ago I was discussing funeral services for a father who was survived by two sons. When I asked the son who was making the arrangements where the family would sit *Shivah*, I was requested to make no public announcement because the sons would not sit together in one house. The reason? Their wives stopped talking to each other years ago over some invitation which was not reciprocated. At least, that's what he thought it was. By now, he was not quite sure what had caused the split in the family. He could not remember the source of the conflict, but whatever it was, neither brother could forget it.

Many a marriage could stand a healthy dose of forgetting. One man complained to his friend that whenever his wife gets angry she becomes historical. "You mean hysterical," the friend corrected him. "No," said the husband, "I mean historical. She starts listing everything I did wrong in the last 27 years."

Lewis E. Lawes, who served many years as the warden of Sing Sing, once said that our prisons are filled with people who could not or would not forget.

So many lives are cluttered with all kinds of destructive memories. They carry accumulated resentments, hurts, sorrows and disappointments suffered in the arena of life. The price for such remembering is exorbitant. It includes our emotional and mental health. When the Torah admonishes us not to "bear a grudge," it is urging us for our own sake to use our God-given power to forget.

An anonymous poet put into rhyme some thoughts about forgetting we would do well to remember:

> "This world would be for us a happier place
> And there would be less of regretting
> If we would remember to practice with grace,
> The very fine art of forgetting."

Of God and Thurman Munson

At the funeral service for Thurman Munson, one of his Yankee teammates delivered a sensitive eulogy that included these words: "We don't know why God took Thurman from us, but we do know that as long as we wear the Yankee uniform he won't be too far from us."

I know these words were meant to comfort a shocked and bereaved family and to provide some solace for the millions of us who were knit together in the "brotherhood of pain" over the sudden death of a great baseball hero in the very prime of his life.

I confess, however, that, for this Yankee fan at least, there was no solace in the words, "We don't know why God took Thurman from us." Those words trouble me more than they console me. They seem to say that God willed the tragic accident that claimed Thurman's life, that it was His doing and His purpose that this career of extraordinary brilliance be abruptly and prematurely terminated.

I am not unfamiliar with such expressions of piety. I have heard colleagues of all faiths utter them in times of tragedy. But I often wonder whether these spokesmen for God do not cost Him more friends than they make. I find it hard to believe that God would want Diane Munson to be widowed, and three very young, innocent children to be left fatherless. I find it terribly difficult to reconcile a God of mercy and love with a God who "took Thurman from us."

I know it is comforting to believe in times of great misfortune that the event that brings us sorrow is the will of God, but the cost of such comfort is extravagantly high. It affirms God's omnipotence at the expense of His benevolence. It extols His power but diminishes His compassion.

A mature faith in God, I believe, is one that recognizes that we live in an orderly universe of cause and effect, and that all of us – the great and the humble, the celebrated and the obscure, the good and the bad – are subject to its laws. If a jet plane violates the laws of nature, its retribution is swift and impartial. At such a moment it is not God who "takes" a life; it is a law-abiding universe affirming the regularity and the precision with which it abides by the laws of its Creator.

And it is this very dependability of nature that makes intelligent living possible. If the law of gravity could be capriciously suspended, if the sun rose one day in the east and the next day in the north, if winter came one year in December and the following year in July, if apple seeds one year produced apples and the next year plums–life as we know it would be impossible. We would be unable to plan from one moment to the next. Because the universe is reliable, we can learn its laws and use that knowledge for our benefit and enrichment. When we break those laws the price is often broken bodies and broken hearts.

Where, then, is God in this terrible tragedy? God is in the dependability and in the orderliness of the universe He created. God is in the love that Thurman felt for his family. God is in the outpouring of grief that millions of Thurman's admirers felt for his dear ones. God is in the tears that were shed, the caring that was expressed, the sense of impoverishment that flooded so many lives.

God is in the awareness that this tragedy brought home to all of us that we are frail and fragile creatures whose lives hang by a slender thread, and that we do not know how soon it will be too late to do all we were meant to do on this earth.

God is in the healing that will come to all who mourn Thurman; it will come slowly, perhaps too slowly, but ever so surely. God is in the power of the human spirit to rise above tragedy, to go on after sorrow, and even to transmute suffering into song and pain into poetry. God is in the great gift of memory that enables us to keep our loved ones alive and to take them with us as we journey in faith toward a beckoning brighter tomorrow.

V

THE ULTIMATE
WISDOM – CHOOSE LIFE

One of the hallmark verses of the Torah challenges us:
"I have set before you life and death, the blessing
and the curse; choose life . . ."
It is only when we believe that there are indeed moral
choices and that we have the power to make moral
choices that we can truly live meaningful lives.

The Ultimate Wisdom – Choose Life

On Sunday, June 10, 1979, artist Jo Roman, 62, said farewell to a friend, her daughter and her husband. Then she swallowed 33 sleeping pills and washed them down with champagne.

This act of self-destruction was not impulsive. Jo had decided some four years earlier that she would not leave her death to fate. She would end her life on her own terms "probably around age 70." It would be a "rational suicide."

In March 1978 she learned that she had breast cancer and decided that she would end her life in about a year. She shared her decision with her family, friends and a TV film crew which was present when she gathered with her confidants to discuss her decision. About 19 hours of taping went into the making of the one-hour documentary, "Choosing Suicide," which was then aired.

Boris Pasternak has observed that our normal reaction to a suicide victim is to "bow compassionately before his suffering." I suspect, however, that the television viewers felt little compassion for Jo Roman. She shows no evidence of suffering. She is altogether too cool and too calculating for someone contemplating the ultimate act of violence turned upon oneself.

She defends her idea of "rational suicide" (about which she was writing a book) as "an option in life that can be life-liberating and enriching." How the destruction of life can be liberating and enriching totally escapes me. Nor does she help to enlighten me by comparing the decision about "one's life span" to the decision about "whether or not to have children, whether or not to marry." Is the equation really so neat and so casual?

Having trivialized the awesome realities of life and death, she elicits from her friends either endorsements for her decision or the most unconvincing arguments designed to dissuade her. One friend sagely observes. "Just as I'm not very much in favor of easy marriage, I wouldn't be in favor of easy suicide." Some comparison!

Another friend explains why she will not attempt to dissuade her. "If someone said to me, at age 75, 'I'm arthritic and can't type anymore and the quality of my life is different,' I think I would attempt to discuss the issue with them and in some way dissuade them. But not you." So! If you lose your ability to type, that's grounds for suicide. And how about your golf stroke, or your ability to jog?

Still another friend waxes absolutely rhapsodic over the prospect of her "rational suicide." "Your dying is going to be maybe the greatest creative act you ever did. It's like starting a canvas." You can't beat that for encouragement.

Her husband, Mel, is a professor of psychiatry, and we might expect his love for his wife and his professional training to express themselves in strongest opposition. He admits that there are times when the knowledge of Jo's intentions has been "absolutely terrible, when it's been so painful and so difficult . . . that I have felt I just couldn't survive it."

But all this pain is offset by the feeling that the experience has not been without its redemptive features: "I've learned an enormous amount about myself," he assures us.

The lesson apparently was worth the tuition because, he adds, "in some ways it's been extraordinarily inspiring." What about love? "I have felt that out of my concern for her, my love for her, that I would do everything I could to help her fulfill what she wants to do." Strange are the ways of love.

The ultimate justification for Jo's contemplated self-destruction, he puts in these words: "I feel Jo is doing something, not only for herself, she's doing something for me. And for us, meaning the family. It may not be right for others but I'm certainly convinced intellectually that it's right." One member of that family is Jo's daughter, who also has cancer. One can only imagine how helpful her mother's suicide was to her.

Jo justifies her decision to end her life at a time of her choosing by asking rhetorically: "Why should I have pain? I don't want a day of pain. I don't want a minute of pain." Perhaps it was this same fear of pain that prompted her after the death of her first husband to give her daughter and son to a friend who adopted them. Being a parent involves pain. Being human involves pain. Being alive involves pain.

The challenge of life is to go on despite pain, to paint, as Renoir did with fingers crippled by arthritis and to say as he did: "The pain passes, the beauty remains." The challenge of life is to be alive to its beauty, its joy, its infinite possibilities. The challenge of life is to confront it with courage and wonder, to accept it for the precious gift that it is, to make the most of it while it is ours, and to leave the world a little richer for our having been here.

The ultimate meaning and wisdom are to be found not in "Choosing Suicide" but in responding to the biblical command: "Behold I set before you this day life and death . . . and you shall choose life."

To Choose One's Own Way

One of the most harrowing moments in contemporary literature is the one which gives William Styron's novel its title. It is the moment describing Sophie's choice, the most horrible choice a mother could be asked to make – which her two children to turn over to Nazi destruction and which to keep alive.

"I can't choose! I can't choose!" she screams again and again in a voice louder than "hell's pandemonium." "Don't make me choose," she pleads, "I can't choose." It is only when the unrelenting doctor threatens to murder both her children that she blurts out: "Take the baby! Take my little girl."

Sophie's maddening choice was to haunt her for the rest of her life.

The terrible truth is that this piercing moment in fiction is only too accurate a description of what actually happened again and again during the holocaust. William Styron distorted the historical record by making the victim of the Nazi's fiendish cruelty a Polish Christian. In real life it was Jewish mothers who were confronted by such blasphemous choices.

(We might also note in passing that in his book Styron does not have any admirable Jewish characters. His good people are all non-Jews.)

Despite what the Nazis did to corrupt the human power to choose, the fact is that this very capacity to make significant choices is one of our most distinctive human endowments.

The word "intelligence" is derived from two Latin words—"inter" and "legere." "Inter" means between, and "legere" means to choose. Intelligence is the capacity to choose between alternative courses of actions, to make moral decisions.

Translated into theological terms this means that you and I possess freedom of will. This doctrine, which is at the very center of Jewish teaching, has had to fight off formidable opponents throughout history down to our own times.

The pagan religions of antiquity taught that man was forever doomed because he slew some deity. Hinduism viewed man as chained to Karma, the wheel of fate. In Islam man is controlled by Kismet.

When the Israelis were withdrawing from the Sinai, one of the Bedouins, who had lived under Israeli rule since 1967, expressed amazement at the value Israel placed on human life. "I don't understand why you take it so seriously when someone gets ill. Why do you get so excited? It comes from Allah."

In our own society there are many voices which strenuously deny that we are indeed free to make significant choices. Some declare that we are the products of our heredity, others affirm that our environment makes us what we are. You and I may delude ourselves into believing that we have freedom of will to choose our way, but in fact the true determinants of our destiny are beyond our power to control. We are mere puppets being manipulated by a fate not of our own making.

It was this type of thinking that prompted one 24-year-old man to sue his parents for $350,000 for what he called "psychological malparenting." He felt that they had messed up his life beyond repair. All his failures were all their fault. He was the helpless victim of their mistakes.

This evasion of responsibility for one's own life would find no support in Judaism. Rather, it would remind us that we do indeed have choices and that we create our own world by the choices we make.

Interestingly, the newest teachings of psychiatry endorse this view. While they do not deny the enormous influence of many factors we cannot control, they remind us that there is a decisive area where our own free will can enable us to take charge of our lives.

A cartoon, appearing in one of our national magazines, points in this direction. It shows a lawyer talking to his client. The caption reads: "We can't blame your problem on television. I polled the jury, and they all watch the same shows you do."

The glory and the anguish of being human derive from our ability to choose and direct the course of our lives. It is often tempting to throw up our hands and plead helplessness. But that strategy leads only to defeat and failure. Significant living is always characterized by a feeling that human will and determination play a decisive role in shaping human destiny.

Thus, *Living With Loss* by Ramsay and Noorbergen concludes with this sentence: "Ultimately whether grief destroys you or strengthens you is something only you can decide."

Most eloquent testimony of the power of the human will is provided by Dr. Victor Frankl. He wrote, "We who have lived in concentration camps can remember the men who walked through the huts comforting others, giving away their last piece of bread. They may have been few in number but they offer sufficient proof that everything can be taken from man but one thing: the last of the human freedoms – to choose one's attitude in any given set of circumstances – to choose one's own way."

Long, long ago the Torah put the challenge to us most directly. "Behold, I have set before you this day the blessing and the curse, life and death. And you shall choose life."

The Man Who Never Died

In our tradition there is only one person who was spared the universal fate of death. That person was the Prophet Elijah who, according to the Biblical account, ascended to heaven alive in a chariot of fire. That Elijah should have been the only person so uniquely favored constitutes a supreme irony, because at one point in his tumultuous life he wanted so desperately to die.

The prophetic portion we read in our synagogues describes the crisis of despair and hopelessness in Elijah's life.

Elijah had run away from the wrath of the idolatrous Queen Jezebel who had vowed to kill him. On Mount Carmel, Elijah had succeeded in bringing the people back to a thunderous affirmation of faith in the One God. But his triumph was to be very brief. Jezebel was determined to take revenge on Elijah.

Now we find Elijah a fugitive in the wilderness of Beer-Sheba convinced of the failure of his mission and tasting the bitter dregs of disappointment. He has fought the Lord's battles to no avail. "I have been very jealous for the Lord, God of hosts; for the children of Israel have forsaken Your covenant, thrown down Your altars and slain Your prophets with the sword. And I, I alone am left; and they seek to take away my life."

Elijah hiding in the cave is in a black mood. He feels defeated, abandoned and cornered. We can almost sympathize with his soul-wrenching plea: "It is enough, O Lord, now take away my life."

Elijah has had it. Life has crushed him. He can't go on. Now God, just one last favor please. "Take away my life."

Yes, this is the same Elijah who, the Bible tells us, was never to die. He who at one crushing juncture had begged for death, came back from the abyss of despair to live a life which was never to taste death at all.

It seems to me that there is a powerful message here to all of us when we find ourselves overwhelmed by sorrow, heartbreak or disappointment. When we are tempted to utter the ultimate heresy: "I can't go on!" Elijah's life responds: "O yes, you can!" When we pray out of the depths: "Take away my life," Elijah's triumph over surrender commands us: "Take your life and use it!"

Thoughts of Elijah surfaced some years ago when there appeared a newspaper account of an unsigned letter of appreciation received by a gentleman in Herkimer, New York. The sender was a woman whom he had met briefly nine years earlier on an eastbound train from California. He was returning from the Pacific theatre where he had flown 60 missions in his B-25. She had just received a war department telegram informing her that her husband had been killed in action.

When they met in the vestibule of the railroad car he did not even remotely suspect that he had interrupted her attempt to commit suicide by jumping off the speeding train. Her letter made all that quite plain now.

"February 1, 1945, that night I was on the train speeding on a journey that seemed endless. You were on the train, too, speeding to the wife you hadn't seen since the war began. I doubt if you remember me now. The girl in the black dress, sad and lonely, sitting across the aisle.

"If you hadn't come into the vestibule when you did, I'd have opened the door and jumped out. Did I thank you for that and for all the kind things you did for me?

"Two years later I married again. I have a fine husband, two wonderful children and a lovely home. To think that I am so happy now and owe it all to a stranger on the train who helped me through my darkest hours. . . .

"Thanks for saving my life. I'm truly grateful."

The letter was signed only, "Sincerely."

Our anonymous widow was on the verge of a desperate irrevocable act because her world had been shattered and she had seen no possibility of ever finding happiness or even meaning in life. But after the grim, dark hours had passed, the dawn of revived hope broke, and with it came the courage to hold on and tough it out until she would find new opportunities for creative living.

Such is the reward of those who do not surrender, who hold on tenaciously, and respond heroically to the challenging Biblical summons: "And you shall choose life."

It's wondrously instructive to notice that in Hebrew the word *shahor* means "black." With the slightest change of vowels, those same Hebrew letters spell *shahar*, which means "dawn." When we are engulfed by the black night of despair it is worth remembering that if we do not give up, if we cling to the precious thread of life, the blackness will be conquered by the dawn when the sun will be aflame in the east, bright with all sorts of unsuspected possibilities.

Accepting Life's Coercions

The late Rabbi Stephen S. Wise was once seated at a banquet next to a woman who tried to impress him with her exalted lineage. "One of my ancestors," she said proudly, "witnessed the signing of the Declaration of Independence." The rabbi could not resist replying: "My ancestors were present at the giving of the Ten Commandments."

The Festival of Shavuot marks the traditional anniversary of that historic occasion when our ancestors heard the Divine voice proclaim the words which have probably had a profounder benevolent impact on all of subsequent history than any other recorded words – the Ten Commandments.

The revolutionary moment happened some 3200 years ago in a harsh desert under a broiling sun. There was no radio reporter or television camera to record the event. The audience was a motley horde of ex-slaves who had so very recently escaped from centuries of oppression. But that fateful encounter forged them into a people, a people whose primary task it would be to treasure those words, preserve them and live by them.

That they honored faithfully their commitment in the face of the most incredible odds is attested to by the fact that we are here, a vital creative Jewish people preparing once again to observe Shavuot, "The time of the giving of our Torah."

Our Sages speculated on the circumstances under which our ancestors accepted the Torah. According to one tradition, the Almighty offered the Torah to one nation after another who each rejected it because of some prohibition it contained which they found objectionable. When He offered it to our ancestors they eagerly accepted the Torah without even bothering to inquire about its contents.

Another tradition gives a radically different version. It claims that the Almighty inverted Mount Sinai like a bowl over the heads of our ancestors and said to them: "If you accept My Torah well and good; if not this shall be your burial place."

Is it possible to reconcile these two conflicting traditions? Can we give credence to the tradition that our ancestors accepted the Torah willingly, while at the same time believing that they accepted the Torah under ultimate coercion?

Perhaps on deeper reflection the two traditions are indeed compatible. Perhaps they point to a wise strategy for facing life – we must learn to accept what we cannot change, we must translate our coercions into affirmations.

Life is full of coercions. Indeed, life itself is a coercion. As an ancient rabbi long ago told us: "Against your will were you born." And the young never tire of reminding their parents: "I didn't ask to be born." One of Sholom Aleichem's characters makes the wry observation: "The way life is, you're better off not to be born. But who can be so lucky? Maybe one in ten thousand."

The Talmud records a philosophical debate between the schools of Shammai and Hillel on this very question. "Was it better for man to have been created than not to have been created." The discussion continued without resolution for two-and-a-half years. Finally they put the question to a vote and it was decided that it were better for man not to have been created. "However," they added, "having been created let him pay heed to his actions."

Life is indeed a matter of coercion but we must accept it gladly and use it wisely. George Santayana reflected the spirit of our Sages when he wrote: "That life is worth living is the most necessary of assumptions, and were it not assumed, the most impossible of conclusions."

On Shavuot we also recite Yizkor, a reminder of another powerful coercion, death. The Sage who reminded us that we were born against our will didn't fail to add "against your will you will die." Death is cruel. It robs us of our loved ones and ultimately inflicts the crushing assault on human personality – obliteration.

And yet here, too, our Sages taught us to accept this bitter coercion. They gave a remarkable interpretation to the Biblical verse: "And God saw all that He had made and, behold, it was very good." "Very good," they said, refers to death.

What a tremendous affirmation! They weren't thumbing their noses at death, but they understood that death plays a vital role in life. We cherish life precisely because we are aware of its transience. The urge to create, the passion to perfect, the sheer joy of welcoming each day – all the noblest of human enterprises and emotions flourish in the soil of human mortality. They would vanish if life on earth were an endless unrelieved process.

Lastly, let us consider that being a Jew is also a matter of coercion. Except for the welcome converts in our midst, the rest of us did not choose to be born Jewish. We were born that way. How shall we deal with this coercion?

We can lament this fact, be ashamed of it, try to suppress or deny it. Or we can accept it with pride, gratitude and joy in the spirit of the prayer we recite each morning:

> "How fortunate we are!
> How good is our portion!
> How pleasant our lot!
> How beautiful our heritage!"

Fate is what we are given. Destiny is what we make of what is given to us. We cannot choose our fate but we can shape our destiny. And in that choice lies all the difference.

"Don't Blame Me"

He came to see the marriage counsellor about his twenty-year-old marriage which was threatening to fall apart. He enumerated several things that had soured the relationship, and in each instance he put the blame on his wife. Finally, the counsellor asked him: "Do you think that the entire responsibility for your troubles rests with your wife?" He thought for a moment and then replied: "No, not really. She's only fifty percent to blame. The other fifty percent belongs to her mother."

This refusal to accept any personal responsibility for the sorry state of the marriage, this eagerness to blame others for what went wrong in his life, is a fairly common human characteristic. The psychologists call it projection. Anna Russell, the British comedienne-singer, has a little lyric that tells how this face-saving mechanism works:

> "But now I'm happy; I have learned
> The lesson this has taught;
> That everything I do that's wrong
> Is someone else's fault."

The human tendency to avoid moral responsibility for misdeeds is scarcely a modern phenomenon. It is as old as man himself.

When Adam in the Garden of Eden eats from the forbidden tree, God confronts him with the accusing question: "Have you eaten from the tree that I commanded you not to eat?" Adam defends himself by saying: "The woman whom You gave me, she gave me of the tree and I did eat."

Notice what Adam is doing. He is dividing the blame equally between the Almighty and the woman. "The woman whom You gave me. . . ." I didn't ask for her. She was Your idea and Your creation. "She gave me of the tree. . . ." The eating was her idea not mine.

Now before we get the impression that evading moral responsibility is strictly a masculine affliction, we should read further into the Biblical incident. After Adam passes the moral buck to Eve, God asks her: "What is this that you have done?" Not to be outdone Eve replies: "The serpent beguiled me and I did eat."

The Torah doesn't report any conversation between the Almighty and the serpent on this matter. It would have been interesting to hear the serpent's excuse.

Projecting on to others the blame for our actions is one of our most persistent human traits. A newspaper item reported some of the explanations motorists gave to the Nevada police for accidents in which they were involved. A few choice samples follow:

"I pulled away from the side of the road, glanced at my mother-in-law and headed over the embankment."

"A pedestrian hit me and went under my car."

"This guy was all over the road. I had to swerve a number of times before I hit him."

Every age has its own Eves and its own serpents. In an earlier, less sophisticated age, when people believed in astrology, it was heavenly bodies which served as the Eves and the serpents. Shakespeare captured the buck-passing exceedingly well in the words of Edmund in *King Lear*:

"This is the excellent foppery of the world that when we are sick in fortune – often the surfeit of our own behavior – we make guilty of our disasters the sun, the moon, the stars; as if we were villains by necessity, fools by heavenly compulsion . . ."

In our own times we are pictured as the passive victims of genes, reflexes, complexes. We are controlled by heredity or environment or both. Massive forces which you and I are impotent to control buffet us about and make us act as we do.

When Former Budget Director David Stockman made some indiscreet revelations to a journalist, the story was headlined on the cover of a respected magazine in these words: "Schizophrenia Made Stockman Do It." How neat! Don't blame Stockman. The poor fellow is the captive of a dread disease. After the assassination attempt on President Reagan's life in 1981, the cover of *Time* magazine proclaimed the act to be "a moment of madness." Hinckley's jury apparently felt the same way and set him free. When a director of a large New York City bank was arrested for embezzling one million dollars, he said: "I don't know why I did it. Maybe a good psychiatrist can figure it out." Again, he was not to blame. Some mysterious forces were at work compelling him to steal. Let the psychiatrist discover them and hold them responsible. The mood of our time seems to be the old song: "Don't Blame Me."

But our tradition will not let us off the hook so easily. It looks upon us not as robots or puppets, but as free moral agents who know the difference between right and wrong, and who have the capacity to choose right over wrong.

To be sure, our biological inheritance, our childhood experiences, our environmental conditioning do exercise a vital influence upon us. These factors are real and powerful, but the human will is no less powerful.

We are not only shaped by our environment; we shape it. We are not only the creatures of circumstance; we are also the creators of circumstance.

Our genes may determine whether our eyes are blue or brown, but whether we look upon each other with cold indifference or warm compassion is for us to choose.

Our physical height may be biologically determined but our human stature we fashion ourselves.

Our environment determines the language we speak and the pronunciation we use, but whether our words are cruel or gentle, carping or comforting depends squarely upon us. Our passions, appetites and instincts are part of our animal equipment, but whether they rule us or we rule them is left for each of us to determine.

One of the hallmark verses of the Torah tells us: "I have set before you life and death, the blessing and the curse; choose life . . ."

It is only when we believe that there are indeed moral choices and that we have the power to make moral choices that we can truly live meaningful lives.

What Do You See?

The biblical incident which figures most prominently in the Rosh Hashanah service is the story of the *akeda*, the binding of Isaac. We read it as our Torah portion on the second morning, we blow the Shofar which recalls the ram which was destined to take Isaac's place on the altar and we encounter a host of references to this towering episode throughout the liturgy of this day.

Our sages embellished the narrative. They tell us that as Abraham and Isaac and their servants approached Mount Moriah, the divinely designated summit for the sacrifice, Abraham turned to his servants with a question: "Do you see anything in the distance?" They stared and shook their heads. "No, we see only the trackless wastes of the wilderness." Abraham then turned to Isaac with the very same question. "Yes," said the son, "I see a mountain, majestic and beautiful, and a cloud of glory hovers above it." It was at this point that Abraham directed his servants to remain behind while he and Isaac continued on their mission alone.

Here then is our text. Two people facing in the same direction, surveying the identical scene, come up with completely different impressions. One sees only emptiness and barrenness ahead. The second sees the majestic and challenging mountains. The difference obviously lay in the eyes of the beholder.

Skipping the centuries now and coming right here into the synagogue, let us each ask ourselves the question – "What do you see?" As we shall soon realize, this can be a decisive question.

Before we proceed to try to answer it, may I say that, in many vital areas of our lives, a great number of us not only do not see anything, but we scarcely seem to be looking at all. I often wonder during these days how many of us have fully grasped the thought that with the manufacture of the hydrogen bomb, it is now possible for the

human race to commit collective suicide. Nuclear scientists today quote
an entry made in a scientific journal more than eighty-five years ago.
At that time leading scientists predicted that within one hundred years
"man would know of what the atom is constituted. When this time
comes," the journal said, "God with His white beard will come down
to earth swinging a bunch of keys and will say to humanity, the way
they say at five o'clock at the saloon: 'Closing time, Gentlemen!' " We
live at what might become closing time.

We see, therefore, how terribly much is at stake in the issues of
peace and war, and yet so many of us are living behind our personal
iron curtains through which these crucial questions never seem to
penetrate.

One of our national monthly magazines carried a two page
spread boldly captioned: "The Big News from Paris." This was directly after the United Nations Assembly had completed a crucial
meeting in the French capital. Mankind's nervous hopes had been
focused on those deliberations. The headline in the magazine, therefore, compelled attention. Well, what do you think was being trum-
peted as "the big news from Paris?" As you read on, you learned that
"necklines will be lower, skirts somewhat longer and three new
perfumes have been created. . . ." To too many Americans, this is not
only the big news, it is the only important news. Crucial days and
trivial interests! People for whom life's decisive issues are resolved in
the arena of fashion.

Lest I be accused of being a little severe with some of the ladies,
may I hasten to add that I am not unappreciative of sartorial grace, nor
do I minimize the high morale value of a new hat. What I am saying is
that when these things loom too large on our personal horizons, we
simply do not see the things that matter. And this is true whether we
are preoccupied solely by fashion, or sports, or the card tables, or any
other form of recreation. As a matter of fact, the same is true if we
permit the business of making a living to become all consuming. If we
are hypnotized by any of these matters, the vital matters go by default.
Willy Loman's wife put the thing simply in *Death of a Salesman*:
"Attention must be paid."

Unless we pay attention to the things that matter most, whom
shall we blame if demagogues make off with our civil liberties, if our
teen-agers become, not a source of hope but a source of danger; if
Judaism becomes for us an unknown quantity and its majestic voice is

reduced to an inaudible whisper; if the home becomes – as someone cynically remarked – a place to pick up the car keys; if the State of Israel becomes victimized by a hostile State Department policy?

"Where are you looking?" is, therefore, an important preliminary question.

Now, while it is possible for us to avoid looking at certain issues, however crucial they are, there is one thing we cannot avoid facing – life itself. On this day when we pray for life, we might, therefore, each ask ourselves – what do you see in life? Let me break this large question down to three smaller questions.

When you look at your life, do you habitually see reasons for grumbling or gratefulness? Do you feel that you have been short-changed or over-paid? Do you constantly feel your cup is half empty or in the words of the psalmist, "my cup runneth over?"

Matthew Arnold has written that "one thing only has been lent to youth and age in common – it is discontent." Our favorite posture is one of protest and we who have so much, so very, very much, often permit the one thing we lack to blind us to the great wealth we possess.

Whenever I am on the verge of indulging in the unearned luxury of feeling sorry for myself, I recall something the late Rabbi Milton Steinberg said to his congregation in a sermon which was later printed. He told them of the first time he got out of bed after a long illness and was permitted to step out of doors.

As I crossed the threshold, sunlight greeted me. This is my experience – all there is to it. And yet, so long as I live, I shall never forget that moment.

The sky overhead was very blue, very clear and very, very high.

A faint wind blew from off the western plains, cool and yet somehow tinged with warmth – like a dry chilled wine. Everywhere in the firmament above me, in the great vault between earth and sky, on the pavements, the buildings – the golden glow of the sunlight. It touched me, too, with friendship, with warmth, with blessing. And as I basked in its glory there ran through my mind those wonder words of the prophet about the sun which someday shall rise with healing on its wings.

In that instant I looked about me to see whether anyone else showed on his face the joy I felt. But no, there they walked, men and women and children, in the glory of a golden flood, and so far as I could detect, there was none to give it heed. And then I remembered how often I too had been indifferent to sunlight, how often, preoccupied with petty and sometimes mean concerns, I had disregarded it. And I said to myself—how precious is the sunlight but, alas, how careless of it are men. How precious— how careless! This has been a refrain sounding in me ever since.

It rang in my spirit when I entered my own home again after months of absence, when I heard from a nearby room the excited voices of my children at play; when I looked once more on the dear faces of some of my friends; when I was able for the first time to speak again from my pulpit in the name of our faith and tradition, to join in worship of the God who gives us so much of which we are so careless.

Milton Steinberg discovers the sunshine after a heart attack, and the psalmist realizes that his cup runneth over after he walks through the valley of the shadow.

What do you see? The bleak wilderness of discontent or the beautiful mountain of thankfulness?

May I ask another question now?

When you look at life, do you see only your life and your needs, or do you see the lives and the needs of others as well? Do you see life as a campaign of acquisition or as an adventure in sharing? This question is basic because it spills over into every area of life. How do you regard your job or profession? Is it only a means of providing you and your family with your needs and luxuries, or is it also an opportunity to render a service? How do you regard your mate in marriage? Someone created for your comfort and convenience or someone whose life you can enrich and ennoble? How do you regard your fellow-man? Someone whose main function in life is to serve as a stepping-stone to your success or someone with hopes and needs just like yourself?

In *The High and the Mighty,* there is one line spoken very quickly which is especially worth remembering. On the dramatic plane trip, Mr. Joseph is telling the passenger across the aisle how his well-laid plans for a dream trip to Honolulu kept going awry at every point. Nothing seemed to go right. Like the time they came to the hotel at which they had made advance reservations only to find that their room had been given by mistake to another Mr. and Mrs. Joseph from

Ogden, Utah. And Mr. Joseph says: "Well, I figured maybe they had had a dream too."

Do you look upon your fellow man as someone who maybe has had a dream too; who has children who worship him as much as yours do you; who wants his little place in the sun as desperately as you want yours; who hungers for that word of encouragement and appreciation as much as you do; who, in brief, is a man created like yourself in the image of God?

I read some time ago about a little fellow who didn't mean to be impolite to his teacher, but, when he was asked to draw a circle and found himself without a compass and couldn't remember the name of it, he asked: "Miss Jones, may I take your circumference?" Well, I suppose some of us may be a little sensitive about our physical circumference, but that young fellow stumbled upon a vital question. What is your circumference? How large is the area of your concern, whom and what do you include in the circle of your vital interests?

Do you feel, for example, that what happens to Israel is your personal concern? Does its security and economic stability worry you at all, or do you feel that having purchased a bond some time ago and having once belonged to a Zionist organization, you have completely and forever discharged your obligations in that direction?

One of the most moving books I ever read is a thick Hebrew anthology called *G'velay Esh – Scrolls of Fire*. It contains the writings of the boys and girls who fell in Israel's war of liberation. Their pictures in the back of the book remind one of a college year book. One piece there is entitled, "At Your Grave My Brother Ephraim." It was written by Zvi Guber, who entered the Haganah at sixteen and gave his age as seventeen so that he could join.

The eloquent tribute to his fallen brother Ephraim concludes with these words: "My brother, I vow to you: 'My heart will be the candle of your soul and I shall cherish your memory within me like a precious treasure.

'In the very path where you met your death, I shall go, even though it be filled with pain and anguish, even though I knew for certain it is my last road.

'By the holiness of the pain and by the holiness of my love for you I swear this; by the holiness of all that makes life worth living and death worthwhile' "

Three months later, Zvi was killed in action and was buried near

Ephraim. Not far from their grave a new settlement has been built and named "The Village of the Brothers."

What do you see in life? An arid wilderness of selfishness or a challenging mountain of service?

We come now to the last and perhaps most decisive question. When you look at life, do you look with fear or with faith?

It is impossible, of course, to be entirely free of fear. There is literally no one without his share of fears and apprehensions. The bravest of men have a fear of losing loved ones, a fear of losing health and fortune. To a certain extent, of course, our fears are the saving of us. The man who fears failure develops his skills and his talents more fully. The fear of separation from loved ones spurs us on in medical and scientific research and "the beginning of wisdom," the psalmist tells us, "is fear of the Lord." But fear becomes a matter of deep concern when it becomes exaggerated and morbid, when instead of leading to action it creates a paralysis of will, when it succumbs to the very object of its dread.

In a children's book there is the fable of the oriental monarch who met Pestilence going to Baghdad. "What are you going to do there?" "I am going to kill 5,000."

On the way back, the monarch met Pestilence again. "You liar," thundered the monarch, "you killed 25,000." "Oh, no," said Pestilence, "I killed 5,000. It was fear that killed the rest."

Beginning with the month of *Elul* and continuing through *Hoshana Rabba,* we add Psalm 27 to our daily Service. That Psalm might well be our watchword not only for these days but throughout the year.

"The Lord is my light and my salvation, whom shall I fear? The Lord is the fortress of my life of whom shall I be afraid?"

The cardinal irreverence in Judaism is to be afraid of life, for when we fear life we betray a lack of faith in God. Faith in God does not mean to believe that sorrow will never invade our homes, or illness never strike us and our loved ones. Many people who cherish such a naive belief are due for heart-breaking disillusionment. It is these people who will say to you: "When my mother died, I stopped believing in God." They believed the wrong things about God to begin with. To believe in God is to have faith that He will give us, amidst all vicissitudes, the strength to endure, and the power to hold on and see it through, the capacity to translate even our trials and our tribulations into moral and spiritual victories.

What do you see in life – the parched desert of fear or the inspiring mountain of faith?

May I conclude with a very brief parable which will sum up our theme and perhaps help us to remember it.

Two men went out one night to explore the world. One equipped himself with a lighted torch while the other went into the darkness without any light. When the second returned he said: "Wherever I went I found nothing but darkness." But the first one said, "Everywhere I went, I found light."

May God kindle in our hearts the torch of gratitude, the candle of service and the lamp of faith, so that wherever we go during the year ahead we may see light. Amen.

Making the Most of Our Best

A few months after Walter Davis, thirty-three, divorced his wife, Barbara, he enlisted the aid of a computer dating service in his search for a new mate. He filled out a lengthy questionnaire in which he provided a great deal of information about himself and about the qualities he sought in a wife.

The computer ran through thirty thousand prospects and then came up with four names. The first name on the list was that of Barbara, his former wife! She had filed a similar form with the same mate-selecting computer.

This is a story worth pondering. For one thing, it might give pause to some people headed for the overcrowded divorce courts. Before they dissolve a marriage, dismantle a home, and disrupt a family, they could profitably ask themselves whether with more patience, effort, and greater determination they could not make a go of their marriage.

Perhaps Walter's experience can slow them down long enough for them to ask whether what they need is to change their mates or to change themselves. Do they require a change of circumstance or a change of attitude? Is the answer in the computer or within themselves?

These questions are not confined to people who find themselves in a shaky marriage. They touch all of us at the point in our lives at which we are tempted to believe that we really could be happy if our circumstances were other than what they are. "Ah, if I lived in another place, in another time; if only I were attractive or rich; if only I had different parents or different genes; if only things were different."

Becky Sharp in Thackeray's *Vanity Fair* excused her loose morals by saying, "I think I could be a good woman if I had 5,000 pounds a year." Becky was kidding herself, and so are we when we blame our circumstances and shirk our responsibility to make maximum use of the opportunities at hand. Those who find fulfillment in life are those who change what should and can be changed, accept what cannot be changed, and go on from there.

This, I believe, is the meaning of that spectacular encounter Moses experienced at the burning bush. There he was in a bleak, desolate wilderness when he heard the divine command: "Remove your shoes from your feet, for the place on which you stand is holy ground." Holy ground! Here, in this barren, dreary spot? Yes, Moses. Here in this miserable place you can find a mission that will give meaning and purpose to your life.

Elizabeth Barrett Browning had that biblical episode in mind when she wrote:

> Earth's crammed with heaven
> And every common bush afire with God;
> But only he who sees, takes off his shoes,
> The rest sit round it and pluck blackberries.

When we learn to look upon the humble ground on which we stand as holy ground, we have acquired the greatest encouragement we need to fertilize it and make it productive. We discover the poetry that is ambushed in the prosaic, the glory that is embedded in the commonplace, the opportunity that is hidden in the thicket of thorn bushes.

If we wait until circumstances are precisely right for us to achieve and accomplish something, then nothing ever will be achieved or accomplished. Neither we nor circumstances are ever precisely right.

Each of us has heartaches and pains, limitations and handicaps. Each of us has burdens to carry and obstacles to overcome. And as Emerson reminded us, there is a crack in everything that God has made.

Moses himself was a stammerer and a stutterer, a refugee from justice, a member of an enslaved people. Circumstances were scarcely ideal for the assignment he was given. But a grateful humanity holds him in warm remembrance because he did the very best he could, and in the least likely of places he discovered holy ground.

Nor was Moses the only person to achieve mightily despite forbidding circumstances. Lord Byron had a clubfoot; Robert Louis Stevenson had tuberculosis; Charles Darwin was an invalid; Thomas Edison and Ludwig van Beethoven were deaf; George Washington Carver was a black slave; Abraham Lincoln was born in a log cabin to parents who could neither read nor write; and Helen Keller could neither see nor hear.

The verdict of history is clear. Among the humble and great alike, those who achieve success do so not because fate and circumstances are especially kind to them. Often the reverse is true. They succeed because they do not whine over their fate but take whatever has been given to them and go on to make the most of their best.

Say Yes to Life

Stories of two paraplegics were in the news about one week apart. One was Kenneth B. Wright, a high-school football star and, later, an avid wrestler, boxer, hunter, and skin diver. A broken neck sustained in a wrestling match in 1979 left him paralyzed from the chest down. He underwent therapy, and his doctors were hopeful that one day he would be able to walk with the help of braces and crutches.

But, apparently, the former athlete could not reconcile himself to his physical disability. He prevailed upon two of his best friends to take him in his wheelchair to a wooded area, where they left him alone with a twelve-gauge shotgun. After they left, he held the shotgun to his abdomen and pulled the trigger. Kenneth Wright, twenty-four, committed suicide.

The second paraplegic in the news was Jim McGowan. Thirty years ago, at the age of nineteen, Jim was stabbed and left paralyzed from the middle of his chest down. He is now confined to be wheelchair. But he came to our attention recently when he made a successful parachute jump, landing on target in the middle of Lake Wallenpaupack in the Pocono Mountains of Pennsylvania.

Soon afterward, I spoke with Jim and learned a number of other things about him. He lives alone, cooks his own meals, washes his own clothes, and cleans his own house. He drives himself wherever he goes in his specially equipped automobile. He has written three books, and he took the photographs for the first book published on the history of wheelchair sports.

When I asked Jim how he managed to do so much with so little, he answered. "It wasn't easy. I had my years of darkness, and it took a long time to get there. Then I came to the conclusion that I am ultimately responsible for my life. Since I am responsible for my life, I'm going to make it as beautiful as I can."

No shotgun, please.

No one has the right to sit in judgment of the disabled athlete who threw in the towel. Who knows what any one of us would have done in his terrible situation? Long ago, a Jewish sage warned us: "Do not judge your fellow man until you are in his place."

But Jim McGowan's heroic response to the same disability is surely a much-needed reminder of the resilience of the human spirit, of our God-given ability to cope with – and to triumph over – difficult or even impossible-seeming circumstances. One of the heavy burdens of being human is the need to make choices – choices that are often as desperately difficult as they are decisive. Edwin Markham, the twentieth-century American poet, wrote of these agonizing dilemmas:

> I will leave man to make the fateful guess
> Will leave him torn between No and Yes
> Leave him in the tragic loneliness to choose
> With all in life to win or lose.

The most fateful choices are made in tragic loneliness. In the valley of decision, we stand alone, accompanied only by our haunting fears or our stubborn hopes, by dread despair or gritty faith.

Yet, though we appear to stand solitary, in truth we are accompanied by the tall and brave spirits who have stood where we stand and who, when torn between "No" and "Yes" have said "Yes" to life and its infinite possibilities; by those who have had the wisdom to focus not on what they had lost but on what they had left; by those who understood that fate is what life gives to us and that destiny is what we do with what's given; and by those who, therefore, grasped the liberating truth that while we have no control over our fate, we do have an astonishing amount of control over our destiny.

When a blind man was asked by a sympathetic woman, "Doesn't being blind rather color your life?" he answered: "Yes, but, thank God, I can choose the color."

The plane that carried paraplegic Jim McGowan to his historic skydive should also have carried aloft the spirits of the discouraged and the despondent, the defeated and the despairing. If he could soar so high, then who has the right to feel low? To all who find themselves in a time of darkness, Jim's words shine with a luminous radiance: "Since I am responsible for my life, I'm going to make it as beautiful as I can."

To "Walk" through Life Takes More Courage than to "Soar"

One of my favorite biblical verses is Isaiah 40:31: "They that trust in the Lord shall renew their strength. They shall soar with wings as eagles, they shall run and not be weary, they shall walk and not faint."

As we analyze the verse, it seems to get weaker as it unfolds. After all, isn't it a greater achievement to soar with wings as eagles? If we can fly, what kind of an accomplishment is it to run; and if we can run, how much of an achievement is it to walk? The figures of speech used by the prophet seem to be diminishing their impact when he goes from flying to running to walking.

But the truth is that far from getting weaker, his metaphors are actually becoming more powerful.

There are times when everyone can soar with enthusiasm. A new election, a new building, a new rabbi – and there is a buzzing in the community. Everybody is inspired, uplifted. And then a year goes by and those who were scraping the heights may have been reduced to a run because, as a matter of fact, you can't keep soaring. Life, it has been pointed out, isn't all running to a fire.

What happens when we stop flying, and after a few more years we stop running, and all the excitement and the glamor and the glory have vanished? What is needed at that time are the people who can just keep walking, going through the ordinary humdrum, bread-and-butter, unspectacular but life-giving tasks, and keep their loyalty undimmed and undiminished.

We are all capable of enthusiasm. Some of us can be enthusiastic for 30 minutes. Others for 30 days. But the challenge of life is to be enthusiastic for 30 years.

A diamond, it has been pointed out, is just a piece of coal that stayed on the job. Ultimately, those who can stay on the job are the people who are the leaders of the community, and these are the people who give strength to the organization that is blessed enough to claim them as its own. These are the solid pegs that keep our world together.

Not the ephemeral high flyers, not even the swift runners, but the undiscouraged, indefatigable, inexhaustible walkers who keep at the task day after day, week after week, year after year, who retain their faith and renew their strength – these are the people who bless and are blessed.

There are many names for this quality. Perhaps the best is "persistence." It is an indispensable ingredient in every successful life and endeavor.

Calvin Coolidge did not exaggerate when he wrote: "Nothing in the world can take the place of persistence. Talent will not; nothing is more common than unsuccessful men with talent. Genius will not; unrewarded genius is almost a proverb. Education will not; the world is full of educated derelicts. Persistence and determination alone are omnipotent. The slogan 'Press on' has solved and always will solve the problems of the human race."

A host of illustrations of the power of persistence spring readily to mind. In the movie *Madame Curie* there is a scene that remains unforgettable. After the failure of the 487th experiment in the search for radium, Pierre Curie strides across the floor, crying in despair: "It can't be done! It can't be done! Maybe in a hundred years it can be done, but never in our lifetime!"

Madame Curie responds simply: "If it takes a hundred years, it will be a pity, but I dare not do less than work for it as long as I live!" That was the persistence that resulted in the discovery of radium. Here were two great "walkers."

Another celebrated "walker" was the composer George Frederick Handel. Here is what his biographer tells us about him. "His health and his fortunes had reached the lowest ebb. His right side had become paralyzed, and his money was all gone. His creditors seized him and threatened him with imprisonment. For a brief time, he was tempted to give up the fight – but he rebounded again to compose the greatest of his inspirations, the epic *Messiah*."

In Israel there lives an artist by the name of Mordecai Steinberg. In the 1948 War of Independence, he stepped on a mine, which ripped off his legs. One arm was left useless, the other badly crippled. He now paints with his teeth and supports himself by the beauty he depicts on canvas. Not a bad job of "walking" for a man without legs.

The Jewish people has countless achievements to which it can point with justifiable pride. One of our most spectacular achievements has surely been our persistence, our ability to keep walking down the perilous road of history, overcoming all obstacles, defying a host of tyrants and tyrannies, and day after day for 2,000 harsh years acting out with unwavering faith the bold proclamation of the Psalmist: "I shall not die but live and proclaim the works of the Lord."

We are history's most celebrated "walkers." To be a Jew is to know in one's bones that a trying time is no time to stop trying; that when the going gets tough, the tough keep going; and that even a small river can carry a good deal of water to the sea if it just keeps moving.

In times of sorrow and grief, in times of disappointment and defeat, in times of illness and incapacity, we need heavy doses of persistence. Just the ability to hang in there, to hold on, to keep walking. This persistence is nourished by an unwavering faith that God gives us no burden too heavy for us to bear, and each day He renews our strength to triumph over the greatest difficulties.

"Yea though I *walk* through the valley of the shadow. . . ." After we emerge from the valley, we can better appreciate the prophet's words: "They that trust in the Lord shall renew their strength. . . . They shall walk and not faint."

Many Are Strong in the Broken Places

When Glenn Cunningham was a boy of eight, he and his brother attempted to start the fire to heat their school building. A violent kerosene explosion ensued and Glenn's legs were so badly burned that the doctors proposed amputation. His mother would not hear of it.

After six long months in the hospital, a series of extensive skin grafts, and endless hours of massaging by his mother's loving hands, Glenn began to walk and then to run to strengthen his crippled legs. He ran and he ran and he ran, until at age twenty-five he ran straight into a world record for the fastest mile – a record he was to hold for years.

The world applauded Cunningham's courage no less than his skill, for he had provided a thrilling illustration of the truth of Ernest Hemingway's words: "The world breaks everyone, and afterward many are strong in the broken places."

Indeed, there are two truths in Hemingway's statement. The first is that sooner or later we are all broken. Defeat, disappointment, sorrow, and tragedy are the common lot of all people.

If there were an X-ray capable of giving us a picture of the human spirit, we would find that we all show evidence of emotional and psychic fractures. Some of us have suffered the break caused by a deep frustration – a career we sought but did not attain, a loved one we wooed but failed to win. Some of us have scars left by a haunting sense of inadequacy; by physical and mental abuse; by blasted hopes; by unrealized dreams; by losses we cannot recapture or forget.

"Man," the Bible says, "is born to trouble as surely as the sparks fly upward" (Job 5:7). Trouble is not a gate-crasher in the arena of our lives; it has a reserved seat there. Heartache has a passkey to every home in the land.

After Helen Hayes suffered the loss of her young and gifted daughter, Mary, she wrote, "When God afflicts the celebrated of the world, it is His way of saying, 'None is privileged. In My eyes all are equal.' "

But Hemingway talks not only of our common vulnerability to being broken; he reminds us too that we can later become strong in the broken places. Where trouble and suffering are concerned, you and I, like young Glenn, have the power not only to confront and endure them; we can use them constructively and creatively.

I say we *can* use them, not that we necessarily *do* use them. *Many* are strong in the broken places – not *all*. Some are embittered by suffering. Some are overcome by self-pity. "Why did it happen to me?" Some are resentful.

But then there are others who understand that some of the noblest human traits flourish in the soil of suffering. Compassion and kindness, fortitude and patience, sympathy and humility – these are part of the rich harvest that can ripen from the dark seeds of pain.

Whether or not we become strong in the broken places depends ultimately on our attitude toward trouble. If we realize that suffering is our common human lot and that it can help us to grow in spirit and in understanding, then we can indeed use it to grow strong in the broken places.

Finding God in the Wilderness

The fourth book of the Torah is called *Bemidbar*, which means "in the wilderness." The book is largely devoted to the vicissitudes our ancestors endured during those difficult years when they journeyed through the wilderness of Sinai toward the Promised Land that beckoned ahead.

Those years in the wilderness were extraordinarily hazardous. Nature and man conspired so severely against the recently liberated slaves that they often wished they were back in Egypt. There was hunger and there was thirst, there were marauding desert tribes who lived by plunder. The burning sand and sun blistered them by day, the cold desert winds froze them at night. The wilderness was most uncongenial to human habitation. It was fierce, harsh, dangerous.

And yet this book begins with the simple but startling statement: "And the Lord spoke to Moses in the wilderness of Sinai." There in that waste-land, there in the midst of the most perilous terrain and circumstances, God speaks. And not to Moses alone. Indeed, God's most dramatic self-revelation was heard by the entire people in the wilderness of Sinai. Whatever the wilderness was, it was not "God-forsaken." Even there His voice could be heard.

Is there not something profoundly instructive in this phenomenon? Does it not seem to suggest to us that even in life's most forbidding circumstances, or perhaps especially then, we can hear God's voice and feel His presence? Human experience daily confirms this striking truth.

Harry Emerson Fosdick was one of America's greatest preachers and teachers of the reality of God. This is generally acknowledged. What is not too well known is the rocky path by which he climbed to spiritual eminence. When he was a young man he suffered a severe nervous breakdown. Looking back to that terrible time in his life he wrote in later years:

"It was the most terrifying wilderness I ever traveled through. I dreadfully wanted to commit suicide, but instead I made some of the most vital discoveries of my life. My little book, *The Meaning of Prayer,* would never have been written without that time of mourning and grief. I found God in a desert. Why is it that some of life's most revealing insights come to us not from life's loveliness, but from life's difficulties? As a small boy said, 'Why are all the vitamins in spinach and not in ice cream, where they ought to be?' I don't know. You will have to ask God that, but vitamins are in spinach and God is in every wilderness."

Yes, God is in every wilderness but not all people who are in the desert of tribulation hear Him speak. Quite often people turn against God when they are confronted by sickness, tragedy, or the loss of loved ones. Who can dare to estimate how many atheists were created by the Holocaust?

And yet who will deny that there are survivors whose faith in God was either discovered or strengthened in the wilderness of anguish during the black night of incarceration? Reeve Robert Brenner in his excellent book *The Faith and Doubt of Holocaust Survivors* reports the following statement of one survivor: "When I hear of other survivors who say they became atheists because of the death of the six million, I become very excited and angry and I always let them know that it is precisely because of the six million that I became a religious Jew, keeping the commandments and developing in myself a deep faith in God. The six million sacrificed so much, their very lives. How can you betray them again after they've gone by using their death as a justification for becoming a *goy* . . .?"

It is one of life's astonishing paradoxes that we often see more clearly when our eyes are dimmed by tears. In the arid desert soil of suffering there often grow tender shoots of compassion, sympathy and service.

When we ourselves experience suffering we can become more sensitive to the suffering of others. After all, sooner or later do we not all find ourselves in life's wilderness? Does all our vaunted power, prestige and affluence immunize us against those "shafts of outrageous fortune" which are our common destiny?

The wilderness can elicit from us powers of fortitude, patience and endurance. It can strip away our pettiness, our pride, our self-centeredness. It can puncture our illusions of invulnerability and self-sufficiency. It can make us more profoundly aware than ever before how great is our dependence upon Him who, in the words of Isaiah, "gives power to the faint, and to him who has no might He increases strength."

In the wilderness of sorrow we often begin to understand what the Biblical Joseph meant when he said: "God has made me fruitful in the land of my affliction." We understand better too the more profound meaning of what the Torah tells us about Moses: "And Moses entered into the thick darkness for there was God." And we understand also why Chateaubriand, the unbeliever, said after the death of his sister: "I wept and then I believed." Again and again God has been found in the desert.

In Israel we saw a rare cactus plant on which there grows an exquisitely lovely flower. That flower is called *Malkat Halailah* – Queen of the Night – because it has the strange characteristic of blooming only in the darkest part of the night. When the blackness is deepest, the *Malkat Halailah* comes bursting out. We can emulate that flower. In the dark night of suffering and sorrow we can hear God's voice calling to us to robe ourselves in our full human splendor, bedecked in all our God-given glory.

"If"

The Torah portion *Behukkotai* begins with the tiny word "if," which plays such a massive role in our lives. "If" is a little hinge on which the door of destiny swings. A history professor built an impressive case in defense of the observation that if Cleopatra's nose had been one inch longer, the entire history of the world would have been different.

The very structure of the word "life" is a reminder of the vast contingencies with which it is fraught. In the middle of the word *life* there is *if*. In the middle of every life there is a big *if*.

The celebrated artist Whistler had his heart set on a career in the army, but he flunked out of West Point because he failed in chemistry. In later life, he used to say: "If silicon had been a gas, I would have been a major general."

There is indeed a big *if* in the middle of every life. What if . . . if I had married a different woman, if I attended a different school, if I had chosen a different career. . . .

Robert Frost makes this point sharply in a haunting little poem called "The Road Not Taken." Once, while walking through the forest, he came upon a fork where two paths branched out. Naturally, he could take only one of them, but in the poem he wonders what would have happened had he taken the other path. The path he did take, he concludes, "has made all the difference."

Nor is it only our own choices and our own decisions that affect our destinies. During the Nazi Holocaust, when European Jewry was being decimated, many of us asked ourselves: "What if my father had not made the boat?" Our very lives hinged upon a decision made by our fathers, who could not possibly have been aware at the time of the fateful consequences of their choice.

Despite all the uncertainties and the unpredictable contingencies of life, we have to accept it as it is and live it the best way we know. We cannot go through life second-guessing ourselves or wishing that things were other than they are.

In his autobiography, *My Young Years,* the master pianist Artur Rubinstein addressed himself directly to this matter. "Most people," he wrote, "have an unrealistic approach toward happiness because they invariably use the fatal conjunction 'if' as a condition. You hear them say: I would be happy *if* I were rich or *if* this woman loved me, or *if* I had talent, or the most popular 'if' – *if* I had good health. They often attain their goal, but then they discover new 'if's.

"As for myself, I love life for better or for worse, unconditionally."

Perhaps it was this capacity to love life "unconditionally" that enabled Rubinstein to enjoy such a long and fruitful life. But what he calls "the fatal conjunction" does have a crucial role in our lives. We may choose to love life unconditionally, but life itself is full of conditions.

We live in a world of cause and effect, where every action has a reaction. If we want certain results, we must fulfill certain conditions.

This is the central thrust of the *Sidrah Behukkotai,* which begins with "if." *If* you follow the commandments, then there will be serenity and fulfillment. ". . . and you shall lie down and none shall make you afraid." But if you reject the commandments and break the covenant, then there will be misery and suffering. ". . . and you shall flee when none pursues you."

It was this passage and several others like it in the Torah that prompted my revered teacher, Professor Mordecai Kaplan, to observe that "Judaism is neither pessimistic nor optimistic; it is *ifistic.*" It tells us what we can make of our lives *if* we fulfill certain conditions.

This is not a haphazard universe. It is a universe governed by law, and in the moral realm as in the physical realm, nature can be commanded only by being obeyed.

If we want a harvest, we have to plant seeds. If we want good health, we have to follow a program of diet, exercise and self-control that leads to good health. If we want friendship, we must perform acts of friendship. If we want to live serenely, we have to live morally. To be sure, there are some ifs over which we have no control, but in so many crucial areas of life, we, and we alone, do have control.

The Internal Revenue Service received an envelope containing $1,000 in cash and an unsigned note that read: "I am sending you this money because I cannot sleep. If I still cannot sleep, I will send you more."

The sender of that note reminds us of a truth we frequently suppress. Much of what we call insomnia is the work of an offended conscience getting even. The "still small voice" has a nasty way of becoming shrill and raspy just when we're trying to get some sleep.

At such times, we can appreciate one of the rewards the Torah promises us for keeping the commandments – "and you shall lie down and none shall make you afraid."

What the Torah is promising here is built into our very structure as human beings. God so fashioned us that we cannot betray our highest principles with impunity. And when we do indeed live in the way He would have us live and we know we should live, we experience the joy and inner happiness that enrich life, add zest to it and keep it sweet to our taste.

It is worth noting that the Hebrew word for life is also a four-letter word. It is *hayyim*. But unlike its English counterpart, which has *if* in the middle of it, the Hebrew word for life has two *yuds* in the middle. And two *yuds,* as we know, spell the name of God.

If we put God in the vital center of our lives, we can meet any contingency without being defeated or overwhelmed. And we can then live with the certainty that life has meaning, purpose and unlimited possibilities for fulfillment.

Moving Thoughts

I remember how I felt when the Board of Directors voted to move our synagogue to Dresher. I approved of what the Board did. I was convinced that the decision was in the best interests of the Congregation. But, I don't mind confessing that I felt that I had undergone major emotional surgery. The decision was right, but it hurt; it hurt a lot.

I have a long history of being unhappy about moving. I recall so vividly the annual distress I felt every June when I had to move out of the Yeshiva College dormitory at the end of the school year. The separation was always a trauma.

I have sharp memories of the malaise I experienced for weeks at the prospect of moving our family from 19th Street to Old Farm Road. Nineteenth Street had become very noisy and the trucks that thundered by at night made sleep almost impossible. But, it had been our home, the place where we observed Shabbat and Passover and Hanukkah, the place where we made Kiddush and sang Z'mirot, the place where we discussed homework and Synagogue business around the family table, the place where Shira, Reena and Adena grew taller and wiser and prettier. It had been home for so long a time and the thought of leaving it threw a dark shadow over many days and nights.

With that kind of track record, how happy am I supposed to feel at the thought of moving from *my* synagogue? It had been mine in a very special way, in a way that it has belonged to nobody else. I had a not insignificant share in the building of it. I saw every brick laid. I ushered in thirty Rosh Hashonahs and concluded thirty Yom Kippurs on its pulpit. I preached my heart and soul out from its pulpit. Here I shed many a tear, evoked many a laugh. I celebrated some 1500 Sabbaths in my shul, named hundreds of babies, officiated at thousands of Bar and Bat Mitzvah celebrations, united hundreds of brides and grooms, consoled thousands of mourners, congratulated thousands when they marked joyous occasions.

At Washington Lane Shira, Reena and Adena became Bat Mitzvah and were confirmed. Shira and Reena celebrated their weddings here. Here we marked our wedding anniversaries and our congregational anniversaries, thanked God for the arrival of our children's children, Elisha, Ilana, Daron and Daniella. Here we celebrated the publication of my books.

Here I said Kaddish for my father. Here I have said Yizkor for my mother 120 times. Here I have known my moments of greatest exaltation and triumph. Here I have sometimes felt the hand of God upon me, and the hopes of my people sustaining me. Except for the times spent in Israel or out of the city on vacation, there have been only a small handful of days in the last thirty years when I haven't been at Washington Lane and Limekiln Pike.

I have been very fortunate indeed. I have been granted the wish which the psalmist expressed as his sole request: "One thing have I asked of the Lord, this do I yearn for – that I might dwell in the house of the Lord all the days of my life." How then am I supposed to have felt at the prospect of moving?

And yet, I congratulated the Board for its decision. It acted with statesmanship and with courage. The easiest thing to do would have been to do nothing, but, it would have been wrong to do nothing. My late teacher, Professor Abraham J. Heschel, once said: "There's only one goal , but there are many ways of missing it." What is our goal?

Our goal is what it has always been – to be the most effective force for creative, meaningful, Jewish living that we can possibly be. We have to radiate with power the enormous heritage which is ours to transmit. Our ability to remain true to that function had been impaired in our present location because the people who live in the neighborhood of our synagogue are almost all non-Jewish. Therefore, the urgency of doing something constructive prompted our Board to act as it did.

We live at a time when the threat to Jewish survival in this land of unlimited freedom is terribly serious. The challenge of intermarriage is unprecedented. The erosion of assimilation is frightening. We as a congregation have to be more effective than we have ever been before. It was therefore crucial that we be in a location where we could indeed render maximum service, maximum inspiration, maximum leadership. That location was in Dresher. It was excruciatingly hard to leave Washington Lane, but it would be an abdication of responsibility not to do so. This is my solace and this is the source of my strength to face the enormous challenges which flow from the decision of the Board.

The prophet Haggai lived in the sixth century B.C.E., at a time when the people had returned from Babylon and had not yet found the strength to rebuild the Temple in Jerusalem which had been destroyed some seventy years earlier. For some reason, they could not summon up the energy and the courage to do the task that was crying to be accomplished. It was at such a time that the prophet rallied his people to action with the promise: *"The glory of the second Temple will be greater than the first."* If we truly will it, we can see to it that *the glory of the second Temple Sinai will be greater than the first.*

We have more experience now. We have greater wisdom now. And we have our children and our grandchildren in Dresher to urge us on and to work by our side. Many of them have their cherished memories of the sanctuary at Washington Lane either carried forward from childhood or acquired during the twelve years since the merger. What is more, we have the future generations looking to us to preserve and to enrich that which has been given to us. We have every reason and every resource to see to it that *the glory of the second Temple Sinai will be greater than the first.*

In 1952, when I celebrated my tenth anniversary at Temple Sinai, my first and only pulpit, I concluded my expression of appreciation with the hopeful lines from Browning's "Rabbi Ben Ezra" which I am privileged to repeat:

> "Come grow old with me, the best is yet to be,
> The last of life for which the first was made."

VI

LIVING AS A JEW

Those who have gone before us have accumulated a precious legacy for us to enjoy, to enlarge and to transmit. Ours is the privilege to keep faith with the past, to give meaning to our present, to insure our future.

Why "Organized" Religion?

A rabbi who tried to persuade a gentleman to join his congregation was told by the man, "I appreciate the importance of religion, but I don't believe in *organized* religion." To which the rabbi replied, "You'll love our synagogue. It's completely disorganized."

I do not know whether the solicited gentleman joined the "disorganized" synagogue. But he expressed a frequently heard opinion. We have all heard people label "religion" good and "organized religion" as either bad or quite expendable.

These same people would not say, "I believe in medicine but I do not believe in medical schools, hospitals, and clinics."

Nor would they say, "I believe in law and justice but I do not believe in law schools, courts, and police."

Nor, "I love art and beauty but I do not believe in art schools and museums."

If medicine, justice and art are worth fostering, there must be institutions devoted to those purposes. And so it is with religion.

This realization came to us early in Jewish history. In the Torah we read that shortly after our ancestors left Egypt, they were commanded: "Let them build Me a sanctuary so that I may dwell among them" (Exodus 25:8). This injunction was the first effort to "organize" religion, and for more than 3,000 years, in good times and bad, in lands of freedom and oppression, our people were builders of sanctuaries.

What purpose do our sanctuaries, or "organized" synagogues, serve?

Let us list briefly some of the major contributions the synagogue makes to the tone and texture of Jewish life.

The synagogue provides the ideal Jewish setting for worship, where that which is noblest within ourselves reaches out toward that which is highest in the universe – God.

In a noisy world, it enables us to pause periodically to listen to the still small voice of the spirit.

The synagogue provides a place of assembly for the Jewish community and for the many organizations of Jewish youth and adults. It is the recognized address of the Jewish community for Jew and non-Jew alike.

The synagogue is the institution that best preserves the Jewish heritage and most effectively transmits the teachings of the prophets, the wisdom of our Sages and teachers.

The synagogue has been the most potent force for Jewish continuity throughout the vicissitudes of our history. It continues to nourish the Jewish will to survive and to provide joy in living as a Jew.

The synagogue raises to loftiest significance the great milestones from birth to death by clothing them in the warmth of hallowed words and sacred rituals, and by providing a community with which to share these exalted occasions.

The synagogue keeps alive and articulates our people's most treasured memories, our most fervent beliefs and our most cherished hopes.

The synagogue provides a fellowship for Jews who take their heritage seriously and who look to it to provide guidance, solace and inspiration.

The synagogue nurtures our faith in the coming of an era of peace and justice for all people; it gives us the courage to work for God's kingdom and the patience to hopefully wait for it.

The synagogue drapes each human being with highest dignity, confers upon life ultimate meaning, invests the universe with high purpose and sees in Jewish destiny cosmic significance.

The synagogue richly merits the tribute paid to it by Robert T. Herford, a Christian scholar: "In all their long history, the Jewish people have done scarcely anything more wonderful than to create the synagogue. No human institution has a longer continuous history, and none has done more for the uplifting of the human race."

However great was the role of the synagogue in elevating the human race, its role in giving meaning and substance to Jewish life was even greater.

In his autobiography, *Dreamer's Journey Home*, Morris Raphael Cohen makes the following confession:

"In my youth I would not have mentioned this for I then joined in the romantic and uncritical disparagement of all priesthoods to extol the revolutionary or reforming prophets. But as I grew older I began to recognize that while the inspiration of the prophets is necessary, men cannot live on revolutions alone. The preaching of prophets would be merely an emotional indulgence if it did not find embodiment in some law, custom or ritual to make smooth and channelize our daily life."

We might add that the preaching of the prophets also needs embodiment in an institution, and for us that institution is the synagogue.

The synagogue is the central institution which both symbolizes Jewish continuity and which made that continuity possible. When we join a synagogue, we join the mighty company of Jews throughout the ages who took seriously the divine command spoken to our ancestors just as soon as they left Egypt: "Let them build Me a sanctuary so that I may dwell among them."

What Can We Prove by You?

Some time ago, I had the dubious privilege of spending a very long hour in the company of a man who had the distressing habit of repeating a rather popular expression. No matter what topic presented itself for discussion, he was ready with his pet comment: "You can't prove it by me." We ranged over many fields – politics, golf, juvenile delinquency, the weather – and with rare consistency our so-called conversationalist kept injecting, "You can't prove it by me."

Much later that night, long after the human record had been

turned off, the monotonous refrain lingered on. I couldn't expel it from my mind. Suddenly, I realized that in this expression there is summed up the real weakness of Jewish religious life in America.

The sad truth is that there are too many things about Judaism that nobody could prove by the lives of Jews who belong to synagogues.

If someone were to ask: "Is Shabbat, the cornerstone of Judaism, really vital?" how many affiliated Jews would be compelled to answer, "You can't prove it by me?"

If someone were to ask: "Is prayer with the congregation at regular intervals truly necessary?" how many synagogue members would be compelled to answer, "You can't prove it by me?"

If someone were to ask: "Does a child's Jewish education really require a parent's personal example and constant active interest?" how many synagogue Jews would be compelled to answer, "You can't prove it by me?"

If someone were to ask: "Does a Jewish home really give a special tone and quality to life?" how many affiliated Jews would be compelled to answer, "You can't prove it by me?"

If someone were to ask: "Is it true that Judaism is both a way of looking at the world and a way of living in the world–in our shops, our offices, our factories?" how many affiliated Jews would be compelled to answer, "You can't prove it by me?"

I submit that if there were more truths about Judaism that could be proved by those inside the synagogue, there would be fewer Jews outside it.

When our ancestors were commanded to build the first sanctuary in the wilderness, they were told that God's purpose was, "so that I might dwell among them." Our sages, with fine ethical sensitivity, noted that the Bible did not say, "so that I might dwell in the sanctuary," but rather "among them." The sanctuary was not meant to contain God but to radiate Him. The individual Jew was himself to become a sanctuary, a dwelling-place of the Divine.

We have mightily enhanced the physical and spiritual landscape of our community by erecting an impressive sanctuary worthy of the high purposes to which it is dedicated and the rich heritage it embodies. No one knows better than I the mountains of devotion, conscientious and sacrificial love that went into its creation. But all our efforts will be vitiated unless we realize that our true objective as Jews is not to build sanctuaries but to become sanctuaries, to reflect in our lives the glory of God and the grandeur of Judaism.

"Every Jew," said the Belzer Rabbi, "should so conduct himself that his sons will rejoice to say, as Jacob did: 'The God of my Father.'" Rabbi Leib Saras went further. He indicated that your responsibility and mine extends beyond those whose lives have flowed directly from our own. "The good man," he declared, "should himself be the Torah, and people should be able to learn good conduct from observing him."

May we so live that we may merit the tribute spoken of one of Browning's characters:

> "Through such souls alone
> God stooping shows sufficient of his light
> For us in the dark to rise by. And I rise."
>   Amen

Paradoxes of Happiness

The high holy day liturgy is saturated with prayers of extraordinary beauty. One of the most touching of these is the prayer found in the Amidah. "Remember us unto life, O King who delights in life; inscribe us in the book of life for Your sake O King of life."

This is the articulation of our deepest yearning. It flows naturally from the human heart. *Es vill zich leben,* "We want to live." The world is beautiful and it is good to be alive. As we grow older I think we are less inclined to take life for granted. Every year finds our list of comrades and loved ones a little more diminished. Inevitably on Rosh Hashanah we remember those who answered the final summons since last Rosh Hashanah. These reflections sadden us, but they also deepen our gratitude for the elementary blessing of life. As we become more mindful of our human frailty an added sense of urgency creeps into our voices when we pray "Remember us unto life, O King who delights in life." We are in love with life.

But even as we ask for continued life, a haunting question lurks in the background. Are we willing to accept life on any terms? Infinitely precious though life is, are there not conditions which would make life too burdensome, too intolerable? Is mere biological survival enough?

No, we want more than another year of life. As our Rosh Hashanah greetings indicate, we wish each other a happy New Year. We are praying for a happy life. But what is happiness? What can we ourselves do to achieve it? I do not believe that God can give us happiness. God can give us many blessings but whether they bring happiness depends very largely upon us. Happiness is not a gift, it is an achievement.

Before we try to discover what happiness is and how it may be achieved, let us briefly indicate what happiness is not, and where we ought not to seek it.

Despite the exaggerated and distorted emphasis in our lives upon the feverish competition to acquire things – more things, bigger things, better things – happiness is not found in things. If it were, all the rich would be happy. And incidentally, compared to the rest of the world, almost any American is a plutocrat. Once we go beyond providing for our basic needs, possessions can only add to our physical comfort, and there is a vast difference between being comfortable and being happy.

Nor is it found in artificially stimulated merry-making. Some of the saddest sights are those who are forever chasing pleasures. Happiness does not come in liquid form. There is a world of difference between forgetting yourself and fulfilling yourself.

Genuine happiness is not expensive but we often pay exorbitant prices for its imitations.

Nor is it far away. "The foolish man seeks happiness in the distance; the wise grows it under his feet." Indeed Helen Keller who was given such meagre equipment with which to confront life, said "Your success and happiness lie in you." How can we achieve happiness?

I would be less than honest if I were to imply that there is a sure road to happiness, that it is perfectly known to me and that I can put you on it in one easy sermon. None of these is true. But I should like to share with you some of my thoughts on this subject which can perhaps serve as signposts along the road, helping us on our quest.

I would like to sum up my reflections in three paradoxes. The first is this. If we seek happiness, it will elude us. We find it only when we are not looking for it.

The American Declaration of Independence is one of the greatest human documents ever written, but it does contain one misleading phrase – "the pursuit of happiness." It gives the impression that happiness must be pursued, and that if pursued it can be caught. Neither is true. Happiness is a by-product, something you achieve while you are altogether intent on doing something else. The moment you start concentrating on happiness, it fades away. The intense pursuit of happiness is one of the chief sources of unhappiness. When we court happiness too intensely, it is frightened away.

This fundamental truth was captured in the parable of the big dog who saw a little dog chasing his tail and asked him, "Why are you chasing your tail?" "Well," said the puppy, "I have been told that the best thing for a dog is happiness and that happiness is in my tail. Therefore I am chasing it. When I catch it, I shall have happiness."

"Listen son," said the big dog, "I too want happiness and I too have been told that it is to be found in my tail. But I noticed that when I chase after it, it keeps running away from me, but when I go about my business, it comes after me."

This is the secret – going about one's business, totally intent on doing a worthwhile task and never running after the tail. When we keep asking ourselves if we are happy, we are no wiser than if we should pause several times during the day to take our temperature to discover whether we are healthy. In the latter case we are more prone to become sick; in the former we are quite likely to grow miserable.

Some years ago a London newspaper offered prizes for the best answers to this question: "Who are the happiest persons on earth?" Here are three of the answers which were judged the best:

1. A craftsman or artist whistling over a job that is well done.
2. A mother after a busy day bathing her baby.
3. A doctor who has finished a difficult and dangerous operation and saved a human life.

Notice that not one of these people is looking for happiness. Each has an important task at hand and is totally absorbed in performing it. And in the act of going about their business, they have unwittingly opened a door by which happiness has quietly entered. You see, happiness enjoys seeing us about our business. She comes to the farmer in his fields, the worker at his lathe, the writer at his desk, the housewife at her mixing bowl. She is attracted by the smell of sweat, by the sight of overalls, by the sound of tools. She tiptoes in so softly we scarcely take note of her presence. She lays her blessings upon us all unawares.

In his book, *How to Be Happy Though Human,* Dr. W. Beran Wolfe summed up this thought in these words: "If you observe a really happy man, you will find him building a boat, writing a symphony, educating his son, growing double dahlias in his garden or looking for dinosaur eggs in the Gobi Desert. He will not be searching for happiness as if it were a collar button that has rolled under the radiator. He will not be striving for it as a goal in itself."

No, happiness cannot be overtaken by those who pursue her. Happiness is a by-product of cheerful, honest labor dedicated to a worthwhile task.

We proceed now to what I consider a second paradox about happiness. You cannot get happiness unless you give it. The truth is suggested by the Hebrew word for life which is *chayim*–a plural noun. In Hebrew there is no singular noun for one life. Any life is a plural noun, as though to drive home the inescapable fact that life to be good cannot be singular. If we would achieve happiness our lives must spill over into other lives. We must concentrate not on getting but on giving, not on hoarding but on sharing.

Think back for a moment to the three most popular conceptions of a happy person. Not one is in the act of receiving. They are all going out of themselves. The mother is bringing comfort to her baby, the surgeon has saved the life of another and even the craftsman and the artist have contributed a vital part of themselves, their skill or genius, to the creation of something which others will enjoy using or looking at.

John Mason Brown, the well-known critic, said something extremely relevant on this matter: "What happiness is, no person can say for another. But no one, I am convinced, can be happy who lives only for himself. The joy of living comes from immersion in something that we know to be bigger, better, more enduring and worthier than we are."

How I wish that more of us would grasp the full meaning of these words! If only we accepted the explosive significance with which they are charged. We would not say "no" to causes which beg for volunteers. We would not shut our eyes to human need. We would not be perennial seekers after diversion, recreation and escape from which we return to an inner emptiness which will not be filled by self-pampering.

One of the real danger zones in a woman's life is that very period which she eagerly anticipated when the problem of raising children seemed so burdensome. Oh how delightful life will be when Joey is grown and Sue is a young lady. They will become more self-reliant, they will require less physical care and attention. I'll be free: Then what happens? *Gott helft,* the years go by and freedom has dawned. But sad to relate, the anticipated happiness does not come with freedom. On the contrary, the mother will frequently become more unhappy as the children become more independent. Now she wonders whether she is needed. The children seem so self-sufficient it hurts.

If she is wise, she will accept this loosening of the strings as nature's way of preparing the child for responsible adulthood. She will also realize that while she may be less needed physically, her children's dependence upon her for guidance, encouragement and counsel is still exceedingly large. And, most important, if she didn't do so earlier she will begin to search earnestly for an occupation, a cause, or an organization to which she can direct her surplus time and energy. Shortly, the children will leave altogether and her need to give of herself will be even greater. Her happiness depends upon finding a worthy object of her skill, her time and her talents.

What is true of this mother at this particular time is true of all of us at all times. We cannot have happiness unless we give of ourselves. Dr. Albert Schweitzer, one of the truly tall spirits of our time, put the essence of the matter simply: "One thing I know; the only ones among you who will be really happy are those who will have sought and found how to serve."

This is the crucial thing. We make a living by what we get. We make a life by what we give.

The third paradox of happiness flows directly from the second. In fact, it is the second one turned around. If it is true that we cannot get happiness unless we give it, it is also true that we cannot give it without getting it. Happiness has correctly been compared to a perfume. You cannot pour it on others without getting a few drops on yourself.

Few living Americans have enjoyed as many well-deserved honors as has the contralto Marion Anderson. She was selected as America's ambassador of good will to Asia. She was invited to sing in the White

House. She won acclaim from some of the musical immortals – Toscanini and Sibelius. An interviewer once asked her: "Miss Anderson, what was the greatest moment in your life?" Do you know what she answered, this woman of so many great moments? "My greatest moment," she replied, "was the day I went home and told my mother she wouldn't need to take work home anymore." Her greatest moment was associated not with getting but with giving.

We go astray in our quest for happiness because we think of it as something due to us, something the world owes us. Some people we know, are forever complaining, full of grievances against the world because it does not minister to them. The next time you feel this mood sneaking up on you remember you may be suffering from an ingrown ego. Try this prescription. Think of someone at that moment whom you can help. Is there someone whose loneliness you can relieve by a visit? Is there a hospital patient you can cheer with a call? Is there an overdue note of appreciation you can write to someone who helped you over a rough spot? Is there someone hungering for a word of reassurance or encouragement that you can speak? When you are unhappy try doing something for somebody, preferably something involving some inconvenience and time. Life will wear a brighter face when you do because as you give happiness it will come back to bless you.

Meyer Levin, the novelist, made this same observation about the heroine of his book, *Eva*. Eva is an 18 year old girl, a Polish Jewess, who miraculously managed to elude the Nazis and to reach ultimate safety in Israel. In an issue of the *American Zionist,* Meyer Levin wrote that the entire gripping episode is unbelievable but true. And he added this comment: "In Eva's story there is an element that is of utmost importance to me. Eva found it hardest to exert herself to survive when she was alone. Only when she was also helping to save someone else, one of the series of close friends with whom she joined forces in each stage of her adventure – only then did her life-urge emerge at its most powerful." In sharing we not only find happiness, we find the will and the power to live.

We cannot dismiss this theme without adding an important postscript. A vital ingredient of a happy life is the faith that the whole enterprise makes sense, that our lives have a meaning which transcends them and goes beyond our own small life span. Happiness, therefore, involves us not only with each other, but also with God.

"Remember us to life, O King, who delights in life." We are here because God wants us to live and it is He who urges us to fulfill our divinely appointed destiny by living life fully and profoundly. My life is terribly important because it comes from God. I dare not do with it less than my God-given best.

As a Jew I know that living life at its best means being intimately concerned with the destiny of my people, the fate of Israel, the strength of the Jewish community. I die a little bit if I deny their claim upon me and my loyalty to them. Rooted in the soil of my people, I draw strength, sustenance and stature.

Living life at its best means adorning it with the mitzvot of a beautiful tradition. It means Shabbat and prayer, Pesach and Kiddush, Torah study and giving tzdakah. My life becomes hollow and denuded when these fall away. With these as a part of my life, living becomes a holy and meaningful pilgrimage.

Living life at its best means keeping on speaking terms with my conscience, to do nothing to outrage it or to inflict pain upon it. When my acts do violence to my moral or ethical standards, I sustain a loss for which no pleasure or material gain can compensate me, for I shrink in moral stature. When I keep my friendship with the best in me, I achieve a serenity which cloaks life with gentle beauty.

Happiness then is distilled from the way we live with one another, with our people, with our heritage and with ourselves. And so, when we pray "Remember us to life," we add, "O King who delights in life." We want the kind of life in which God can take delight. If God finds delight in our lives, we find life delightful. We will find it happy. God grant us all the wisdom to strive for that kind of life on the New Year.

Our Magnificent Obsession

During a single week one television channel showed *The Ten Commandments,* while other channels featured programs that broke six of them.

This melancholy coincidence illustrates the very observation made by an astute observer of the contemporary scene: "There's no need for a period in punctuation anymore. Nobody stops at anything."

However shabbily the Ten Commandments are treated today, their pronouncement on Mount Sinai some 3,000 years ago was surely one of the most luminous events in all of human history. The world was never quite the same after that incandescent moment when our ancestors stood at the foot of a quaking mountain and, amidst thunder and lightning, heard the Divine words.

Even Hitler felt the powerful impact of that moment–even if only in a perverse way. Referring to his monstrous creation, Nazism, he called it "the great battle for the liberation from the curse of Mount Sinai." He went on to say: "We are fighting against . . . the curse of the so-called Ten Commandments, against them we are fighting."

On the Festival of Shavuot, we celebrate the "birthday" of the Ten Commandments. Far from being a "curse" from which we need "liberation," the commandments are a blessing to which we need deepened rededication.

Shavuot, "the time of the giving of our Torah," has extraordinary significance for our people. It commemorates the event which burned itself into our soul, molded our character, regulated our behavior and shaped our destiny.

Whatever the impact of Sinai on the course of the subsequent history of mankind in general, one thing is certain. For our people something profoundly revolutionary and irreversible happened there. After Sinai the Jewish people would never be the same.

It was at Sinai that our ancestors heard the heavenly verdict: "On this day you have become a people." A horde of ex-slaves, so recently liberated, was elevated into a consecrated people and given a priceless gift–the Torah. And that made all the difference.

We did not become a people when we threw off the chains of Pharaoh; we became a people when we enlisted in the service of God.

Centuries later the Jewish philosopher Saadiah could write with every justification: "Our people is a people only by virtue of our possession of the Torah."

To possess the Torah meant to be possessed by it. Torah for our people became our magnificent obsession. And thus the Torah grew. Other books were added to the original five, the books that became our Bible, then the Mishnah, the Gemara, Responsa, Commentaries; the works of grammarians, philosophers, mystics, kabbalists, rationalists–all inspired by Torah and included within it.

It was to the study of this entire body of literature that Judaism applied the rabbinic verdict: "The merit of Torah study is equal to all the Commandments."

Torah study was to begin as soon as a child was old enough to read, and the process was to continue throughout life. Only death could interrupt it.

We who appeared on the stage of history carrying a Book earned the proud designation – the People of the Book. We carried the Book and the Book carried us. It gave us strength to resist, courage to persevere, and a special dimension of joy in living.

One of the real threats to Jewish survival in America derives from the growing distance between the People of the Book and the books of our people. More and more of our people know less and less about the rich heritage of our people accumulated over long centuries of spiritual and intellectual creativity. Ignorance leads to indifference and indifference leads to loss of identity. An empty sack cannot stand.

The words of Ahad Ha'am are no less true in contemporary America than they were in early twentieth-century Russia where they were written: "Learning! Learning! Learning! That is the secret of Jewish survival."

Long before Ahad Ha'am, our Sages emphasized the crucial centrality of study in two rhetorical questions: "If you have acquired knowledge what do you lack? If you lack knowledge what have you acquired?"

Rabbis Harold Kushner and Jack Riemer have summoned us to study and acquaint ourselves with our extravagant legacy. Their words are especially meaningful as we approach Shavuot and once again face Mount Sinai:

"We owe it to our ancestors to keep Torah alive;
They struggled and suffered to preserve our way of life;
They knew this to be their most precious gift to us.

We owe it to our children to keep Torah alive;
For why should they be spiritual paupers
When the riches of this heritage can be theirs?

We owe it to the world to keep Torah alive;
This is a message which the world needs to hear.

We owe it to God to continue as a people,
To share His dream, to bear witness to His sovereignty,
And to live the words of Torah."

The Secret of Our Immortality

When you come into a traditional synagogue on Simhat Torah evening, the sights and the sounds that will greet you will make you wonder whether you are, in fact, in a house of worship. The mood will range from gay to wild. The atmosphere will be charged with celebration. The reason? – Rejoicing in the Torah.

Here is what Herman Wouk, the renowned novelist, has written about this uniquely Jewish festival: "Nobody who has been in a synagogue during Simhat Torah needs to be told what it is like. For one who has never seen it, description will be pale. The manner varies from the exalted frenzy of the Hasidic congregations to the decorous dancing and singing in the elegant Manhattan synagogues. The essence everywhere is the same: excitement, singing, joking, joy within the usually solemn precincts of worship.

"Seven times, chanting processions circle the synagogue with all the Holy Torah Scrolls. Flag-waving children march behind in cheery disorder. . . . A powerful jubilation irradiates the synagogue. The time comes when the rabbi is himself drawn into the rejoicing and solemnly dances with a Holy Scroll in his arms. My grandfather, patriarchal and reserved all year long, was still performing this dance in his 90s, a few shuffling, tottering steps, his face alight with pleasure as he clasped the Torah in his old arms" (*This Is My God,* pages 79–80).

What is it that the flag-waving children and the tottering patriarch celebrate on Simhat Torah? They are celebrating first the privilege of having reached the annual conclusion of the Torah reading cycle. On Simhat Torah we read publicly the last verses of the Book of Deuteronomy. Then we begin immediately to read the Torah once again from Chapter 1, verse 1 of the Book of Genesis. Thus, we demonstrate our unending obligation to study Torah and to draw continuous inspiration from the living words of our sacred Scriptures.

Judaism is vitally concerned that we serve God with heart, soul and might. But it has been no less insistent that we serve Him too with our minds – with minds that stay open and keep growing.

As we grow older it is very tempting to develop a permanent mind set. But minds, like parachutes, are valuable only when open.

To shut the windows of the mind is to court mental and spiritual suffocation. We must literally never stop going to school, broadening our horizons and expanding our knowledge.

This is the distinctive Jewish contribution to mental hygiene – the unparalleled emphasis upon study as a process that only death ought to terminate.

As long as we keep our minds open and alert, as long as we are willing to try a new skill, entertain a new thought, develop a new friend, surrender an old prejudice – so long do we remain vital people, so long do we gain ground and move forward in the search for more abundant life.

On Simhat Torah we celebrate, too, the privilege that has been ours to be God's messengers on an exalted and perilous errand – to be the carriers of His word to humanity. The Torah earned for us the title "The People of the Book." The Torah is our mark of nobility, the central symbol of our historical adventure, the most potent source of our strength and the guarantor of our survival.

In 1898, Mark Twain wrote an article in *Harper's* magazine entitled "Concerning the Jews." There the following passage appears: "All things are mortal but the Jew; all other forces pass, but he remains. What is the secret of his immortality?"

The answer to Mark Twain's question is given every evening in our prayers: "The words of the Torah are our life and the length of our days." Should you enter a synagogue this evening you are very likely to hear these words chanted in Hebrew in joyous affirmation. And then your heart will guess the truth that you have discovered the secret of our immortality.

Using the Past Wisely

Nostalgia, it has been said, is when we find the present tense and the past perfect. Current difficulties cast a retroactive glow of happiness on the past, and conceal its pains and its problems. Distance in time as in space lends enchantment.

The Torah portion *Hukkat* describes two severe attacks of nostalgia—two of many that our ancestors suffered in the wilderness. When they ran short of water or became fed up with a steady diet of manna they looked back to the "good old days" before Moses led them into this predicament.

"Why did you make us leave Egypt to die in the wilderness? There is no bread and no water, and we have come to loathe this miserable food." "We remember the fish we used to eat in Egypt free, the cucumbers and the melons and the leeks and the onions and the garlic. But now our soul is dried up; we have nothing except this manna to look to."

Oh the glory that was Egypt! The grandeur we left behind!

Conveniently edited out of their rosy memories was the degradation of slavery, the brutality of arbitrary whippings, the bricks without straw, the groans of broken bodies, the decree consigning every male Hebrew infant to death at birth. "Boy, did we have fish and cucumbers and garlic in Egypt!" Forgotten of course was the fact that these foods were flavored with bitter tears and eaten with the bread of affliction.

The tendency to romanticize the past and to denigrate the present did not begin with our ancestors in the wilderness. The oldest piece of writing in existence is a cuneiform script on a piece of papyrus some 6,000 years old. It contains this complaint: "Alas, times are not what they used to be. Everyone wants to write a book and children are no longer obedient to their parents."

And when do you think the following commentary on the younger generation was written? "Our youth now love luxury, they have bad manners, contempt for authority; they show disrespect for elders, and they love to chatter instead of exercise. Children are now tyrants, not the servants of their household. They no longer rise when elders enter the room. They contradict their parents, chatter before company, gobble up their food and tyrannize their teachers."

No, this is not the report of a principal to the school board on the behavior of high school students in the inner city; it is a lament of Socrates written some 2,400 years ago!

In the "good old days" they also longed for the good old days. Perhaps the best thing we can say about the good old days is that they cannot come back. If we doubt it, let's try to read this page tonight by an oil lamp.

After a lifetime of studying America's past, Otto Bettmann's verdict in 1974 was a book called *The Good Old Days – They Were Terrible*.

And let's not forget that one day the very days which now fill us with so much discontent and grumbling will one day be considered "the good old days."

Despite the nostalgia that filled our ancestors in the wilderness the whole thrust of Judaism is to look forward not backward. Our messiah has not yet come. Moses is told by the Almighty to command the complaining Israelites in the wilderness: "Sanctify yourselves for tomorrow!" The road to fulfillment leads not to yesterday but to tomorrow.

Having said all this we ought to hasten to add that if we should not deify the past neither should we denigrate it. Unless we know where we come from we do not know who we are and where we should be facing. A generation without Jewish memories is a generation without Jewish hopes. To be sure we cannot and should not live in the past; but the past can and should live in us.

In his poignant autobiography *Growing Up,* Russell Baker talks about the thoughts that came to him as a result of his visits with his bedridden mother who is in her 80s. "These hopeless end-of-the-line visits with my mother made me wish I had not thrown off my own past so carelessly. We all come from the past, and children ought to know what it was that went into their making, to know that life is a braided cord of humanity stretching up from time long gone, and that it cannot be defined by a single journey from diaper to shroud."

A moving illustration of this truth was contained in a lengthy article in the *Wall Street Journal* on the incredible scope of Jewish fundraising in America. Imbedded in the story was the account of a Jew from Washington who recently became active in Jewish affairs. During his first trip to Israel he visited Yad Vashem, the magnificent and moving Holocaust memorial in Jerusalem. "There," we are told, he "noticed a small wooden *menorah* that had been made by a doomed inmate. Since that trip, lighting the Sabbath candles has become a Friday night ritual" in his home.

This is the way to use our past to enrich our present and to guarantee our future.

Creeds and Deeds

One of the most risky real estate deals in history is described in the weekly prophetic portion for the *Sidrah Behar*. The piece of land was in Jerusalem. What made the purchase so speculative was the timing.

The year was 586 before the Common Era, and Jerusalem was under an unbreakable siege by the powerful Babylonian armies. The destruction of the city and the exile of its inhabitants were imminent. Indeed, Jeremiah himself had predicted these events and had gotten himself thrown into prison for his efforts.

At this perilous time, God advises Jeremiah to purchase a plot of land. This land was a field in the city of Anatot, and it was the property of Hanamel, the son of his father's brother. Hanamel was apparently compelled by circumstances to sell it, and according to the prevailing Biblical law, Jeremiah as a kinsman was obliged to purchase the field so that it should not pass from the family.

But the purchase of the field at this particular time would have, in addition, a crucial symbolic significance. It would dramatically give expression to the faith that after the destruction and exile which were now unavoidable, there would be return and rebirth.

But how can Jeremiah convince the people not to despair? How can they be persuaded to cling to so frail and fragile a hope? Only one way. Buy the field. Risk some silver and save a people. Jeremiah's personal faith in his people's future restoration would be of little consequence unless he acted on that faith.

A truth leaps at us from this dramatic transaction. The value of our beliefs is reflected in how we behave. Our convictions become concrete where they are converted into conduct. Our creeds become vital when they shape our deeds.

An interesting historical parallel to Jeremiah's purchase is found centuries later during Hannibal's invasion of Italy. At that critical time one Roman patriot bought at full price in public auction the ground on which Hannibal's army was encamped.

A somewhat similar gesture of faith in our own people's future came to the surface following the Six Day War in June 1967. The first major cultural event following the conclusion of the war was a concert on the recently recaptured Mount Scopus.

One of the passengers on the bus which climbed Mount Scopus gave the driver a ticket he had purchased in 1948 before Mount Scopus had been captured by the Arabs. He had held on to the ticket for nineteen years, confident that he would one day be able to use it.

So many of our beliefs lie asleep in the quiet dormitory of our minds. They never awake in action. Little wonder that they matter so little.

A national poll a while ago showed that the overwhelming majority of Americans believe in God. But when they were asked whether it made any difference in their behavior more than half said it did not.

These figures justify the complaint of Dr. Melvin E. Wheatley: "Great hosts of people worship a God of religion who is not at all the God of all life. He is a pious presence in the sacraments but an impudent intruder in the science lab. He is a point of reference for prayers, but an unemployed consultant on business contracts."

Religion, to be alive, must be acted out in the arena of life. Its concern is not only to keep the Sabbath holy, but to keep the weekdays honest.

One of our teachers at the rabbinical seminary cautioned us that the feast of the sermon is always followed by spiritual indigestion unless it is followed by religious exercise. And then he added: "Remember, one kind act will teach more love of God than a thousand sermons."

The matter was summed up best by a prophet whose literary remains are only three chapters in our Bible. But he put us in his everlasting debt in three Hebrew words which are translated: "The righteous shall live by his faith" (Habakkuk 2:4).

On Keeping Kosher

In a biography of the late Dr. Stephen Wise, there is a fascinating incident which provides a telling commentary on the powerful role that the laws of *Kashrut* have played in our history from the time they were promulgated in the Torah down to modern times.

When the American Standard Bible Committee, a Protestant group, was preparing to work on a new translation of the Hebrew

Bible, the committee invited the well-known Jewish Biblical scholar, Dr. Harry Orlinsky, to join in the endeavor. For a variety of reasons, Dr. Orlinsky was reluctant to do so. When the invitation was repeated, Dr. Orlinsky, who was then a member of the faculty of the Jewish Institute of Religion, decided to ask its president, Dr. Stephen Wise, for his advice.

Dr. Wise urged Dr. Orlinsky to accept the invitation but to remember that he was going to serve on that committee as the representative of the Jewish people. Therefore, Dr. Orlinsky was not to work with the committee on the Sabbath nor was he to partake of *trefah* food in the company of his Christian colleagues.

What is so striking about this conversation is that fact that Stephen Wise himself, as a leader of Reform Judaism, was not especially observant of the traditional laws relating to Shabbat or *Kashrut*. But he understood how crucial Shabbat and *Kashrut* observance had always been in Jewish life and he wanted Dr. Orlinsky to honor these sancta when he worked with Christians as a representative of the Jewish people.

As a student of Jewish history, Dr. Wise knew well how often Jews made great sacrifices to observe *Kashrut*. One of the first recorded Jewish martyrs was the aged scribe Eliezer. When the Greeks at the time of the Maccabees attempted to compel him to eat pig's flesh, he permitted himself to be killed rather than transgress the laws of the Torah.

The historian Josephus tells of the Essenes, who during the war against the Romans, though "racked and twisted, burnt and broken, and made to pass through every instrument of torture in order to induce them to blaspheme their lawgiver or to eat some forbidden thing, refused to yield to either demand, nor even once did they cringe to their persecutors or shed a tear."

And so it went down the centuries. During the Inquisition many Marranos in Spain risked their lives to obtain Kosher meat. This was considered an act of heresy and could be punished by death.

At the time of the Crusades even forced conversions could not separate many Jews from their observance of the Dietary Laws. Thus a contemporary chronicler wrote: "It is fitting that I should recount their praise, for whatever they ate . . . they did at the peril of their lives. They would ritually slaughter animals for food according to the Jewish tradition."

Countless incidents of fidelity to the Dietary Laws at great personal peril are also part of the spiritual legacy of the black night in the Nazi kingdom of evil.

The Talmud tells us that those *Mitzvot* for which our people risked their very lives became especially dear to them. Who will deny that the *Mitzvah* of *Kashrut* is most prominent among them?

Modern times have not dealt kindly with the Dietary Laws. They are derided as constituting a religion of "pot-and-pan-theism." Originally, it is claimed, they were a valuable safeguard to health, but today government agencies assure the quality of the food we eat. The truth is that in urging upon us the observance of *Kashrut*, the Torah links it not to healthiness but to holiness.

Further, it is argued, the Dietary Laws prevent social and political integration. Their observance is an unnecessary burden. And besides, it is expensive to keep them.

But if I read the signs correctly, *Kashrut* is making a comeback. It's becoming quite kosher to keep Kosher.

Before each of the Jewish holidays, American newspapers pass along to their readers Kosher recipes for traditional holiday foods. Stockholders of major corporations are given the option of selecting a Kosher lunch at the annual meeting. All airlines and many ships offer Kosher meals, as do many non-Jewish hospitals.

It is almost routine today for the White House to serve a Kosher meal whenever the function is in honor of an Israeli dignitary.

Kashrut has also become more widely practiced among Reform rabbis. Today it is no longer unusual to meet a Reform rabbi whose home is Kosher.

A celebrated sociologist once observed that what the children of immigrants wish to forget, the grandchildren wish to remember. In many instances this is proving true as it relates to *Kashrut*. Why do the grandchildren reclaim the discarded practices? Let one of the grandchildren give the answer.

In *Sh'ma,* a fine biweekly magazine, Andy and Marian Bowman wrote a piece entitled: ". . . And So We Became Kosher." She is a former special education teacher "now raising a family," and he is the Chief Federal Public Defender for the State of Connecticut. Here is what they wrote in part:

"It's a wonderful feeling to know that any Jew can come to our home and eat with us without feeling uncomfortable. It's also wonderful to feel that we have undertaken a discipline in our home which is peculiarly Jewish in nature, for we believe that *Kashrut* is an act of faith.

". . . to us the extra attention that we pay to eating in our Kosher home gives us a feeling of warmth and closeness to a heritage we take pride in and to a people to whose survival we are dedicated. It is our way of expressing who and what we are in a basic, personal and positive away."

The Bigness of Little Laws

The Torah portion *Yitro* describes the most decisive event in Jewish history – that incandescent moment when our ancestors stood at the foot of a quaking and smoking Mount Sinai and heard the majestic Ten Commandments proclaimed amidst thunder and lightning.

The spectacular grandeur of the setting was a fitting backdrop for the impressive pronouncements. They proclaimed the fundamental teachings of our faith – absolute monotheism, uncompromising opposition to idolatry, the holiness of Shabbat, the sanctity of human life and marriage, the inviolable rights of our neighbors.

The moment was massive and so were the laws to which it gave birth.

By contrast, so many of the laws which are promulgated in the following *Sidrah, Mishpatim,* appear almost trivial. They appear to be too petty for the Almighty to bother with them. They deal with wounds inflicted during arguments, the treatment of slaves, oxen that gore, livestock which graze in a neighbor's field, gossiping. Not very exalted subjects, are they? It is almost beneath God's dignity to talk about them.

And yet our Sages made the pointed comment: "As the Ten Commandments came from Sinai, so did these laws come from Sinai." They are no less significant. They are no less sacred.

What prompted our Sages to throw the full authority of Sinai behind the "little laws"?

There were two reasons. The first was historical. In the Temple in Jerusalem the order of daily worship included the recitation of the Ten Commandments (Mishnah Tamid 5:1). However, after the rise of Christianity the reading of the Ten Commandments at daily services was discontinued. The early Christians contended that only these commandments were given at Sinai and none other. Therefore the other laws had no divine sanction (Palestinian Talmud, Berakhot 3c).

To decentralize the Ten Commandments, the Sages removed them from the regular order of worship; the Sages then augmented the authority of the "little laws" by explicitly claiming for them Sinaitic origin.

There was a second reason for emphasizing the significance of the "little laws." Our Sages correctly suspected that the "little laws" might too easily be disregarded. Small duties are too frequently dismissed as inconsequential. Be careful, our Sages were admonishing us, these too are from Sinai, these too are sacred. Guard them well.

I think that our generation needs desperately to be alerted to the importance of the little laws. Being a Jew has too often in our history been fraught with the most fateful consequences, and demanded the ultimate in sacrifice and courage. Loyalty to Judaism was frequently spelled out in acts of martyrdom and *Kiddush Hashem*. But what is demanded of us? Heroism? Self-sacrifice? Martyrdom? Scarcely!

Loyalty to Judaism for us has to be spelled out in humble acts, undramatic tasks, unspectacular little deeds.

Beginning the meal with a *"B'rakhah"* is a little deed.

Attending a synagogue service is a little deed.

Enrolling in a class of Jewish studies, reading a Jewish book, adorning the home with Jewish symbolism, owning and playing records of Jewish music – these are little deeds.

Enjoying a Shabbat meal as a family, lighting the Shabbat candles, reciting the *Kiddush,* subscribing to a Jewish magazine, buying an Israel Bond, joining a Jewish organization – all these are little deeds.

And yet it is precisely in our faithfulness to these little deeds that our loyalty to Judaism is reflected, the texture of our lives is woven and the very future of Judaism in America will be determined.

Judaism in America will not be defeated by great acts of betrayal. It will be undermined by small acts of negligence. For want of a nail the kingdom was lost!

Judaism will not be saved by any headline-making, breathtaking deeds of valor. It will be sustained by high fidelity to little *mitzvot*.

"Piety," wrote Rabbi Leo Baeck, "especially Jewish piety, respects the little act, the little man, the little matter, the little task, the
little duty. Through the little, religion meets the greatness that lies
behind."

The little act, the little task performed regularly and faithfully by
little people – this is what gives tone, content and character to a society.
We are not called upon to perform extraordinary things. We are asked
to perform ordinary things, little things, with extraordinary fidelity.

In her darkness Helen Keller saw a shining truth which can guide
each of us. "I long to accomplish a great and noble task, but it is my
chief duty and joy to accomplish humble tasks as though they were
great and noble . . . For the world is moved along, not only by the
mighty shoves of its heroes, but also by the aggregate of tiny pushes of
each honest worker."

Let us each contribute our tiny pushes. That's how the world is
moved along.

The Day that Blesses

With the announcement that the *Reader's Digest* has condensed the
Bible to sixty percent of its original length, one wit said that he was
eager to see which four commandments we don't have to worry about
anymore.

In our time we have to worry about all of the Ten Commandments more than ever before. The contemporary moral climate is not
too congenial to the observance of these time-hallowed precepts.

Of all the commandments it may be the fourth, "Remember the
Sabbath Day to keep it holy," that we have to worry about the most.
A nationwide poll rating the commandments in order of significance
put the Sabbath Commandment at the very bottom of the list. Would
the results have been any different had the poll been conducted exclusively among Jews? I wonder.

In any event, it is worth noting that of all the holy days on the
Jewish calendar, only the Sabbath was included among the Ten
Commandments. None of the Festivals, not even Rosh Hashanah or

Yom Kippur, was accorded such an honor. Moreover, the observance of Shabbat is enjoined in the Torah no fewer than twelve times.

Our Sages lavished extraordinary affection upon the Sabbath. They personified it as a beautiful bride, a lovely princess, a gracious queen. Above all, it was a priceless gift from God, a precious link between the paradise that was lost and the paradise that was yet to come.

So deeply did the Sabbath enter into the soul of the Jew and so profound was its influence that Israel Zangwill could speak of it as "the hub of the Jew's universe." Ahad Ha'am saw in it a most potent force for Jewish survival: "One can say without exaggeration that more than the Jew has kept the Sabbath, the Sabbath has kept the Jew." And Abraham Joshua Heschel in his lyrical volume, *The Sabbath,* celebrating the exquisite beauty and magnificent splendor of that holy day, called it a majestic cathedral in time.

If we want to grasp the benevolent influence of the Sabbath we have to see how it impacts on the lives of people. A number of illustrations rush to mind. Henrietta Szold, the founder of Hadassah, would begin her day at 4:30 A.M., end it at midnight, and work busily all the intervening hours. When a close friend once asked her how she was able to work this way, she answered: "There are two reasons: one, I keep the Sabbath; and two, my cast iron stomach." She went on to add that when she lit her candles on Friday she put aside all business and cares and entered into the pure delight of the Sabbath. This day renewed her for the week ahead.

In his book, *This Is My God,* Herman Wouk described how on Friday afternoon he would leave his work on Broadway where he was preparing a play: "Leaving the gloomy theatre, the littered coffee cups, the shouting stagehands, the bedevilled director, I have come home. It has been a startling change, very like a brief return from the wars. My wife and my boys, whose existence I have almost forgotten, are waiting for me, dressed in holiday clothes, and looking to me marvelously attractive. . . .

"Saturday is healing for the whole week. The telephone is silent. I can think, read, study, walk, or do nothing. It is an oasis of quiet. When night falls I go back to the wonderful nerve-racking Broadway game. Often I make my best contribution of the week then and there.

"One Saturday night my producer said to me: 'I don't envy you your religion, but I envy you your Sabbath.' "

Sam Levenson, the celebrated comedian, once gave us a remark-able insight into what Shabbat meant to the ordinary Jew, the Jew who struggled to eke out a living. Writing of his father, he tells us:

"Now when it came to Papa, he dealt in two times: sacred time and profane time. Making a living, being a sweatshop slave 16 hours a day, this was profane time. But came 'Erev Shabbos' with the candles lit on the table, and I could see my father change from a sweatshop slave into an angelic figure who had something to do with eternity and sacred time.

"Suddenly the wrinkles came out of his face, and he became again a holy man who was related to the whole universe and to God's destiny for man – which was greater than sitting over a sewing ma-chine in a sweatshop."

Some questions: Do you and I need Shabbat less than Henrietta Szold, Herman Wouk or Sam Levenson's Papa?

In these harried, hurried and harassed times, do we not urgently require some of the spiritual and emotional therapy the Shabbat offers?

At a time when a national magazine designates the computer as "the man of the year" is there not a desperate need to have Shabbat restore our eroded humanity, reaffirm our God-given dignity?

At a time when the integrity of the Jewish family has been seriously undermined, do we not need more than ever before the powerful help of Shabbat to preserve the cohesiveness and promote the togetherness of the family?

At a time when so many worries gnaw at us, so many problems weigh on us, and so many cares feed on us, can we afford to dispense with the joy and the delight the Shabbat can bring us?

The Shabbat, the Torah tells us, is the day that God blessed. It is more. It is the day that blesses those who have the wisdom to observe it.

Coming Home

At vacation time the freeway near the University of California in Berkeley is lined with students trying to hitch rides home. The students usually display large signs with their destinations printed in bold letters. Despite the intense competition for rides, one student got a lift almost as soon as he held up his sign. It said: "Mom's Waiting."

That young man exploited one of our most profound and most enduring loves—the love of home. The mere mention of the word evokes an almost mystic reverence and misty nostalgia. Home is one of the largest words in our emotional vocabulary.

Home is Mom waiting, home is comfort when bruised, home is sorrow eased and joy enlarged, home is childhood and growing up, home is hot food and warm beds, snow etching faces on the window and the morning sun announcing the time to get up. "Home," as Robert Frost said, "is the place where, when you have to go there, they have to take you in."

The homing instinct in birds has been well documented. In *The Territorial Imperative,* Robert Ardrey tells about a bird known as the Manx Shearwater from Skokholm Island off the Coast of Wales. A Cambridge scientist transported it by airplane from its native habitat to Harvard University. There it was tagged and released. The Shearwater was back in its burrow on Skokholm Island twelve-and-one-half days later. The bird had flown 3,050 miles covering an average of 244 miles per day!

Is there also a homing instinct in human beings? Every indication points to its existence. How else can we explain the opening passage of the *Sidrah Vayishlach,* where we find Jacob returning home after an absence of some twenty years? After all, home for Jacob means facing his brother Esau who had vowed to kill him. That is why Jacob fled from his home in the first place. Coming home means not only jeopardizing his own life but also the lives of his wives and children. Despite the awesome risk of coming home, Jacob throws all caution aside and faces homeward. Why? Was it because the homing instinct in him is too strong to be denied?

Was it also the homing instinct that kept alive in our people the love for *Eretz Yisrael* through the long, hard centuries down the drafty corridors of history? Wherever we traveled we took with us the hope for return to the land of our origins. We echoed that hope in our daily prayers, and "home" was the direction we faced when we offered those prayers.

In July of 1967, a group of Conservative rabbis and their wives arrived in Israel on a pilgrimage. Avraham Fradkin greeted them with these words: "Welcome to Israel! Welcome home!" Avraham was right. Israel is the place where a Jew feels at home even though he has never been there before. There is within us a latent spark that bursts into a warming flame upon contact with this niggardly piece of geography. Israel is many things to many peoples and faiths. But to the Jew alone it is home, and it is the homing instinct that has brought us back to our ancestral land.

The homing instinct works upon Jews in other ways. It has helped to bring many an alienated Jew back to his people. Former Supreme Court Justice Felix Frankfurter was for a brief time active in Zionism under the influence of Louis D. Brandeis. For years before his death however he had virtually no association with Jewish life. As for the Jewish religion, he claimed to have left the Synagogue at the age of 15, never to return.

But when he was ailing in his advanced years he instructed a good friend, Garson Kanin, about his own funeral arrangements. He asked that one of the participants in the funeral service be a certain close friend "who is also a practicing Orthodox Jew. He knows Hebrew perfectly well and will know exactly what to say."

"Do you mean a prayer of some sort?"

"Well, of course, you nut, what else would he say in Hebrew?"

"Then you mean the Kaddish?"

"Oh, I don't know and neither do you, but he'll know and he'll do it beautifully. Let me explain. I came into the world a Jew; I think it is fitting that I should leave as a Jew. I don't want to be one of those pretenders and turn my back on a great and noble heritage."

And there is still another way that the homing instinct affects us. It is suggested by our reaction to E.T. Adults no less than children were taken by this ugly extra-terrestrial little creature whose vocabulary consists of a single word–"home." There is a deep sadness in his watery eyes as he points his bony finger toward the heavens indicating the source of his distress–home-sickness. Why did he touch us so? Is it because, like E.T., we too are longing for home? Homesickness can afflict even those of us who are secure in our own terrestrial homes.

In "The Bella Lingua," John Cheever offers a revealing insight into our human condition. One of his characters says: "Fifty percent of the people in the world are homesick all the time. . . . You don't really long for another country. You long for something in yourself that you don't have, or haven't been able to find."

What is this something for which we long in our homesickness even when we are at home? The poet Wordsworth gave us a clue to our malaise when he said "trailing clouds of glory we come, from God who is our home." The longing, the yearning that we can't define is for the very source of our being, God.

Dr. Louis Finkelstein has spoken directly to this theme. Despite all our unprecedented affluence, he noted, there is among us restlessness, confusion, increasing neuroses and general unhappiness.

"Living in a gilded palace, as it were, we are still miserable, for we are essentially orphans, having lost that most precious of all values in life, the sense of the Fatherhood of God. . . .

"More than ever then do we become homesick; homesick not for our houses or for our countries, but homesick for the universal Parent of all of us, for that deep affection which is at the heart of the universe itself, for the mercy of God. . . ."

Dr. Finkelstein invites us to come home. It's an invitation we would be wise to accept.

On Being Impractical

When a congregant was informed by her rabbi one year that the first Hanukkah candle would be lit that year on the evening of December 10th, she exclaimed, "Hanukkah is surely early this year!" "No, it isn't," the rabbi hastened to assure her. "Hanukkah is precisely on time. It begins this year, as it always does, on the 25th day of the Hebrew month Kislev."

Whenever Hanukkah comes it brings a soft glow and warmth which help take the edge off December's frosty bite. And the flickering candles have a special bit of wisdom they would share with us.

After we recite the blessings which accompany the lighting of the candles, we add a prayer in which there is this striking sentence: "These candles are sacred and we are not permitted to put them to any use; we may only look upon them."

Let's understand what the prayer declares. We may not use the Hanukkah candles for any practical purpose. We may not read by their light. We may not use them to light the Shabbat candles. In fact we may not use one Hanukkah candle to light another one. That is why we use the *Shamash* candle.

How terribly impractical all this sounds especially to us who live in a utilitarian society, who measure the value of all things by one pragmatic question: "What is it good for?" The light of the Hanukkah candles, tradition tells us, is not to be used for anything; it is just for looking.

It figures. After all, how practical were the people to whom we owe the festival of Hanukkah? They were the most impractical people. There were others, much more practical, who said: "Why resist the Syrians, the bearers of the proud Greek culture? They are the wave of the future. Why should we be different? Why can't we be just like everybody else?"

These practical people were called Hellenists. They spoke the Greek language, dressed like Greeks, participated in Greek sports, adopted Greek names, neglected Hebrew, Shabbat, *Yom Tov,* and gradually replaced them by pagan observances. Had these practical people prevailed they would have sounded the death-knell of Judaism.

Happily there were some very impractical Jews in the year 168 B.C.E. Mattathias spoke for them when he declared: "Though all the heathen within the bounds of the royal domain obey him [Antiochus] and each one forsakes the worship of his fathers . . . yet will I, my sons and my brothers walk in the covenant of our fathers."

This may be the real miracle of Hanukkah – that there were enough impractical people who believed that security purchased at the cost of conscience is too dearly purchased; impractical people, ill-trained and ill-equipped who dared to take on a foe far more mighty and more numerous; impractical people who followed the line of most resistance and, like the saying goes, "would rather fight than switch."

And if we are here more than 2,100 years later still celebrating Hanukkah it is because in all the intervening years there were enough impractical Jewish mothers and fathers, humble, nameless heroes and heroines, who often at great peril and in the most forbidding circumstances, kindled the Hanukkah lights, looked at them and knew who they were and what was expected of them.

A streak of impracticality runs through Jewish thought as well as Jewish history. Thus one of the truly unique Jewish contributions is the concept of *"Torah lishmah"* – study of Torah for its own sake. We are urged to engage in a discipline of study which leads to no trade or profession, which has no utilitarian purpose, which we may not use "as a spade with which to dig" – to use the rabbinic phrase. Torah study directed to no practical end is one of our tradition's most hallowed *Mitzvot*.

We are also urged to serve God without any practical purpose in mind. Our performance of His will should be motivated solely by our love of Him and not by any hope that we will be repaid by material blessings. Thus we are admonished in *Pirkei Avot* (Ethics of Our Fathers): "Be not like servants who serve their Master for the sake of receiving a reward. Be rather like those servants who serve their Master without expecting a reward." A *Mitzvah* is not an investment on which dividends are expected. "The reward of the *Mitzvah* is the *Mitzvah* itself." Beyond that, it has no practical value.

When we stop to think about the matter we realize how deeply indebted we are to impractical people. Giving charity is impractical. After all, why should anyone voluntarily part with possessions acquired at the cost of time and toil? Giving time to one's synagogue or community is impractical. The time could be used for one's own entertainment, recreation or relaxation. Visiting the sick, comforting the bereaved, performing acts of kindness and thoughtfulness are all impractical – the time and energy could be better invested in furthering our own pursuits. Yet who will deny that it is precisely these impractical acts which humanize our lives and add a dimension of holiness to our existence?

So as we kindle the Hanukkah lights, let's just look at them. Remember, they have no practical value. Or do they?

Purim's Sobering Lessons

"Purim iz nit kein yom tov und kadoches iz nit kein krenk." "Purim is not a festival and fever is no disease." This Yiddish folk adage contains a mighty dose of disrespect, or at least irreverence, for the festival of Purim.

The Book of Esther, which contains the story of Purim, is a

Biblical book that does not contain as much as a single mention of God's name. And the book had to go through quite a struggle before it became part of the Bible.

The hero and heroine in the story, Mordecai and Esther, have names that sound suspiciously like Marduk and Istar, Babylonian deities.

And most damaging to Purim's claim to honor is the disconcerting fact that few modern scholars are prepared to accept the Purim story as authentic history. The narrative appears too contrived to be accorded credibility. It is more likely the product of a creative imagination than the chronicle of an historian.

Despite the aspersions that were cast on Purim, this spiritual vagabond of questionable legitimacy, the Jews welcomed Purim with a warmth and gaiety they did not lavish upon the more austere holidays with untainted pedigrees.

Perhaps the Jew could more readily identify with Purim because he too was considered a vagabond among the nations, he too was vilified, he too had his legitimacy challenged. Whatever the reason, the Jew welcomed Purim into his home and heart, and made its arrival the occasion for a degree of merrymaking he never permitted himself in the presence of the more respectable visitors.

Moreover, the tradition which is so heavily committed to sobriety made it almost obligatory to consume so much alcohol on Purim that one could no longer distinguish "blessed be Mordecai" from "cursed be Haman."

(Characteristically, before the Jew was allowed to overindulge, he was obliged to remember the poor with gifts. Somewhat reminiscent is the sign at a mid-city bar: "If you are drinking to forget, please pay in advance.")

Even the synagogue whose sanctity was so inviolate all year round, became on Purim the scene of noisy celebrations that were decidedly off limits on other festivals.

Thus Purim, in spite of its humble rank among the festivals, this buck-private among the brass, received a thunderous reception from a people who were usually harried and harassed, and welcomed an opportunity to make merry.

And perhaps Purim was welcomed because it served other purposes as well. Amidst the mandated inebriety, the Jew absorbed from Purim some very sobering lessons.

He stood taller when he read of the courage of Mordecai who would not bow down or kneel before Haman. Here was this prime minister, next to the king the most powerful representative of a most powerful empire, before whom all bowed in submissive obeisance. One person alone, Mordecai, denies him adoration. The Sages embellished the narrative by explaining the reason for Mordecai's refusal to bow before Haman. Haman, they say, wore an idol on his chest, thus Mordecai's very faith in God was at stake. He risked the wrath of a vengeful prime minister rather than appear to compromise his most cherished belief.

Has this not been the role of the Jew through the centuries? Has he not been the perpetual dissenter against every political and religious totalitarianism that secular and religious rules have sought to impose? When Hellenism or Rome or the church or the mosque demanded complete conformity and tried to impose a coercive uniformity, was it not the Jew who alone resisted these imperialisms, the Jew who served as the lone heckler in a mass chorus, the Jew who was repeatedly the Mordecai who would not bow down?

There was another lesson the Jew absorbed from Purim. The Purim story taught him how inextricably the destiny of the individual Jew is intertwined with the fate of all Jews. Here, Haman was offended by a single person, Mordecai. But when he learns that Mordecai is a Jew "it seemed contemptible in his eyes to lay hands on Mordecai alone. . . . Wherefore Haman sought to destroy all the Jews that were throughout the whole kingdom of Ahasuerus." A single Jews pricks his pride and Haman is ready to destroy them all.

Mordecai himself stresses the same theme of Jewish interdependence a little later in the story. When he urges Esther to intercede with the king on behalf of her people she hesitates because she says that she risks losing her life by coming to the king uninvited. Whereupon Mordecai warns her: "Do not think that you will escape in the king's house more than all the Jews." Esther's special status will not exempt her from the fate of her people. Tyranny draws no distinctions between Jews. Even when we do not share a common faith we share a common fate. Elementary wisdom, therefore, dictates that our single destiny should strengthen the bonds of concern, compassion and caring for each other.

The last thing that Purim taught the Jew was an unwavering faith in Jewish survival. It was this faith that Mordecai expressed when he told Esther that if she does not act to save her people "help and rescue will come to the Jews from somewhere else." Mordecai did not say, nor perhaps did he know, where that "somewhere else" was. One thing he knew for sure. His people would live on. They are an eternal people whom no tyrant can defeat and no empire can vanquish. "I shall not die but live and declare the works of the Lord," says the Psalmist.

And so it has been. Many a tyrant who attempted to destroy the Jewish people is remembered only because he linked his name malevolently with the story of an undying people.

Purim's message, unfortunately, was always timely. Always there lurked some threat to Jewish survival, and the Jew was reassured and strengthened by the bright hope and sparkling faith of Purim.

So treasured are the lessons of Purim that the great Maimonides taught that when the Messiah comes all the festivals will be abolished—except Purim.

Historians might question whether the events of the Purim story are authentic. For us, Jews, Purim's lessons remain abidingly true.

Remembrance Rock

Among Carl Sandburg's literary works there is a sprawling novel called, *Remembrance Rock,* which breathes the clean fresh air of healthy patriotism. Its central character is Judge Orville Brand Windom, a thoughtful and sensitive man. The title of the book, *Remembrance Rock,* refers to a tall rugged boulder which stands in the center of the Judge's cedar-shaded garden. He likes to go there to meditate from time to time because he has placed some precious dust under the rock.

First he put there a handful of dust from Plymouth, Massachusetts in honor of the pilgrim fathers. Alongside it he placed a Colonial silver snuffbox filled with earth from Valley Forge. Then came a little box of soil from Cemetery Ridge at Gettysburg where his father fought, and side by side with that, a handful of earth which he brought back from the Argonne in France where his son fell in the first World War. This precious dust he has reverently gathered around his Remembrance Rock because he does not want to forget the hard road over which this great nation has come.

The Yizkor hour is for us a huge Remembrance Rock in time. It stands at the center of our most tender sentiments. To it, we have each brought in the clenched fist of memory some dust which is personally sacred–the dust beneath which a loved one sleeps, the dust we have moistened with our tears, hallowed by our love. In this sense the Yizkor hour is a most intimate and private moment. A daughter remembers her mother, a wife her husband, a father his son. Remembering, like sorrowing, is a profoundly solitary experience. We recall, as we weep, alone.

And yet there are strong bonds that draw us to each other even in our aloneness. For one thing, we are part of one congregation, listening to one voice, and we will soon join in one prayer. We are sitting together, we will rise together, and together we will each try, with varying degrees of success, to stifle our sobs.

Much stronger than these physical bonds, however, are the firmer though invisible bonds of memories which link us to each other as Jews. In addition to our individual memories as members of a family, we have collective memories as members of our people. The same prayerbook which contains the prayers into which we will soon insert the names of our own beloved dead also contains the prayers which evoke the names of our common ancestors: Abraham, Isaac and Jacob, Moses and Aaron, Rebecca and Hannah, Isaiah and Jeremiah, and the ten martyrs who died *al kiddush haShem*. Under our Remembrance Rock there is, as under Judge Windom's rock, soil which is sacred to us as individuals and soil which our people's past has sanctified. And today, on this Day of Atonement, when we feel most intensely a sense of "at-one-ment" with each other and with fellow Jews throughout the world. I should like to gather together some precious Jewish bags of soil and consider briefly the lessons that each has to offer.

The first bag of soil that we Jews keep under our Remembrance Rock comes from the slave pits of Egypt. "And you shall remember that you were a slave in the land of Egypt." In no less than fifty passages in the five books of Moses alone, Egypt is the geographical point of reference. In the Ten Commandments, in the grace after meals, in the Kiddush of the Sabbath and festivals, we remember Egypt. On Passover we take our entire families with us on an annual eight-day excursion back to Egypt. We re-enact the drama and try to recapture even the bitter taste of bondage and the salty flavor of the slave's tears. Why this excessive fixation upon the painful chapter in our earliest history?

The answer I feel gives us a clue to the genius of our people. We are a people who learned very early how to utilize every experience creatively, to distill from every event, no matter how barren and forbidding it appeared, some vital lesson. Indeed, we learned that there are certain lessons which are taught only in the school of suffering, and that if we mastered these lessons well, even our suffering need not have been in vain.

And so in Egypt we digested with our bread of poverty, the understanding of what it means to be denied and downtrodden. Slavery taught us sympathy for those who are stripped of their manhood, compassion for those who toil without hope. The taskmaster's lash which scarred our bent backs burned into our souls the fearful awareness that cruelty not only degrades the slave, it also dehumanizes the master.

These are lessons we are often tempted to forget during these fateful days when the American Black is struggling to harmonize America's deed with the American dream, its great promise to him with its inadequate performance. Too often we consider ourselves uninvolved in this struggle, or what is worse, we sometimes carelessly throw another log of prejudice on the fire of intolerance. Is it for this that we suffered in Egypt?

I had a deeply moving experience as I read the report of a colleague who was one of the Freedom Riders who rode into the South in a mixed group of Blacks and Whites using together the eating facilities, the bathrooms, the water-fountains, the buses which were segregated. "I would drink from the Negro water and the Negroes would drink from the white water. I would drink the colored Coca-Colas and they would drink the white Coca-Colas." This was their first task, to disobey the segregation signs.

Their second task was to address groups of Blacks in different Southern communities, to give them hope and courage. "Don't let anyone step on you" he urged them. "Don't let anyone push you down. Stand up like a man. It's better to stand up for one minute – erect – than to crawl on your hands and knees for your whole life."

"I would tell them," he goes on, " 'I am a Jew' and I would stress this. I wanted them to know Jews are fighting for them. 'I am a Jew and

I have come to tell you that we understand how you feel. We too have suffered, but by acting to gain our rights as equal citizens, we have gained those rights. You must do the same. We know what hatred and persecution can do, and you are persecuted.' "

As I read these words, I felt that this was the authentic voice of our people talking out of the profound depths of the Jewish soul. These were the sentiments nurtured on the words of the Haggadah which admonish us at every Seder that every Jew must look upon himself as though he personally experienced the anguish of bondage and the joy of liberation. A Jew can never be neutral when human dignity is under attack. To keep the faith with our ancestors, to be true to ourselves, we must lend our voices and contribute our efforts to the ongoing struggle for the extension of human equality and freedom. Our whole history has uniquely sensitized us to make a distinctive contribution to the vitalization of American democracy. Under our Remembrance Rock, a bag of Egyptian soil is indispensable.

A second bag of soil I would bring from Mount Sinai. It was at Sinai that we were given a code by which to live and a purpose for which to live. It was at Sinai that we became a unique and holy people. It was at Sinai that we first heard the immortal words we were destined to speak to all men. It was at Sinai that great heavenly sparks kindled in the Jewish soul an eternal flame by which all humanity has been warmed. "As long as the world lasts," wrote Matthew Arnold, "all who want to make progress in righteousness will come to Israel for inspiration, as the people who have the sense for righteousness most glowing and strongest."

We listen to these extravagant words of praise from a non-Jewish scholar and we are understandably uplifted. It is astonishing that so small a people should have made so enormous a contribution. It is immensely gratifying to be able to say with Chaim Weizmann: "We may be sons of peddlers but we are the grandsons of prophets." But what are we ourselves doing with the legacy of Sinai? To what extent are we trying to familiarize ourselves with it, to learn what guidance it has for our anxious times, what direction it can offer to a generation which seems to have lost its capacity for telling right from wrong, what is its message to a world hovering on the brink of thermonuclear self-annihilation? To what extent do we permit that legacy to shape our lives? How much evidence of it do we find in our homes, in our places of business, in our lying down and our rising up? Do we teach it diligently to our children? Do we speak of it when we sit at home or walk by the way? How many distinctively Jewish acts do we perform in a day, a week, a year? "How strange," Dr. Heschel has exclaimed, "to be a Jew and to go astray on God's perilous errands." Unless we keep alive the legacy of Sinai, what meaning is there to the Jewish past, what likelihood is there for a Jewish future? And if our past is without meaning and our future without hope, what sense does it make to be a Jew at all?

But we do want to be Jews. That is why we build and support synagogues. That is why we send our children to religious schools. That is why we look for colleges for our children with a large Jewish population. That is why we are so relieved when our son informs us that he has found a "nice Jewish girl." That is why we search out Jewish neighborhoods, Jewish swim clubs, Jewish country clubs, Jewish organizations and Jewish causes. All this is evidence of our genuine yearning to perpetuate our Jewishness. This yearning must be translated daily into positive acts of loyalty. To live on with dignity, with direction, with distinction, we must draw regularly upon those unique moral and ethical values which are embodied in our legacy, values which teach us what to cherish in the world, how to look upon the world, how to live in the world. Every noble instinct within us cries out that we place under our Remembrance Rock a bag of soil from Mount Sinai.

Another bag I would place under our Remembrance Rock but this one would be filled not with soil but with ashes–ashes from the crematoria of Auschwitz and Bergen-Belsen and Dachau.

I know that no one wants to remember the six million. Germany wants to forget, the world would much prefer not being reminded and we ourselves find the whole subject as painful as it is incomprehensible. To invoke the memories of those who perished in the gas chambers, the ovens and in the heaving graves is to reopen unhealed wounds, to raise questions which cannot be answered without a two-fold assault both upon our sanity and our humanity.

But remember the six million we must. That is the very least we owe them–the immortality which remembrance confers. If we do not remember them, they die a second time. Would we not then be accomplices in the program of obliteration the enemy launched? If we say no Yizkor who will be their refuge against oblivion?

Nor is it for their sake alone that we must remember them. The world needs to be reminded. After the close of the Eichmann trial, the *New York Times* asked editorially: "What was the object and justification of the trial?" The answer it gave to this question is worth pondering. "It was and it is to do all that can be done to eradicate an evil thing out of our civilization . . .a thing so incredibly wicked that it would not have been believable of modern man if it had not actually occurred. This evil, this wickedness began with intolerance and hate in a few men's hearts. It spread until it almost wrecked the world. Now the obligation is to remember, not in hate, not in the spirit of revenge, but so that this spirit cannot ever flourish again so long as man remains on earth. And to this end, let us begin, each of us, by looking into our own hearts."

These are words that could bear reprinting periodically in newspapers throughout the world which has recently witnessed in many places the reappearance of this malignancy. In South America, in South Africa, in Algeria, in Britain, even here at home, the bigots have begun to emerge from the sewers apparently believing that men have forgotten that the last time intolerance "almost wrecked the world." We must never weary of reminding the world of the six million so that there be no repetition of the catastrophic madness.

In some quarters the lesson seems to have been well learned. A highly provocative editorial appeared in the weekly, *America,* which is published by Jesuit priests. The burden of the message was a "warning" to American Jews that their support of the Supreme Court decision outlawing the New York Regents prayer in public schools might lead to an outbreak of anti-Semitism in this country. The statement precipitated a Niagara of protest not only from accredited spokesmen of the Jewish community but, what is most heartening, from respected voices in the Protestant and Catholic communities as well. Particularly noteworthy was the stinging rebuke administered to *America,* by *Commonweal,* which is published by Catholic laymen. "If there is any real danger of anti-Semitism among Catholics," *Commonweal* wrote, "then it is *Catholics* who ought to be warned. . . . Indeed, 'warned' is too mild a word. They ought to be told as sharply as possible of the sin of any form of anti-Semitism." *Commonweal* apparently has not forgotten the Six Million.

We must remember them for their sake, for the sake of the world and not least, for our own sake. Yes, for our own sake. If it is true as I said earlier that we learned how to use our Egypt, so that the agony of slavery was redeemed by the deepened moral sensitivity we derived from it, then we can use even our Dachau if, from it, we the living derive a deeper loyalty to our people and to our faith.

There are two things, it seems to me, that we can do. In the first place we need more Jews. We need larger Jewish families. To all young people still planning their families I say: Every Jewish child that is born constitutes our most dramatic frustration of the enemies of our people. Our answer to death is life. *Lo amut kee echeyeh,* "I shall not die but live." This is a great country with plenty of room for healthy children to grow in, and no group has given America more intelligent children, more sober and more law-abiding children than we have. As we raise larger families, America will be the richer, our lives will be the fuller, and our people's future more secure.

In addition to needing more Jews, we need better Jews – that means us, you and I. With more than one-third of our people destroyed, we must each take upon ourselves an added measure of responsibility. The prayers they might have offered, we must offer. The books they might have created and read, we must create and read. The *Shabbat* candles they would have kindled, we must kindle. The *tzedakah* they would have given, we must give. Every day, in every way, we must be more devout, more devoted, more dedicated. Our honored dead could not save their own lives but if we and all men remember them, they may be able to save and to deepen ours.

Alongside the bag of ashes, we place our last little sack – this one containing soil from the Land of Israel. This little bag of soil has a long and honorable history. One of the most cherished hopes of the Jew in Eastern Europe was that he could spend his last years in the beloved holy land so that he could at the end be laid to rest in its bosom. Understandably, few were privileged to see the fulfillment of this remote hope. The next best thing was to obtain a sack of holy land soil from an occasional traveler. The Jew who was fortunate enough to obtain it considered it a veritable treasure. Now he could instruct his children to put this soil on his grave so that he could sleep the everlasting sleep under the sacred soil. If the Jew could not be buried in the land itself he could at least have some of the land placed over him at the end of the journey. Thus the bag of soil was something which one set aside for use at death.

In our day, the sack of Israel's soil is a symbol of life – life emerging out of the ashes, life for a people and its language, life for a culture and a religious civilization, pulsating vitality restored to a people upon contact with the earth which had nourished its earliest and most enduring achievements. Suddenly an old people is young again. The winter of annihilation has been followed by the spring of rebirth. The weary, heavy footsteps on the wanderer's road now give way to young, sturdy feet dancing in the valley of Jezreel. The eyes darkened with fear now are ablaze with hope. The bent backs are straight. Israel itself is the most glowing tribute to the Six Million, for it was born out of their agony, it has welcomed and comforted their surviving kin and, above all, it is the most effective defense against a repetition of the holocaust.

And who can find the words to capture what Israel has meant to us? Many of us have already been privileged to behold the miracle of Israel reborn with our own eyes. Thousands of our American young people have walked its dusty roads with a renewed sense of pride. All of us have found new hope, new streams of strength flowing to us in refreshing abundance out of Zion. The bag of its earth becomes for us a witness of the bonds of enduring love which bind us to the Yishuv, to its destiny, to its tomorrow.

This, then, dear friends, is what I would place under our Remembrance Rock. Some soil from Egypt to teach us compassion, some soil from Sinai to reaffirm our convictions, some ashes from the crematoria to strengthen our commitments and some soil from the Land of Israel to proclaim our comradeship with our Israeli brethren. If it is at such a rock that we gather regularly to meditate quietly, then I believe that when the time comes for our loved ones to add the remembrance of us to the memories they cherish, we may be for them a source of tender benediction.

Jewish Income and Taxes

This is being written in the middle of March when Americans are performing the painful civic duty of sharing a substantial portion of their earnings with Uncle Sam. By the time this will be read, I trust we shall all have recovered sufficiently to view the subject of taxes with calm objectivity.

With this hope in mind, I'd like to raise a hypothetical question: "If the Jewish community had the power to impose an income tax upon its members, what Jewish income would we have to declare? What satisfaction, inspiration, meaning or enrichment have we derived from Judaism during the past year?"

Note that I am not asking how much we have paid in taxes to the Synagogue, to Allied, to B'nai B'rith, to Israel, to an institution of higher Jewish learning. At the moment I am not appealing for Jewish *giving*. Right now I am deeply concerned with Jewish *receiving*. The sad fact is that for many of our people their Jewish income tax is disproportionately high. While they give generously, they receive meagerly. Where Jewish life is concerned, too many of us are in the low income brackets.

Here are some of the leading items every Jew ought to be able to declare as his spiritual income from Judaism:

1. A sense of life's worthwhileness and high potential worth.
2. A feeling of personal dignity as a creature of the Divine.
3. An awareness of belonging to a proud people and participating in a significant adventure.
4. A high ethical sensitivity which restrains and directs.
5. A round of holidays and a system of ritual which raise existence into living and redeem life from monotony and drabness.

Let us concentrate on raising our spiritual income.

We Can't Live on Miracles

A popular folk saying in Israel is that if you don't believe in miracles you're not a realist. Believing in miracles comes naturally to the descendants of a people whose entire existence has been one continuous miracle, whose rebirth out of the ashes of the Holocaust was one of history's most spectacular miracles.

But there is another piece of folk wisdom which comes in the form of a question and answer. Why do we eat latkes on Hanukkah?

Because on miracles alone you can't live. Israel's first president, Chaim Weizmann, was one of the most prominent contributors to its rebirth, and he spoke out of the depths of personal experience when he said: "Miracles sometimes occur but one has to work terribly hard for them."

He was cautioning us against believing in miracles too much, against depending upon them so heavily that we forget that so many of God's miracles are man made, that there is an enormous human component that goes into the making of a miracle.

Hanukkah itself provides a dramatic illustration of this truth. The word itself means "dedication," and at the heart of the festival is the joy of the rededication of the Temple in Jerusalem after the incredible victory of the vastly outnumbered Maccabees over the Syrians who had defiled it. But the rededication of the Temple would have been impossible if there had not been a powerful dedication on the part of the Jewish people to their heritage and their faith.

If the truth be told, not all Jews at that time had this sense of dedication. There were in fact the Hellenists who were quite content to throw in the *Tallit*. They adopted the Greek gods, the Greek language, Greek sports, Greek modes of dress, Greek names. Hebrew was neglected. The Sabbath and Jewish festivals were gradually replaced by pagan observances. Some of the Hellenists even underwent a painful surgical procedure to undo the circumcision so that they might appear in the public arena in the nude!

Had these Hellenists prevailed there would have been no resistance, no war, no Temple, no Jewish religion, no miracle. But because there were enough Jews who cared enough about preserving Judaism, their distinctive way of life, and their own spiritual identity, they decided that "they would rather fight than switch." Without their own fierce dedication there would have been no Temple dedication. Yes, miracles sometimes happen but we have to work hard to make them happen.

This is a truth worth pondering. People often say they don't believe in miracles, and yet their behavior, or lack of it, indicates that they believe in miracles too much. They expect good things to happen without any effort on their part. No toil, no travail, no sacrifice, no surrender of comfort or leisure or pleasure; just relying on miracles to happen.

Some time ago, there was a popular song which assured us that "wishing will make it so." Our own experience raises serious doubt about that glib optimism. A wish-bone rarely accomplishes a thing until it is joined to the back-bone and the finger-bone.

Long ago our Sages, who surely could not be accused of lacking faith in God, warned us: "We may not rely on miracles." They knew that wishing will not make it so unless we are prepared to work with God to translate those wishes into reality, those desires into deeds.

A pupil once asked his rabbi why the Almighty endowed man with skepticism. "After all," he asked, "we have been taught that everything He created has some beneficial purpose, but what possible purpose could skepticism serve? It only leads to doubt and denial of faith."

The rabbi was ready with his answer. "There are times," he answered, "when it is better not to have too much faith in the Almighty. When a poor man comes to you for help because he and his children are hungry, do not send him away with the assurance that the *Ribbono Shel Olam* (Master of the Universe) will perform some miracle for him. That is when you use your skepticism. Act independently. You help the poor man yourself."

Let's not depend on miracles.

If we want Israel to be strong, secure and safe, what are we doing to make that wish come true?

If we want our children to be comfortable in their Jewishness, proud of their past and committed to its future, what are we doing to make that wish come true?

If we want the Jewish home to fulfill its historic role of shaping Jewish values and transmitting Jewish teachings, what are we doing to make that wish come true?

If we want the name Jew to stand for honesty, integrity and generosity, what are we doing to make that wish come true?

If we want creative Jewish survival to continue into the un-charted future, what are we doing to make that wish come true?

The court philosopher, we are told, had just completed his lecture on miracles, and after the applause ended the king turned to him with the challenge: "Show me a miracle." The philosopher reflected briefly and answered: "Sire, the Jews."

Jewish survival in the face of the most monstrous odds and towering threats has indeed been a massive miracle. The real miracle that we celebrate on Hanukkah is not the tiny cruse of oil that lasted so much longer than expected. The fact that we are still celebrating Hanukkah twenty-one and a half centuries later – that is the miracle. But that miracle was not made possible by casual Jews. Casual Jews too easily become Jewish casualties. In every age the miracle was renewed by the dedication, devotion and sacrificial love of men and women who cared enough to give their very best.

So at Hanukkah time, it's quite all right to believe in miracles, but let the latke remind us, that on miracles alone you can't live.

Nothing There

On Columbus Day we honor Columbus for his intrepid role in discovering America. Even before Columbus there was a theory that if you traveled westward on the Atlantic far enough you would reach land. Well, a group of Portuguese sailors sailed out on the Atlantic about 50 or 100 miles and then returned and pronounced their considered judgment: "There's nothing there."

Mind you, a whole new world was out there for those who had the courage and the perseverance to sail on, and here they were after an abortive effort rendering the verdict: Nothing there!

The mistake of the Portuguese sailors did not die with them. In so many vital areas of life we too make abbreviated voyages of discovery, turn back and pronounce: Nothing is there!

Consider, for example, how many Americans resemble the Portuguese sailors where marriage is concerned. We've heard a theory that if we sail on the sea of matrimony we will discover the continent of fulfillment and happiness. And so we launch our boats, venture forth briefly, run into a few squalls or choppy seas and head for shore muttering dejectedly: Nothing there!

Living in an age that has taught us to expect to get what we want when we want it, we are altogether unprepared for the patience, the adjustment, the experimentation, the faith, that marriage requires. When the seas are choppy and the winds grow turbulent that's when the mastery of the helmsman is tested. It is easy and tempting to head for the shore and cry: Nothing there! But the prize is in the other direction.

There is another important area where we resemble the Portuguese sailors. More of us than are aware of it are guilty of underestimating ourselves. We may never put it into words but we often pass that kind of damning judgment on ourselves. Nothing there!

We avoid taking on new duties for fear that we will be unable to discharge them adequately. We run away from challenges because we have little confidence in our ability to meet them squarely. So often after a great emergency has come and found us equal to the heavy demands laid upon us, we explain: "I didn't know I had that in me."

Let us persevere in our voyage of self-discovery, and we will be delighted to discover more courage, more strength, more resilience of spirit than we ever suspected we possessed. There is indeed something there.

Where our religion is concerned, too many of us have passed the hasty verdict: Nothing there! I have heard otherwise intelligent and judicious people deliver themselves of conclusions that have no visible means of support. Thus a man turns his back on his ancestral faith because: "I went to a service once and it left me cold." Another abandons the precious legacy of centuries because "religion is superstition." Shades of the Portuguese sailors.

Sail on, dear friends, on the sea of knowledge. Probe, study and find out why our people has ever found our faith "a tree of life to those who grasp hold of it." There is indeed something great and powerful there!

How Much Is the Bible Worth?

The Bible was in the news some time ago. A copy of the Gutenberg Bible was sold for $2.4 million. Even in a time of inflation, $2.4 million is still a lot of shekels. In fact, it was a record price for a single book or manuscript.

As I read of all that money changing hands for a copy of the Bible, I dreamed of how perfectly lovely life could be if the Jewish people were paid royalties on the tens of millions of copies of our Bible that are sold every year. If the royalties were paid retroactively, tiny Israel could even help its good friend America balance its budget.

A more sober reaction to the item about the sale of the Gutenberg Bible took the form of a question. How much is a copy of the Bible really worth?

There is no shortage of testimonials to the Bible. It has been called "the great book of consolation for humanity," "the Magna Charta of the poor and the oppressed," "the great medicine chest of humanity."

The Hebrew Bible played a unique role in the destiny of the Jewish people. It earned them the proud title "The People of the Book." They had a double claim to that designation, for they not only created the Bible, the Bible in turn helped to create and shape them.

Heinrich Heine grasped a subtle truth when he said that for the Jews their Bible was their "portable homeland." What soil, flag, sovereignty, and country are to other peoples, the Bible was to the Jews. It gave them the power *with* which to live, the pattern *by* which to live, and the purpose *for* which to live.

Well, then, how much is a copy of the Bible really worth?

As a rare and precious volume, it may be worth $2.4 million. But that copy of the Bible will never be used. It will probably be displayed in a heavily secured showcase that will keep it beyond the touch of human hands.

Nor is a Bible worth much if it is gathering dust on the home shelf. It has been estimated that if all the neglected Bibles were dusted simultaneously, we would have a record dust storm.

The clue to the real worth of the Bible is found in the complaint of Dr. Samuel Sandmel, who wrote: "More people praise the Bible than read it, more read it than understand it, and more understand it than follow it."

If we read the Bible and understand it and follow it, then it becomes truly priceless.

What Keeps the Jew Alive?

Some time ago the syndicated columnist Sydney Harris wrote a piece on the mystery of Jewish survival. Here is how he explained it:

"What has kept the Jewish people alive throughout the centuries has been the awesome paradox of persecution. Left alone to live their lives and practice their beliefs they inevitably tend to dwindle in numbers, to disperse and dilute their ethnic identification.

"Then every so often in history there comes along a devastating persecution that has the very opposite effect of its intention. It militates and mobilizes these people, reminds them of their unique heritage that is regarded as both a blessing and a burden, and re-animates their faith and their sense of identity."

In this reading of Jewish history Sydney Harris is not alone. Many historians have attributed our perseverance to persecution. Thus Lewis Browne, writing during the Hitler era, declared: "We are not so much voluntary Jews as involuntary non-Gentiles. . . . Let us be and we will cease to be."

Even our Sages seemed to find in Jewish persecution strong impetus to more intensive Jewish living. They noted that we are told that the Israelites fleeing from Egypt are pursued by Pharaoh, who is about to overtake them. The verb form the Torah uses is *"hikriv"* which means "he *brought* near" rather than *"karav,"* "he *came* near," and they deduce from this that the Torah wants us to know that the pursuing Pharaoh *brought* the Israelites nearer to God. In their mortal dread of the avenging tyrant, "they lifted their eyes heavenward, they did penance, and they prayed." Thus Pharaoh's threat accomplished more for the Israelites "than one hundred fasts and prayers."

For all its many advocates, the theory that anti-Semitism keeps Judaism alive is at best a half-truth. The truth is that it is anti-Semitism that threatens Jewish survival. Throughout history it was persecution that decimated Jewish communities, and made escape from Jewishness an attractive alternative. It is anti-Semitism which forever makes the Jew a soliloquizing Hamlet asking: "To be or not to be?" Why remain Jewish in a world where the vicious, the sick, the misinformed repeatedly make it so dangerous to be Jewish?

Why is there no Christian problem of survival? Why is there no Moslem problem of survival? The answer is obvious. It is the persistent efforts to destroy the Jew which create the problem of Jewish survival. Even when it is not actively destroying Jewish lives, anti-Semitism still lurks as a menacing threat, eroding Jewish morale, gnawing away at Jewish security.

If Judaism has survived it is not *because* of anti-Semitism but *despite* it. Anti-Semitism did not strengthen us, it tested our strength. A person who survives a bout of double pneumonia cannot be said to have survived because of the illness. The illness tested his resistance, and his survival demonstrates his ability to triumph over the disease germs that threatened his life.

The Jew survived because he possessed an indestructible will to live. His perennial slogan was from the Psalmist: "I shall not die but live and I shall declare the works of the Lord."

A reading of Jewish history will indicate that freedom and toleration need not be inimical to healthy Jewish living. On the contrary, Judaism has enjoyed its most creative periods in periods free from persecution.

The Bible itself is the product of a free people living in its own land, determining its own destiny. That massive product of Jewish genius and intellectual ferment, the Talmud, was created at a time of substantial freedom, and it was only the fear of looming danger that prompted its codification.

Rashi's commentaries, the words of Yehudah Halevi, Ibn Gabirol and almost all the great classics of our heritage were the products of eras when Jews enjoyed freedom and security. The explosion of Jewish spiritual and literary creativity in America and in Israel today provides further overwhelming evidence of Judaism's compatibility with freedom.

To be sure, the freedom to live Judaism also implies the freedom to leave Judaism. That is the price of freedom, and we must be prepared to reckon with it. We cannot depend on, much less hope for, anti-Semitism to keep Jews in the fold. A Judaism that was kept alive by its enemies who would not let it die, would scarcely be worth preserving.

Judaism will survive as it always has, proudly and creatively, because its adherents find meaning in their Jewishness, identify with its teachings, find joy in its festivals and holy days, and understand in the depths of their own souls why generations of Jews have resisted every tyranny to remain true to themselves and to their God.

Ours is a tradition ripe with the wisdom of years, strengthened by a thousand anvils. Judaism was a venerable faith before other powerful religions were born. For it, millions were innocently martyred. By it, millions more have nobly and compassionately lived. Despite its antiquity, it evidences none of the infirmities of age. It remains throbbing and dynamic, capable of sustaining its adherents and enriching with its unique genius the larger human family. If we will strive to possess that which is rightfully ours we will enjoy an abundant inheritance past generations have stored up for us to enjoy. And then we will understand why generations of Jews have proclaimed daily in their morning prayers:

> "How fortunate are we!
> How good is our portion!
> How pleasant is our lot!
> How beautiful our heritage!"

The Gifts We Withhold

Under the influence of the TV presentation of *Roots,* one young man developed a burning desire to learn his own genealogy. However, he lacked the necessary funds to engage someone to perform this service for him. Whereupon he consulted a wise friend and asked him if he knew a way that he could have his family background traced without money. "That's easy," his friend assured him, "all you have to do is run for public office."

Those who aspire to leadership must be prepared to have their past meticulously scrutinized under a probing microscope. And that is not all. As we read in the case of Moses in the *Sidrah, Korah,* leaders must also be prepared to have their motives impugned, their integrity questioned and even their right to lead radically challenged.

Such a challenge to Moses' leadership was led by Korah. Some of the charges he leveled against Moses are cited in the Torah itself. Our Sages elaborated further on the confrontation. They pictured Korah as trying to discredit Moses by mocking his teachings.

Here is one dialogue: "You Moses have taught us 'Do not rob the poor for he is poor.' That's ridiculous! How can one possibly rob from the poor? Since he is poor there is nothing to rob from him!"

To this taunt Moses replied: "Yes, it is possible to rob the poor. The charity we are obliged to give to the poor man is rightfully his. When we fail to give it to him we are indeed robbing him."

A profoundly sensitive truth is contained in the answer of Moses. Robbing does not necessarily involve taking from another what already belongs to that person; sometimes we rob by failing to give that person what he needs. We impoverish others by the gifts we withhold from them, by the support we fail to extend. We can rob without taking. We can rob by not giving.

This kind of robbery never shows up in the crime statistics and is punishable by no court of justice. But upon reflection we realize that it is far more prevalent than we suspect. And not only where material things are concerned.

Consider, for example, how often we withhold a word of appreciation and encouragement to those who desperately need to be praised and given a lift. How quick we are to criticize, but slow to compliment. One little boy on his first day in nursery school was asked by the teacher what his name was. He replied: "Billy don't."

Thomas Carlyle's wife was a highly gifted person, one of the most clever women in England in her time. She loved her husband dearly, and to the extent that he was capable of loving any woman other than his mother, he loved her too. After her death, he read this entry in her diary: "Carlyle never praises me. If he says nothing I have to be content that things are all right."

He had been living for decades with a woman whose heart hungered and ached for a word of appreciation – a word which this prolific writer of words had never been kind enough to utter. Did he not rob her by failing to give her what she so much needed to have?

There is also a specifically Jewish dimension to this form of robbery. Consider, for example, Jewish parents who deny their children what rightfully belongs to them – their Jewish heritage.

Some time ago the late Paul Cowan, author of the book *An Orphan In History,* addressed our congregation. During the course of his remarks he spoke of the de-Judaized atmosphere in which he grew up.

His father had changed his name from Cohen to Cowan. In his parents' home they had an elaborate Christmas celebration, not a word or gesture about Hanukkah. At Easter the family gathered for a dinner of ham and sweet potatoes. Paul and his brother attended Choate, an Episcopalian prep school, where he learned stately Christian hymns and litanies by heart. Paul had no Bar Mitvah, never entered a synagogue, and while he was growing up he didn't remember knowing anyone who kept Kosher or observed Shabbat.

By a fortuitous combination of circumstances Paul found his own way to the heritage that had been kept from him. His book is subtitled: "Retrieving A Jewish Legacy." Though both his parents were killed in a tragic fire, he was an "orphan" no longer. Paul and his wife Rachel who converted to Judaism were active, practicing Jews.

Thus Paul writes: "There's no question that my deepening awareness of being Jewish has given me a more secure sense of my own identity. It has eased my loneliness in America by teaching me that I do have a home in a tradition I love."

As we read Paul's moving story we rejoice over his rewarding discovery of his Jewish identity and heritage. But how many Paul Cowans have not been so fortunate? How many did not retrieve their Jewish legacy? How many were robbed of their spiritual inheritance and remain Orphans in History?

Being a Jewish parent is an awesome responsibility, for we are each a link between the hundred Jewish generations that have preceded us and whatever Jewish generations will follow us. Those who have gone before us have accumulated a precious legacy for us to enjoy, to enlarge and to transmit. Ours is the privilege to keep faith with the past, to give meaning to our present, to insure our future.

To fulfill these tasks we must make certain that our children receive what belongs to them – a rich, vibrant and meaningful Jewish heritage. They must never feel like "orphans." They are related to some of the tallest giants of the spirit who ever walked this earth.

Promises to Keep

Kol Nidre speaks of broken promises and unfulfilled vows. Who among us can confront a God of Judgment before Whom nothing is hidden, without a stabbing sense of remorse over the promises we did not keep, the vows we did not fulfill?

Among the best known and most frequently quoted lines of Robert Frost are these: "The woods are lovely, dark and deep. But I have promises to keep . . . and miles to go before I sleep. . . ." Not long before his death, Frost was asked after a public lecture, what promises he had in mind when he wrote those lines. The poet smiled softly and replied, "Oh, promises to myself and promises to my ancestors."

We too have promises to keep – to ourselves and to our ancestors.

Let us deal first with some of the promises to ourselves that Kol Nidre calls to mind. And, of course, I am not thinking only of promises we actually put into words or write out over our signatures. George Chapman was correct when he said: "Promise is most given when least is said." Some of the most sacred promises are made without words in the silent sanctuary of the soul.

Have we kept the promises we have made to ourselves? Every one of us is endowed at birth with all sorts of magnificent possibilities and potentialities. There is a capacity for idealism, a yearning for truth and beauty and nobility, a sensitivity to the hurt of others and to the dreams and needs of our fellow man. In the hopeful dawn of youth we feel these stirrings within us and we promise to bring them to life. And yet so often as the years pass by we permit these promises to be swept under the rug of expediency. We chalk them up to immaturity and we go on to live "more realistically."

Let's face it! We have not made the most of ourselves. We have not cultivated all our latent thoughtfulness and kindness and ability. We have not been as devoted, as tolerant, as forgiving as we could have been and should have been.

How well have we kept the promise inherent in our parenthood, the unspoken promise that forms itself in the heart of the father and mother of every new-born babe, to set a noble example, to establish a pattern of life which accentuates the importance of values and principles? The very fact of being a parent implies a host of unspoken and unwritten obligations to our children. The fourth commandment urges children to honor father and mother. The unwritten commandment for father and mother is to make themselves worthy of honor and to make it easy for their children to fulfill the fourth commandment. But do we always act in such a way as to be worthy of being honored? If our children did exactly as we do – not as we say but as we do – what would happen to the most precious ideals of our faith? What would happen to charity and compassion, to study and prayer, to *yiddishkeit* and *menshlechkeit,* and to all the things we know are the enduring things and the ennobling things and the traditional hallmarks of the Jew?

The director of Jewish Communal Affairs of the American

Jewish Committee wrote an article entitled: "Jewish Family Values—Are They Breaking Down or Changing?" In the course of his paper he refers to a study made of college students who were asked: "What is the most important thing in life?" Three-fourths of the Catholic students said, "to live in accordance with my religious beliefs," and half of the Protestant students said, "to make the world a better place in which to live." Half the Jewish students answered, "my own personal happiness" or "economic independence."

When I read these lines, I could not believe my eyes. Incredulously, I reread them to make sure that I had read and understood correctly. The answers of our Christian friends seemed to have been copied off our papers. For it is we who throughout the centuries have been speaking of Torah and commandments as our very life and the length of our days, the subject of our most intensive thought by day and by night. It is we who pray thrice daily in the Alaynu "to perfect the world according to the kingdom of the Almighty." And if half of our young people consider their own personal happiness or economic independence as the most important thing in life, I'm afraid that too many of us have forgotten the promise that parenthood implies. There is a searing character to the rhetorical question the poet asks:

> "How shall we teach a child to reach beyond himself and touch the stars? We who have stooped so much."

We have promises to keep . . . and miles to go before we sleep.

Like Robert Frost, we have promises not only to ourselves but also promises to our ancestors. Judaism has been enormously preoccupied with promises.

To us Jews promises are a crucial dimension of our collective existence. When a male child is eight days old, there is engraved upon his flesh the mark of the promise. *Brit* means covenant; covenant means an agreement, a binding promise. Jewish history begins with a promise. The first words spoken by God to the first Jew are words of promise. "I will make thee a great nation and I will bless thee. And I will make thy name great and be thou a blessing."

This was God's promise to Abraham, and Abraham in turn promised to worship God and to serve Him. The circumcision became the mark of that mutual promise. At Sinai the covenant was renewed. Before Moses died he reaffirmed the mutual promise, and he added these fateful words: "Not with you only do I make this covenant and this vow, but with him who stands here today with us before the Lord our God and also with him that is not here with us this day." Our Sages understood these words to constitute a binding commitment for the generations yet unborn, so that every child who is born is ipso facto committed to a promise. Never mind that you were not there yourself; never mind that you did not give your own word in person. To be a Jew is to be born under the weight and the glory of a sacred promise, the promise of God to the Jew, the promise of the Jew to his God.

Unless we understand the crucial role which promises have played in Jewish thought we cannot begin to understand Jewish history at all. If the Jew refused to be lured away from his ancestral faith either by the threat of force or the promise of reward, if he remained constant in the face of unspeakable cruelty and indescribable brutality, if he would not bend the knee before any earthly despots who were armed with crushing might, it is because he believed in a God who was a "Zocher Ha-brit," One who would remember the promise. And he, the Jew, had a promise to remember too. He had a task to perform, and he would not quit before he had seen it through.

We cannot begin to understand the whole incredible story of the rebirth of Israel unless we understand the role of the promise—"To your seed shall I give this land." What mattered it that the Jew was scattered to the winds, to the far-flung corners of the globe? What mattered it that strangers ruled over the land with an iron grip? What mattered it that he had never seen the land with his own eyes? He was convinced, despite the most imposing evidence to the contrary, that one day the promise would be kept. "To your seed shall I give this land."

At the heart of Jewish history is a promise, a promise renewed with every child that is born, a promise renewed with every Sabbath that is kept. "And the children of Israel shall keep the Sabbath, to observe the Sabbath throughout the generations, 'Brit Olam,' an everlasting promise." The Jew did not accept the cynical observation of Jonathan Swift that "promises and pie crusts are made to be broken." The promise was made to be kept. God would keep His promise to the Jew, and the Jew would keep his promise to God. And what is more, we have demonstrated most convincingly that you can live on promises. We have done it!

But it would be dangerous if this conviction of the eternity of the

Jewish people were to lull us into a false sense of security. I do believe with all my heart that we are an "Am Olam," a people with eternity stamped on our souls. But while the Jewish people as a whole will survive, individual segments of that people can disappear. We know that important Jewish communities have disappeared in the past. We ought to be sensitive to those problems which threaten our very existence.

Our most crucial problems each begin with the letter "I". We suffer from ignorance, from indifference and from intermarriage. The three are related one to the other. Where there is ignorance of Jewish texts and tradition, there is likely to be indifference to Jewish sanctities and symbols and Jewish survival. Both together make a fertile soil for intermarriage.

We need to declare war on Jewish poverty. We, who comprise the most affluent Jewish community anywhere in the world, are stricken by spiritual and intellectual poverty. Judaism is rich and we are paupers.

What a pity it would be if after the long and grueling relay over history's most brutal obstacle course, we who now carry the baton of Jewish life, should forget the message and the promise. What was it that gave significance to the struggle, inspired courage in long, dark nights, evoked heroism from ordinary people and conferred a touch of glory upon a story without its equal in the annals of any other people? To be a Jew means to be the possessor of a very special message, the bearer of a very sacred promise, the embodiment of a unique way of life. It is a way of life which encompasses Shabbat and Kashrut, work and worship, charity and compassion, honesty and holiness, a love of man and a love of God.

We have promises to keep and miles to go before we sleep . . .

If we are to keep faith with the promises to ourselves and to our ancestors we have to keep faith with the Synagogue.

The Synagogue is the keeper of that light and you and I have promised to mind that light.

As we keep faith with those who have gone before us, we preserve the faith for those who come after us.

As we keep the promise to our ancestors, we transmit a future of promise to our descendants.

As we keep our promise to God we merit His faithfulness to the promise we read every day of the year at morning services.

"And as for Me, this is My covenant with them, saith the Lord. My spirit which is upon you and My words which I have put into your mouth shall not depart from your mouth, nor from the mouth of your children, nor from the mouth of your children's children, from this time and forever."

Amen

What Israel Means to Us

As Jews who are profoundly involved in Israel's destiny, we tend to look at the State from the perspective of daily crises. We live by the headlines. And because good news is no news and usually goes unreported, Israel provides every loyal Jew with more than a fair share of heartaches. A characteristic Jewish telegram, one wit tells us, reads as follows: "Start worrying. Letter follows."

But when we mark once again an anniversary of Israel's rebirth, we are not only entitled to the joy that all celebrations bring, but we also owe it to ourselves to look at Israel in its larger perspective. What is the real meaning of Israel to world Jewry?

Coming so soon after the Holocaust, the first thing that Israel did was to take the "krechtz" out of Jewish living. The State has given Jews everywhere a mighty banner around which to rally–a banner, not a tombstone. It has made Jews everywhere feel, as did our ancestors for other reasons, that being a Jew is a proud privilege.

A specific example is Karl Shapiro, a most gifted American poet. Until the rebirth of Israel, he was cited as an illustration of a tendency to total assimilation in American Jewry. In fact, his poetry echoed Christian motifs and reflected Jewish self-hatred. Again and again he struck out against his people. But came the birth of Israel and within a month Karl Shapiro wrote in *The New Yorker*: "When I think of the liberation of Zion, I hear the drop of chains . . . I feel the weight of prisons in my skull falling away. . . . When I see the name of Israel high in print the fences crumble in my flesh. . . . I say my name aloud for the first time unconsciously. . . . Speak the name of the land, speak the name only of the living land."

Yes, "the name of the living land," and this alone, could awaken the dormant yearning in estranged Jewish hearts. Jews everywhere have heard the drop of chains and have felt the weight of prisons fall away. They walk the earth with a newly discovered sense of pride and self-respect. In brief, Israel has not only taken many Jews out of exile; it has already taken the exile out of the Jew. That is the first meaning of Israel.

Israel has done something more for us – something so subtle that it could easily be overlooked. It has reversed the 2000-year-old role of the Jew on the stage of history. For the past two millennia the Jew's external history has been shaped for him by other nations. Coercion, subjugation, oppression, persecution, exile, martydom – these were the involuntary roles assigned to him. For 2,000 years, Jewish history has been not the story of what the Jew did, as much as what was done to him. This motif of helplessness and passivity reached its frightening crescendo in the death of the Six Million.

Seen against this background, the rebirth of Israel points to a new role that the Jew has chosen for himself. He is saying to the world: "No more shall my destiny be shaped by the unkind hands of others. I have had enough – dear world, too much – of playing the anvil for your hammer blows. Once upon a time my ancestors called themselves Maccabees because 'Maccab' means a hammer. Once again I shall beat out my own destiny. I shall forge for myself the instruments of my salvation. I shall honestly, stubbornly and unflinchingly rebuild myself in body and spirit on my ancestral soil, which bloomed when my fathers tilled it, lay waste for centuries in alien hands, and awakened once more to the tender caress of loving hands."

That is the meaning of Israel. That is the central meaning. A people is on the march, not a forced march, but a self-willed march. It has gotten off its knees, straightened shoulders stooped by the burdens of the long night of exile, and stands erect. The spirit of the Maccabees has been rekindled. Israel has redeemed not only the land but also itself.

Finally, the rebirth of Israel has meant the rebirth of our faith in the power of ideals. It has reaffirmed our faith in the reality of spiritual forces in the world. It has rekindled our belief in miracles.

Who would have dared to believe possible what we have seen with our own eyes? Any "realistic" student of history could have advanced a thousand cogent reasons to deny the possibility of such a consummation. For here was a people divorced from its land for almost

2000 years and exposed to the corrosive acids of human brutality, a people whose very existence was called into question by a historian who labeled it a "fossil," a people whose dreams of restoration had been mocked by circumstances and even repudiated by many of its own members. That such a people could achieve the fulfillment of its most cherished and long-deferred hope at the precise moment when the hand of despair lay most heavily upon it – this is an achievement to convert the most skeptical and cynical into passionate believers in the invincibility of the human spirit when wedded to an imperishable ideal.

In the face of a miracle of such incredible dimensions, our will to believe receives most powerful stimulation. The rebirth of Israel has rekindled the faith of decent men and women everywhere that ultimately it is "not by might and not by power but by My spirit, says the Lord of Hosts."

Thus, on the anniversary of Israel's rebirth, we salute our brethren. We say to them: "Thank you for making us proud of you and thereby restoring to us our sense of pride. Thank you, too, for charting a new and more dignified role for our people. And, above all, thank you for reviving our faith in all that is beautiful and worthwhile in life."

The Spirit of Power vs. the Power of the Spirit

Hanukkah tells a story of military valor and epic bravery. It focuses attention upon a dramatic crisis in Jewish history when freedom cried out for dedicated men to protect it against rude hands. It celebrates valiant people who answered the cry.

While Jews alone celebrate Hanukkah, its message is charged with deep significance for freedom-loving people everywhere. It recalls the first struggle in history when people fought not for material possessions, but for ideals – especially the ideal of human liberty. It calls to mind the first instance when people spurned security purchased at the cost of conscience, when the human spirit refused to be intimidated by force.

So Hanukkah is a powerful inspiration for all people to resist tyranny.

How vastly different human history might have been if the Maccabees had lost their war and Judaism had disappeared 21 centuries ago. Could Christianity and Mohammedanism have been born centuries later? Could a faith long dead have yielded any spiritual offspring?

Thus the Church and the Mosque, no less than the Synagogue, owe their existence to the Maccabees.

Hannukkah means "dedication," and it underscores not so much the military achievement as the spiritual victory – the rededication of the Temple. The victory on the field of battle was crucial but the ultimate triumph lay in the inner temple of the spirit – in the hearts and minds of people.

To underscore this aspect of Hanukkah, tradition prescribed for the Sabbath of Hanukkah the prophetic reading which contains the words: "Not by might nor by power but by My spirit, says the Lord of Hosts" (Zachariah 4:6). Hanukkah commemorates not the spirit of power, but the power of the spirit.

In answer to the question: "Why do we celebrate Hanukkah?" our Sages told the legend of the small flask of oil which was found in the desecrated Temple in Jerusalem after the enemy had been driven out. Containing sufficient oil for only one day, it miraculously lasted for eight.

Here we can find a clue to the destiny of our people and our faith. By every known standard, we should have "burned ourselves out" long centuries ago. Time and again, we have heard our final doom pronounced. Yet time and again, through courage and loyalty, we have found the necessary fuel to keep alive the flames of faith and hope. Hanukkah summons us in our day to act as worthy heirs of a dedicated people.

VII

REACHING FOR THE HIGHEST

*Here, ultimately, may be the reason that you and I are
here on this earth. God needs us, each of us.
We are joined with Him in a great partnership.*

Is the Universe the Result of Chance?

When the first Soviet cosmonaut returned from orbiting the earth he announced rather triumphantly that he had looked all around in outer space but he saw no God. That, as far as he was concerned, settled the matter of God's existence. Since he saw no God up there, there obviously is no God up there or down here or anywhere . Atheism at last had been empirically vindicated!

I remember my reaction to that bit of nonsense when it was proclaimed. I thought of the surgeon who had just completed an operation and said to his nurse: "Well, you didn't see any soul inside there, did you?"

"No, doctor," she replied, "and you didn't see the pain you were trying to get rid of, did you?"

The things that count for most, cannot be counted. The things that weigh most cannot be weighed, or measured or seen. Love and longing, gratitude and grief, friendship and frustration, aspiration and anguish –what human eye has ever seen them? And are there any things in life more real, more powerful, than these invisible things?

Far from being disturbed by the cosmonant's report, I was cheered by it. Had he come back with the news that he had seen God I would have been dismayed. The God I believe in cannot be seen because he has no bodily existence–though He exists in every body.

But however we conceive of God, if we deny Him, one of the

important consequences of that denial is that the universe becomes a matter of chance. No mind created it; it just happened. How plausible is that?

Julian Huxley, a celebrated zoologist, once calculated the odds against a horse developing in evolution from a one-celled protozoan purely by chance. The staggering figure he came to was 1 out of a number consisting of 3 million zeroes. Just to write that number would require 1,500 pages! And this stops with the horse, long before man appears with his mind and soul.

The belief that this orderly universe just happened, without any mind fashioning it, is as probable as a claim that no mind created the *Encyclopaedia Britannica;* it resulted from an explosion in a printing factory and the letters just happened to arrange themselves in that order.

It was not a clergyman but Darwin who said: "If we consider the whole universe, the mind refuses to look upon it as the outcome of chance."

When the American astronauts were speeding through space, they took turns reading the opening chapter of Genesis. A six-cent stamp was issued to commemorate the historic flight. It carried the words: "In the beginning God . . ."

The Unreachable Promised Land

"And the Lord said unto Moses: 'This is the land which I swore to Abraham, Isaac and Jacob . . . I have let you see it with your own eyes, but you shall not cross there.' So Moses the servant of the Lord died in the land of Moab, at the command of the Lord" (Deuteronomy 34:4-5).

Whenever I come to this passage in the Torah, I recall the sense of disappointment that filled me when, as a child, I read this Biblical story for the first time. How cruel was the sense of frustration I shared with Moses. He had dedicated his very life to a single goal which drew him irresistibly on. To achieve it, he had led his people through four perilous decades, inspiring them with courage, battling their recurrent doubts, buttressing their sagging faith, keeping steadfastly before them the vision of the ultimate destination – the Promised Land. When, at last, he stands with them on the very threshhold of fulfillment, Moses is permitted only a glimpse of the Promised Land, before death rudely intervenes to claim him.

To have struggled so long for an overarching goal only to be halted at the precise moment when it is virtually within reach – that appeared to be too depressing a climax to so noble a human adventure. It seemed to betray the very faith by which Moses himself had lived. It seemed to empty the vision which Moses had so resolutely championed.

Our Rabbis in the Midrash in their amplification of this closing chapter in the life of Moses added greater poignancy to it. They picture Moses as pleading fervently with God to permit him to enter the land, if not as a person then at least as a bird or in the form of some other animal; if not alive, then dead. But all in vain. The bitter decree is irreversible.

With maturity, however, the sense of disappointment was mellowed by the realization that in the untimely death of Moses the Bible was conveying an inescapable truth of human experience. The great always die too soon. For it is in the essence of greatness that it sets up for itself goals which are too large to be achieved in any lifetime, however long. Big people are unsatisfied with small objectives. Every Moses inevitably leaves his final Jordan uncrossed.

Dean Stanley amplified this thought when he wrote: "To labor and not see the end of our labors, to sow and not to reap, to be removed from this earthly scene before our work has been appreciated . . . is a law so common in the highest characters of history, that none can be said to be altogether exempt from its operation."

I am tempted to make the generalization that it is only small people who reach their Promised Land in their lifetime. If a man is concerned only with acquiring a new home, or a higher income bracket, or a political office, or financial security in his twilight years – he can very well reach his Promised Land. But what of the man whose Promised Land is the defeat of disease, the melting of prejudice, the triumph of democracy, the fortification of Judaism – is he likely to reach his destination? And yet who will deny that it is in the very striving after these goals that life acquires its highest significance?

Our Sages seem to have been pointing in this direction when they said that every Jew is obliged to participate in "a *Mitzvah* which is designed for the generations." They were apparently talking about goals which in their very nature defy easy attainment, dreams so large that the road to their realization must be long and arduous.

Perhaps we have here a clue to what Oscar Wilde meant in his paradoxical comment: "There are two tragedies in life. One is not getting what you want. The other is getting what you want." We should be suspicious of Promised Lands which are too easily reached. They may not be worth the journey.

"A man's reach should exceed his grasp or what's a heaven for?"

How to Measure a Person

In his autobiography entitled *Wayward Child*, Addison Gayle Jr. recalls a childhood incident that left an enduring mark. The time was the '40s and the place was Newport News, Virginia.

A young black boy is told by his father that he is running for Congress. The lad asks his father whether he expects to win.

"What kind of a question is that?" his father replies. "Of course I won't win. Those pecks would never let a black man win."

"Why you running, then?"

"So that some day *you* can win."

That day young Addison learned an important lesson. High aspiration has its own rewards even though the results are not immediately apparent.

This truth is vividly illustrated in the Haftarah assigned to the Torah portion *Pekudei*.

When King Solomon dedicates the magnificent Temple he built in Jerusalem, he recalls that his father, King David, had wanted "to build a house for the Lord, the God of Israel," but he was denied the privilege. That very desire, however, was found praiseworthy by God. ". . . You did well that it was in your heart." God further assures him that his son "shall build the house for My name" (I Kings 8:17–19).

The aspiration of the father became the achievement of the son. Moreover, the father himself became a better human being for the high goal that he had pursued. "You did well that it was in your heart."

So much of life compels us to occupy ourselves with our small daily needs and concerns. There are mundane chores to be done, assignments to be met, routine duties to be carried out. In addition there is the perpetual demand to make ends meet. All of these pedestrian concerns tend to lower our sights, to narrow the range of our vision. In our preoccupation with immediates we tend to lose sight of ultimates.

The *Plodder's Petition* echoes a prayer we might each offer from time to time:

> "Lord let me not be too content
> With life in trifling service spent.
> Make me aspire!
> When days with petty cares are filled,
> Let me with fleeting thoughts be thrilled,
> Of something higher."
>
> (Helen Gilbert)

Our genuine need for thoughts of "something higher" is something we all feel in our finer moments. "A map of the world," wrote Oscar Wilde, "that does not include Utopia, is not worth glancing at." We need long-range goals to keep from being frustrated by short-range failures. We need our Utopias to keep life from becoming coarsened. When Emerson urged: "Hitch your wagon to a star," he knew that wagons cannot reach stars, but the very effort might keep the wagon from getting mired in the gutter.

A good measure of a human being is not in what he achieves as much as in what he strives to achieve. A man can be measured by the size of his goals. He who aims high and fails is in many ways a taller person than he who aims low and succeeds.

It is no small consolation to earn the Divine verdict: "You did well that it was in your heart."

What Is in the Middle of Your Life?

We come to our synagogue on Rosh Hashanah from a world packed with pressure and tight with tension. The synagogue appears to us like

an island of serenity in an angry ocean. How fittingly might we apply
to it the beautiful lines of the poet:

> "In the heart of the cyclone tearing the sky
> And flinging the clouds and the towers by
> Is a place of central calm.
> So here in the rush of earthly things
> There is a place where the spirit sings
> In the hollow of God's palm."

Having torn ourselves away from "the rush of earthly things,"
and having assembled in this "place where the spirit sings," let us use
this moment of spiritual refuge to think together about the major motif
of these prayers we have been uttering as well as of the unspoken
thoughts which have filled our yearning hearts these past few hours.

We have been praying for nothing less than life itself. However
differently we may each look upon it, however diverse the purposes to
which we intend to put it, it is life itself, more life, for which we are
asking. And our earnestness is commensurate with the prize.

But even while we pray for life, we are all mindful of the perils
and uncertainties of life. The very spelling of the word calls attention to
the vast contingencies with which life is fraught. In the very middle of
the word LIFE, there is IF. In the middle of every life there is a big IF.

Robert Frost makes this point sharply in a haunting little poem
called "The Road Not Taken." Once while walking through the forest
he came upon a fork where two paths branched out. Naturally, he
could take only one but in the poem he wonders what would have
happened had he taken the other path.

> "I shall be telling this with a sigh
> Somewhere ages and ages hence
> Two roads diverged in a wood, and I
>   took the one less travelled by
> And that has made all the difference."

A man chooses a road that leads to a career or to the selection of
a life's mate or to a crucial decision in his business, and then in an
introspective moment he thinks of "the road not taken." What would

have happened if I had taken the other road. How vastly different my life might be today!

The famous artist Whistler had his heart set upon a career in the army but he was dropped from West Point because he failed in chemistry. In later life he used to say: "If silicon had been a gas, I should have been a major-general."

Yes! The big IF in the middle of every life. How often do you and I in our reveries walk along the road not taken.

Nor is it only our own decisions and our own choices which affect our destinies. During the Nazi holocaust, when European Jewry was being decimated, I would ask myself repeatedly: "What if my father had not made the boat?" My very life hinged literally upon a decision made by my father who could not possibly have been aware at the time of the fateful consequences of his choice.

This thought came back to me a while ago when I watched on television the dramatic reconstruction of *A Night To Remember*–the last stirring hours in the life of the proud Titanic. The tragedy claimed the lives of over 1,500 people including 102 women and 54 children. After the gripping presentation was over, the narrator added a tone of poignancy to the disaster by saying:

> If the Titanic had heeded any of the 6 iceberg warnings that it had received;
> If it had hit the iceberg 16 seconds sooner or 16 seconds later;
> If the Californian had heeded the Titanic's agonized cries for help;
> If the Titanic had carried more lifeboats;
> If its water-tight cabins were one story higher;
> If the night were moonlit;
> If any of these contingencies had occurred, the disaster might have been averted.

The enormous IFs in the middle of 1,500 lives!

Once we realize how central a position IF occupies in our life as we look backwards, it takes only the most superficial reflection to grasp the role of IF in our life as we look ahead. Indeed, overwhelming uncertainty has become the dominant mood of our time. Only at political conventions is the road to the future pictured with dogmatic assurance as peaceful and unbroken. Sober students of our time have, with compelling evidence, labeled our age as the Age of Anxiety. Living as we do during the era of the alphabetical bombs, we can understand why Quincy Howe has written that "the 20th century has put the human race on trial for its life."

But even apart from the added hazards of this nuclear Age of Anxiety, life at Rosh Hashanah time has always presented a series of big IFs to any Jew who surveyed the year ahead against the background of his prayerbook. On each of the three Holy Days, life's precariousness and perils are spelled out with terrifying realism.

> "Who shall live and who shall die
> Who shall perish by fire and who by water
> Who shall have rest and who shall go wandering
> Who shall be tranquil and who shall be disturbed
> Who shall be at ease and who shall be afflicted
> Who shall become poor and who shall wax rich
> Who shall be brought low and who shall be exalted."

The only thing in life, it would appear, of which we may be reasonably certain, is its uncertainty. As we peer into the future, the IF in the middle of life looms large indeed.

And yet, is that all we can say about life? Can it be that the only thing we can say with assurance is that there is nothing we can say with assurance? Is life to be reduced to a series of haphazard contingencies which we are powerless to control and helpless to change? Must life pivot on so unstable a center? Must we face tomorrow with only a huge, baffling question mark to sustain us?

In our innermost hearts you and I know that at the center of our life there can be something more than IF. And that plus, that added element, is indicated by the Hebrew word for life. That word as we know is "chayim." Like its English counterpart, it is also a four lettered word. But what is in the middle of "chayim?" The two middle letters of *chayim* are two *yuds,* and two *yuds,* as we know, spell the name of God.

The antidote to a life befogged by uncertainty is a life rooted in God.

If life is not to sag under the burden of heavy hazards, it must be supported by the stout beams of great affirmations.

IF reduces life to a question mark.
God punctuates life with an exclamation point.
IF makes us helpless bystanders.
God makes us intelligent co-workers.
IF leads us to despair,
God whispers courage.

And so, no sooner have we finished reciting all the uncertainties in the *Uvrosh Hashanah* prayer than we exclaim: "But You are ever our living God and King." Given God as the vital center of our lives, we can meet every contingency of life without being defeated or overwhelmed. This is the central meaning of these Holy Days. This is the theme of the 27th psalm which is read during this entire penitential season. "The Lord is my light and my salvation, whom shall I fear? The Lord is the stronghold of my life, of whom shall I be afraid?"

Let us see what it means to put God at the center in times of trouble. Does it mean that faith in God grants us and our children immunity to polio, keeps us from crippling accidents, or assures us uninterrupted prosperity? To be sure, there are some people whose faith is as naive as that. They are what we might call God's fair-weather friends. When the sun of good-fortune smiles down on them, they are enrolled among the believers. But let a heavy cloud gather on their personal horizon, then they feel betrayed, their belief has been splintered.

There are others however, for whom faith becomes a stimulant to heroic responses to the severest challenges of adversity. They do not expect God to keep them from trouble, but rather to enable them to accept it when necessary and surmount it when possible.

A little while ago, I heard a radio address delivered by a man who had lost both legs and had gone on to create for himself a useful career at the head of an organization called "Abilities Incorporated." This organization employs only handicapped people. After the speaker told how he had learned to go on despite his own handicap, he concluded with the following declamation written by another but which he had adopted for himself:

I asked God for strength, that I might achieve,
I was made weak, that I might learn humbly to obey. . . .
I asked for health that I might do greater things,

> I was given infirmity, that I might do better things. . . .
> I asked for riches, that I might be happy,
> I was given poverty that I might be wise. . . .
> I asked for power, that I might have the praise of men,
> I was given weakness, that I might feel the need of God. . . .
> I asked for all things, that I might enjoy life,
> I was given life, that I might enjoy all things. . . .
> I got nothing that I asked for – but everything I had hoped
>   for,
> Almost despite myself, my unspoken prayers were an-
>   swered.
> I am among all men, most richly blessed.

That man had made of God the vital center in his life in the time of trouble.

But life as we know is not only a series of burdens. It also has its great hours of achievement and success. As the prayer reminds us, IF can also be a series of pleasant possibilities –

> Who shall live?
> Who shall have rest?
> Who shall be tranquil?
> Who shall be at ease?
> Who shall wax rich?
> Who shall be exalted?

What does it mean to put God at the center of life in the time of triumph?

Well, at first blush, this problem doesn't seem quite so pressing. When we are well and prosperous we can manage quite well ourselves, thank you. A solvent business-man rarely advertises for partners.

On second glance, however, we notice that the prosperous man is not always the happy man. Success in any field does not necessarily bring the fulfilment it promises. Someone has reversed the popular slogan, "Nothing succeeds like success," to make it say: "Nothing fails like success." This revised version contains a genuine psychological insight. For it is only after we succeed in attaining any material goal that we realize that, by itself, it can never bring happiness. Those of us who are today earning what appeared to us in our lean college days astronomical figures, are we basically happier than we were then? Is there necessarily more contentment in the modern well-appointed split-level home than there was in the unfurnished flat in which the marriage began? Is it merely a coincidence that the Age of Anxiety has coincided with the Age of Abundance, or is it true, as Tolstoy said, that discontent is not the result of man's needs but of man's abundance? The Psalmist spoke of an affliction God sometimes visits upon the successful: "And He gave them what they asked for but He sent a hunger into their souls."

To put God at the center of life in the time of triumph means to recognize that basically we are spiritual creatures, and no matter how we pamper our bodies it shall avail us not at all unless we also nourish our souls. And it means something else too – something a famous rabbi once taught a former pupil.

The pupil of the Hafetz Hayim had ventured forth from the Yeshiva, gone to a distant town, and prospered in the business world. Some years later, the rabbi was passing through this town and naturally the business man came to visit his teacher.

"What are you doing?" the rabbi asked solicitously.

"Thank you," his pupil answered, "I'm doing quite well. My business has grown, I have many employees, my financial rating is very high."

The conversation turned to other matters. In a little while the rabbi asked again: "What are you doing?"

It seemed strange that the rabbi should repeat the question he had already answered. But the rabbi was growing older. His memory apparently was not what it used to be.

"Thank you," the pupil said a second time, "I have a nice family, a lovely wife and fine children who are growing beautifully."

Again the conversation drifted into other channels. After they had roamed over a variety of subjects, the rabbi asked a third time:

"What are you doing?"

This time the pupil could not longer contain himself. "Rabbi," he protested, "you have already asked this very question three times!"

"Yes, my son" the rabbi said in mild rebuke. "I have asked three times but you have not answered the question even once. I have asked 'What are you doing?' You tell me of your prosperity, your family.

That's not your doing. That is God's doing. I asked you what are *you* doing? How much charity are you giving? What are you doing for your people? Now tell me, my son, what are you doing? *Vos tust du?*"

To make God the vital center of our lives in the hour of triumph means to regard ourselves under obligation to return to Him a portion of the physical and financial means with which He has blessed us.

For last, I have left what I consider to be the supreme significance of making God the vital center of our lives. To do so, is not only to arm us with a strategy of action for any specific life situation. To put God in the middle of life means to make the whole enterprise, the whole business of life meaningful. Unless God is at work at the very core of life, what sense does the whole thing make?

Basically, the anxiety of our time derives in profound measure not so much from the uncertainty as to what life will bring us, as from the uncertainty as to what life means. Is life worthwhile? Does it have any intrinsic value?

We find evidence of this groping in least expected places. Let John Steinbeck in his book *Sweet Thursday* bear testimony. "Where does discontent start?" he asks. "You are warm enough but you shiver. You are fed, yet hunger gnaws you. You have been loved, but your yearning wanders in new fields. And to prod all these, there's time. . . . The end of life is now not so terribly far away – you can see it the way you see the finish line when you come into the stretch, and your mind says: 'What has my life meant so far, and what can it mean in the time left to me? What have I contributed to the Great Ledger? What am I worth?' "

Not all of us are as articulate as Steinbeck but isn't he really giving voice to the most crucial questions which agitate us? "What has my life meant so far? What can it mean? What am I worth?"

Those who have discarded a belief in God will give us no comforting answers. You and I are here for no conceivable purpose, going nowhere in particular on a journey which is full of sound and fury but signifies absolutely nothing. You and I are, as one of them put it, "only a bundle of cellular matter on its way to becoming manure," and life, in the words of another, "is a nightmare between two nothings." This is one set of answers we can give Steinbeck's piercing questions.

But when God becomes the vital center of our lives, we get an entirely different set of answers. Your life and mine become infinitely precious because there is a spark of divinity aglow within us. "Each one of us is a priceless bit of mosaic in the design of God's universe." We are but little lower than the angels. We are here at God's orders rendering a command performance. And what we do with our lives is of everlasting significance. Life is an unending adventure towards the goal of becoming human.

Zochraynu l'chayim melech chofetz b'chayim, "Remember us to life, O King, because You want us to live."

The cyclone of which we spoke at the beginning derives its extraordinary driving power because, as the poet said, in its heart "is a place of central calm." If we are to live our lives with courage, with compassion and with conviction we need God in our hearts to give our lives a place of central calm.

> "And I said to the man who stood at the gate to the year:
> 'Give me a light that I may tread safely into the unknown.'
>
> And he replied:
>
> Go out into the darkness and put your hand into the Hand of God.
> That shall be to you better than light and safer than a known way!"
>
> (M. Louise Haskins)

What Faith Cannot Do

The word *faith* is widely used as a synonym for "religion." Thus we might refer to a Christian as a "member of the Christian faith." A Jew is often described as belonging "to the Jewish faith." Thus, "faith" and "religion" are so intimately related that a clergyman is expected to extol the power of faith and to expound on what faith can do for us. So, for a change, perhaps it might be helpful to think about those things that faith cannot do for us. If we are not to abuse our faith or misuse it, we ought to be aware of its limitations.

The first thing that faith cannot do for us is exempt us from thinking. To believe does not mean to suspend our critical faculties. Tertullian, the third-century religious writer, uttered the famous statement: "I believe because it is absurd." The queen in Lewis Carroll's *Through the Looking Glass* has the same conception of what it means to believe. When she tells Alice that she is one hundred and one years, five months, and one day old, Alice says, "I cannot believe that." "Can't you?" says the queen. "Try again. Draw a long breath and shut your eyes."

No, true faith does not require us to believe the absurd, or to shut our eyes to the realities of life, the discoveries of science, or the evidence of reason. Albert Einstein put it accurately: "Science without religion is lame: religion without science is blind." Moreover, those who believe absurdities will practice atrocities. One of God's greatest gifts to us is the power of reason, and when we use it properly we pay highest tribute to Him who, in the words of our prayer book, "mercifully endows the human being with understanding."

In the second place, faith cannot exempt us from toil. To believe in God does not mean to sit back and wait for Him to do for us what we must do for ourselves. An old adage offers sound advice: "Trust in God, but row away from the rocks."

Faith is not meant to be a narcotic but a stimulant; it is a call to action, not a substitute for it. Faith does not mean that "God's in His Heaven, all's right with the world." It does mean that God who is in Heaven urges us to work with Him in righting what is wrong with the world.

Lastly, faith cannot exempt us from trouble. It does not shield us against sorrow or suffering. Our belief in God grants us no immunity against cancer or heart disease or death on the highway.

How often have I heard people say: "When my mother died, I stopped believing in God." "He was such a good person. Why did this tragedy happen to him?"

Many of us have a faith that shrinks when it is washed in the waters of adversity. We forget that trouble and sorrow have a passkey to every home in the land; no one is exempt from suffering. To believe in God does not mean that we and those who are dear to us will be spared those burdens that are the common lot of all of us.

To believe in Him does mean that we should live by His commandments so that our deeds bring no harvest of pain, remorse, or fear.

Our faith should also give us the strength to go on in the face of adversity and to fortify us with the understanding that we may even emerge from our trials wiser and more humane because of what we have endured.

Man Is Always in God's Presence

When Martin Buber died at 87 years of age, the Jewish people lost one of its most renowned religious thinkers, and the world lost one of its most influential philosophers.

"Man," he wrote, "is always in God's presence, and God should always be present to man." In these words, Buber summed up one of our basic needs – the need for the constant awareness that wherever we are, we are in God's presence.

We need a sense of His presence when life is kind, when we prosper and taste the heady wine of success, when we are sorely tempted to that greatest of all idolatries – self deification. At such a time we need to be reminded of the bountiful Source of all our gifts of body and mind, without which we should be as helpless infants. We could not achieve if we did not first receive.

We need the awareness of His presence when we lie in a sick bed. Finding ourselves in a hospital room is often frightening and demoralizing. Our privacy is invaded. Our weakness is emphasized. Our dependence is magnified. Our fears are given free play. In the aloneness of a hospital room, we need the comforting Presence to reassure us, to abide with us through the long dark night.

We need His presence when we are overcome with bereavement. Friends perform small courtesies, soft acts of compassion. But in the heart of the mourner there is an emptiness that friends cannot fill; which can be filled only by the presence of God. "Yea, though I walk through the valley of the shadow of death, I fear no evil for You are with me" (Psalms 23:4).

We need the awareness of His presence as we grow older, when we have said many a goodbye, when the friends on the other side outnumber those on this side, and the thought of death, our death, closes in on us. The thought frightens us but if we have the Presence with us, should we be afraid?

Perhaps if we had possessed consciousness we would have been afraid of being born, of surrendering that secure and comfortable prenatal world for the unknown world outside. But the world into which we were born was ready to look after our needs. There were loving arms to enfold us, open hearts to admit us, soft lips to kiss us.

Will God, who provided all things for us at the entrance desert us at the exit? Does He not know how much we are still children who frighten easily, and will He not be there to see that we are not left alone in our new surroundings? Can we really travel beyond the range of His care and His concern? Is there any place devoid of His presence?

"Man is always in God's presence, and God should always be present to man."

Humility – A Lost Virtue

Some time ago, a very prominent television personality discharged a singing member of his staff and gave as his reason: "He lost his humility." If the discharged star was somewhat devoid of humility before his dismissal, we have reason to fear that he has even less today, because this accusation and the resulting dismissal projected the young man into instantaneous prominence and financial success. The alleged loss of humility thus proved no real deterrent to our singer.

In many people's minds, there was some lingering confusion as to who was really deficient in humility – the accused or the accuser. Somehow, the virtue called "humility" is one which the possessor must carry without being too conscious of it. The moment a person becomes aware of his humility, he loses it. For then it is very tempting to say, as Gilbert and Sullivan's Mikado did: "You have no idea how poor an opinion I have of myself and how little I deserve it." The Hasidic Rebbe Mendele of Kotzk made the penetrating observation that of all the *mitzvot* in the Torah, the *mitzvah* of humility is the only one which does not require conscious intent. On the contrary, the presence of such self consciousness negates humility entirely.

You can understand my reluctance to deal with this theme. To call attention to a lack of humility is almost tantamount to convicting oneself of the same fault.

Moreover, ours is a society singularly incongenial to the flowering of humility. This is the age which has created the high-pressure publicity agent and promoted advertising into one of America's major industries. Neither of these developments was triggered by an excess of modesty. Indeed, if a sense of humility ever descended upon Madison Avenue, many a publicity and press agent would be stricken with total disability and we should probably never know again the touching musical tributes to soap suds or the heart-warming poems in praise of dog food.

In recommending a man for a job or an applicant for admission to a school, we are apt to call attention to his reliability, industry, integrity, intelligence. Rarely, if ever, would we think of including humility among his attractive qualities. For humility in our time is almost a lost virtue.

And yet, humility runs like a golden thread throughout the Jewish pattern of righteous living. Indeed, among the Hasidim, humility was regarded as the top rung on the ladder of perfection.

Consider, for example, the biblical profile of Moses. In many real ways, he is the central hero of the Jewish drama. It was he who planted in the heavy hearts of a down-trodden slave people the yearning to be free. It was he who led them triumphantly, in spite of themselves, out of Egypt. It was he who served as God's agent for the Revelation at Sinai. It was he, again, who led them for some forty years through the fierce and forbidding desert–a journey made more difficult by the nostalgic backward glances towards Egypt which the rabble rousers among the people were perpetually casting. There were so many noteworthy qualities of Moses that the Bible could have singled out for praise; and yet there is only one direct compliment which Scripture pays Moses: "The man Moses was very humble, above all the men who are on the face of the earth." This is the quality, above all others, to which the Torah called direct attention.

Nor is this an isolated tribute to the role of humility. It serves as the climax of Micah's eloquent summation of man's highest duties: "What does the Lord require of you? Only to do justice, to love mercy and to walk humbly with your God."

In rabbinic writings, there are also many impressive indications of how highly humility was cherished by the molders of our tradition. "Why was man created last in the order of Creation?" the Sages ask. And they answer, "In order that, should he ever become too proud, he might be reminded that the tiniest flea preceded him in the divine scheme of things." In another *Midrash,* we are told that God revealed himself to Moses in a lowly bush and not in a tall, stately tree, precisely because of the modest size of the bush. Again, He chose Sinai, the smallest of the mountains in that region, to teach us that humility is a requisite for experiencing God's presence. Elsewhere, we are told that the prophet Isaiah compared the words of the Torah to water, because, "just as water forsakes the high places and flows down to the low ones, so do the words of the Torah find a resting place only in a person of humble spirit." Another Sage, Rabbi Levitas of Jabneh, counseled, "Be exceedingly humble, for what is the hope of mortals but the grave."

Does this mean that Judaism considers it sinful for a human being to feel a sense of pride? Scarcely. Who will condemn the look of quiet pride that settles on the faces of parents as their sons chant their Bar Mitzvah blessings and Haftarah? Who will question the right of a mother to be proud as her lovely daughter and her nervous husband come down the aisle leading to the canopy? The father who raises a decent family, the mother who prepares a tasty meal, the shoemaker who makes a beaten pair of shoes look wearable again, the secretary whose letter is neat and evenly spaced, the Jew who contemplates his inheritance and finds it noble – all these have their moments of pride, and who will challenge their right to them?

Moreover, there is often virtue in pride. A man may be too proud to demean himself. He may have too high an opinion of himself to resort to dishonesty or betrayal or compromise with principle. "Pride," it has been rightly said, "makes some men ridiculous and prevents others from becoming so." There is the kind of pride that prompts a man not to turn his nose up, but to keep his chin up and to carry his honor high. When a Jew of yesterday was tempted to perform an unseemly act, he would instinctively protest: *"Es passt nit far a yid –* this is conduct unbecoming a Jew." His pride prevented him from debasing himself. Even the Hasidim, who valued humility so highly, taught that there are moments when pride becomes a duty. "When the Evil Inclination approaches, whispering in your ear: 'You are unworthy to fulfill the Torah,' you must say: 'I am worthy.' " We all need a strong measure of such pride.

What our tradition opposes so strongly is the pride which causes a man to be so dazzled by the splendor of his own brilliance that he sees no one else; the pride which tempts a man into the blasphemy and folly of thinking of himself as a self-made man and worshipping his creator.

This, as our Sages saw it, was the cardinal sin of Pharaoh, as indeed of all tyrants. He suffered from an inflated sense of his own importance. Pharaoh, our Sages say, played the role of God. *"Anee v'afsee od*–There is none as exalted as I am," he proclaimed. "The Nile is my own. I have made it for myself." It was, therefore, our Sages say, that the first plague to be visited upon Egypt was the plague which turned the waters of the Nile into blood. This was designed to teach Pharaoh an object lesson in humility.

How shall we be saved from that kind of consuming pride? How can we derive satisfaction from our work without being blinded by a vision of ourselves? How can we cultivate a mood of humility in a society given to proclaiming aloud one's virtues–real and imaginary?

It seems to me that, in the first place, we have to maintain a sense of proportion and a sense of perspective.

After repeated failures, man finally conquered the forbidding heights of Mt. Everest. For a few brief moments of exaltation, man stood on the top and looked down. It was, of course, a magnificent victory of the indomitable human spirit, which has refused to accept limits on its vast capacities.

And yet I wonder if ever a man had a right to feel any more insignificant than did those intrepid climbers, alone in the howling vastness of space. Who among us has not stood on a mountain and felt, with the psalmist, an exaggerated awareness of our microscopic size? "When I behold the heavens, the work of Your hands, the moon and the stars which You have created, what is man that You are mindful of him, or the son of man that You take account of him?" How small they must have felt up there in their moment of greatest triumph. This is what Pascal had in mind when he said, "When he consults himself, man knows he is great. When he contemplates the universe around him, he knows that he is little, and his ultimate greatness consists of his knowledge of his littleness." When we feel a powerful sense of our own importance creeping up on us, it might be very salutary to run for the nearest mountain.

Well, I suppose, we might be ready to concede, in our more

generous moments, that we are not as big as the infinite universe, but our pride usually feeds on the knowledge or the illusion that we are so much better than other people. The truth is that, in spite of the preamble to the Declaration of Independence, all men are not created equal. In George Orwell's *Nineteen Eighty-four,* the worker's building displays an inscription which declares: "All men are equal, only some men are more equal than others." There is a vast difference between a Heifetz and the usher who shows a ticket bearer to his seat in the concert hall. There is an enormous gap between a George Bernard Shaw and the salesgirl who sells his book in the department store. There is an impressive discrepancy between an Arthur Szyk, who captured in color the grandeur and pathos of Jewish life, and the man who buys the master's painting for his study. Seen through human eyes, we are indeed not equal at all.

And yet, before God, how small we all are! This, I believe, is why the prophet Micah suggested that we walk humbly with our God. When we walk with God it must be humbly. For what, after all, is the music of a Heifetz before Him Who taught the brooks to murmur, the leaves to whisper, the wind to howl, the birds to sing and the baby to cry? How impressive is a Shaw compared to the Divine Playwright whose dramas touch everything, and whose cast of characters include every human being? How significant is the brush of a Szyk alongside the One who paints sunsets daily and touches the leaves of autumn with intoxicating colors? How large is our knowledge compared with the Infinite wisdom? How big is our goodness alongside of the unspeakable mercy of God? "A mountain shames a molehill until they are both humbled by the stars." Phillips Brooks was dispensing very sound spiritual advice when he said, "The true way to be humble is not to stoop until you are smaller than yourself, but to stand at your real height against some higher nature that will show you what the real smallness of your greatness is."

This leaves one last point, which is perhaps most decisive. To every one of our accomplishments an infinite number of people, past and present, have made their contribution. Let us take an example that I know best – this sermon. Of course I wrote it myself. Well – almost myself.

In retrospect, I see that I have quoted the Bible, the Mishnah, the Talmud, a television star, Gilbert and Sullivan, Pascal and Brooks, among others. Apart from these, the sermon is all my own, except, of course, that there were certain Rebbes who taught me to read the Bible and the Talmud, and there were the teachers who taught me to read English. There were also some people who inspired me to become a rabbi. And then there is the small matter of some 150 generations of Jews who struggled to keep the tradition alive.

Oh, yes, it is difficult to preach at 9:45 P.M. on an empty stomach, so we ought to consider the Shabbat meal we ate before these late services tonight. There was the farmer who raised the chicken, the *Shochet* who slaughtered it, the butcher who sold it, the delivery boy who brought it, the *rebbetzin* who *koshered* it and cooked it, and our three daughters who made it tastier by their constant chatter. Shall I take you through the whole meal – wine, *challah,* vegetables, dessert and all? No less than eighty people are involved between the time that wheat is planted and a loaf of bread appears on my table.

In fairness, I suppose we ought to include also those who built the Synagogue and pulpit, those who provided the flowers, the heat, you trusting people who came to listen, the babysitters who released some of you. Shall I go on? Come to think of it, I have not even mentioned the most important ingredients that went into the preaching of this sermon: the health and strength I need to speak.

On second thought, many a hand wrote this sermon tonight, and if I cannot even write a sermon alone, how can I even in my most self-intoxicated moments dare to consider myself a self-made man?

Humility, then, is simply a matter of fairness, of getting our sights adjusted. We must learn to see ourselves in true relationship to the world, to our fellowman, and to God. If we get our spiritual lenses refracted we can then more easily follow the counsel of Jeremiah:

"Thus saith the Lord:

> Let not the wise man glory in his wisdom.
> Neither let the mighty man glory in his might.
> Neither let the rich man glory in his riches.
> But let him that glories glory in this:
> That he understands and knows Me,
> That I am the Lord Who exercises mercy,
> Justice and righteousness in the earth
> For in these things I delight
> Says the Lord."

Humbly let us pray:

Father of the strong and the weak beforewW hom even the strongest is weak;

Lord of all wisdom and knowledge before Whom even the wisest is as a speechless child;

You who fills the heavens and reveals Yourself in a lowly bush;

You who dwells in the high places and with him who is of a humble spirit;

Fill us with the pride that keeps us from self-humiliation,

Purge us from the pride which leads to self-exaltation.

Keep us mindful that we are only human,

So that we might be most human.

Impress upon us our littleness, so that we may strive for true greatness.

Encourage us to measure ourselves against the stars so that we might be tempted to reach for them.

Help us to see how we lean upon You and upon one another so that we truly fulfill the injunction of Your Prophet: "to do justice, love mercy and to walk humbly before You."

Amen.

Things God Cannot Do without Us

One of the most thrilling passages in the Bible is the one with which it opens. It transports us to the very beginning of things, to the fresh dawn of creation   when we hear the Divine voice summoning order out of chaos, light out of darkness, life out of the unchartered void. After six days of creation, we read: "And God saw everything that He had made, and behold it was very good" (Genesis 1:31). "Very good" – but not perfect.

A young man who was depressed by the evil, the suffering, the misery of the world complained to his rabbi: "Why did God ever make such a world? Why, I could make a better world than this myself." His rabbi answered quietly: "That is exactly the reason God put you in this world – to make it a better world. Now go ahead and do your part."

In the rabbi's answer, we come upon a subtle truth that is frequently overlooked. We always talk of our dependence upon God.

We seem to forget that God also depends on us. There are so many things He cannot do without us. "Man," taught the ancient sages, is "a partner to the Holy One, blessed be He, in the work of creation." And, may I add, not a silent partner, either.

Now I don't know why God put us in an unfinished world. Perhaps life would have no purpose in a finished world. But here we are in a world crying to be made better and God asking us to do these jobs with Him because He cannot do them alone.

God cannot make a peaceful world unless we, His children, help Him by rooting out the hatred from our hearts, the prejudice from our minds, the injustice from our society.

God cannot build a happy home unless husband and wife work with Him by bringing to it a spirit of sharing, mutual respect, a binding loyalty, constancy, and compassion.

God cannot give us a peaceful night's sleep unless we cooperate with Him by doing an honest day's work.

God cannot forgive our sins unless we help Him by genuine contrition for what has been, and firm resolve for what we mean to accomplish.

God heals the sick, but not without the surgeon's hand, the doctor's medicine, the nurse's vigilance, the encouragement of loved ones and friends.

God brings forth bread from the earth, but not without the farmer who prepares the soil, plants the seed, harvests the crop.

God helps the poor with the charity we give, cheers the lonely with the visits we make, comforts the bereaved with the words we speak, guides our children with the examples we set, ennobles our lives with the good deeds we perform.

And here, ultimately, may be the reason that you and I are here on this earth. God needs us, each of us. We are joined with Him in a great partnership.

Believing and Behaving

The Bible portion *Emor* contains a very crucial verse: "You shall not profane My Holy name; but I will be hallowed among the people of Israel" (Leviticus 22:32).

This verse has been called "Israel's miniature Bible." It has had a profound impact on the fabric of Judaism and the faith of the Jew. The verse contains both a negative idea and a positive one.

The negative idea is that we must refrain from doing anything that tarnishes the honor of Judaism or the glory of God. Any misdeed is not only an offense against another human being; it constitutes at the same time a blemish upon God's holy name. God's reputation is, as it were, in our hands; we must be exceedingly careful to do nothing to taint or diminish it.

The rabbis in the Talmud were especially strong in their warning that an offense against a non-Jew was doubly sinful because it conveyed a false impression of the ethical and moral standards that Judaism demands of its adherents. Thus, it also profanes God's holy name.

The positive idea urged upon us by the second half of the verse is that we act in such a way that we will "hallow" God's name. This idea is embodied in the concept "Kiddush Hashem." Literally, it means hallowing or sanctifying the divine name. We are enjoined to enhance the glory of God by the way we live and conduct ourselves.

Historically, Kiddush Hashem has been associated with Jewish martyrdom. "Martyrdom" is derived from a term which means "bearing witness." By his willingness to die for his faith rather than abandon it or compromise it or exchange it, the Jew felt that he was bearing the ultimate witness to the preciousness of his faith in the one God.

Unhappily, Jewish history is all too laden with evidence of this kind of Kiddush Hashem. But Kiddush Hashem is not reserved for the dramatic act of surrendering one's life. Kiddush Hashem also is achieved through the quality of our daily lives. We must live with the constant awareness that our acts, day-by-day, have the power of enhancing God's name.

An example of Kiddush Hashem is provided by Rabbi Simeon ben Shetach, who lived during the early part of the 1st century. One day, he commissioned his disciples to buy for him a donkey from an Arab. When they brought him the animal, they happily announced that they had found a precious stone which the former owner had apparently forgotten in the donkey's collar. The rabbi, however, protested: "I purchased a donkey and not a precious stone. Return the gem to its owner." When his disciples reluctantly performed the master's command, the Arab exclaimed: "Praise be the God of Simeon ben Shetach." This was an act of true Kiddush Hashem.

Faith in God cannot be an unobtrusive idea quietly asleep in the dormitory of our mind. It has to be acted out in the arena of everyday life. Faith in God is not merely an idea the mind possesses; it is an idea that possesses the mind. Faith in God is demonstrated not in diction but in action; not in our creeds but in our deeds. What we believe is illustrated in how we behave.

To each of us there has been given the unique privilege of beautifying our lives by sanctifying His name.

One Little Boy

Some time ago there appeared in West Germany a book written by a German-Jewish journalist who used for her illustrations the actual drawings made in the Nazi concentration camps by the Jewish children whose story she tells. The appearance of the book inspired an editorial in *The New York Times*. The editorial was entitled, "One Little Boy." It began by asking a series of questions:

"Why the search for Nazis 20 years after World War II? Why does bitterness still burn as a hot coal in the hearts of millions throughout the world? Why can so many decent human beings not find in their hearts the capacity to forgive and forget?

"A story in this newspaper yesterday suggests one of the reasons. There has just been published in Germany a book entitled, *For Theirs Was the Hell*. It is a documented account of the fate which befell some of the 1.2 million Jewish children under 16 years of age in Hitler's concentration camps. These few sentences from the story are enough:

" 'Then the guard ordered the children to fold their clothes neatly and march into the gas chamber and crematorium. One little boy, less than two years old, was too little to climb the steps. So the guard took the child in her arms and carried him into the chamber.'

"There is the reason – one little boy."

The editorial was quite correct. Six Million Jews is an incomprehensible figure. The lips can say it in a moment; the mind cannot absorb it in a lifetime. "1.2 million children under 16!" The figure is staggering, but it still says nothing to the heart. One little boy, however, crawls into the heart, and we understand the enormity of the outrage, the unspeakable magnitude of the disaster. Six Million is a statistic. One little boy too little to climb the steps breathes the agony of life and the anguish of death, and we understand.

I don't suppose that this is an ideal beginning for a Rosh Hashanah sermon. But then again, we haven't lived through ideal times, nor are we yet living in the best of all possible worlds. And there is a very direct connection between that one little boy and the central message of Rosh Hashanah.

As a matter of fact, the Torah reading for Rosh Hashanah begins with the birth of one little boy. The name of the boy is Isaac. He was extremely important to the development of Judaism. God had promised Abraham that He would make his name great and that He would be the father of a mighty multitude, as numerous as the sands of the sea and the stars of heaven. His descendants would be enlisted in Divine service, teaching men to believe in the One God, the God of justice and mercy and truth.

But this entire promise hinged upon one little boy; for without that child to carry the message and the commitment there would be no future. One little boy was the key to tomorrow and to all the centuries between Abraham and ourselves.

Significantly, the Haftarah for this morning also deals with the birth of one little boy. The name of the boy was Samuel, who was to leave an enormous imprint upon Jewish thought and life through the two books of our Bible which bear his name and reflect the passion of the first of the great prophets after Moses.

Isn't it strange, when we stop to think of it, that both the Torah reading and the Haftarah should focus so sharply upon the single individual precisely on Rosh Hashanah where our concern seems to be with the whole world? *"Hayom Harat Olam*—on this day the world came into being." Our scope on this day is as wide as the whole universe.

"And therefore, O Lord our God, let Your awe be manifest in all Your works and a reverence for You fill *all* that You have created, so that *all* Your creatures may know You and *all* mankind bow down to acknowledge You."

On Rosh Hashanah the canvas is the entire world, and the subject is all mankind, and yet the Torah reading and the Haftarah reading each talk about, one little boy.

There is enormous wisdom compressed into this preoccupation of Rosh Hashanah with the solitary individual. For our purposes, I would like to call attention to *three* specific implications which have direct and immediate relevance to us in our time.

In the first place, it drives home to us the fundamental Jewish teaching that every human being is unique. In a world where there are four billion of us crowding a shrinking globe, and where so much justified concern is being devoted to the prevention of the uncontrolled multiplication of the human species, it is difficult to preserve a sense of awe and wonder and mystery in the presence of the individual human being.

In a world where machines can outperform us to a distressing degree, it is not easy to maintain a sense of reverence for the human personality. A computer in England trying to determine the respective odds on the player and the banker in a card game called baccarat, took 45 minutes to complete the calculations involving more than one billion separate operations. An Einstein could not have done this task alone if he lived to be 1,000 years.

In a world where men tend more and more to be reduced to statistical data, efficiency is frequently purchased at the cost of our humanity. One college president (Dr. Howard R. Bowen of Grinnell College) recently decried what he called "the tyranny of numbers."

"In describing a particular student," he wrote, "we often say something like this: 'Steven Martin, oh yes, he was 35th in a high school class of 280, he scored 553 on the verbal and 610 on the quantitative College Board tests, his college grade-point average was 2.85 and he scored 275 on the Graduate Record Examination!' There you have the biography of Steven Martin reduced to the stark essentials. No nonsense about his curiosity, his moral fiber, his dreams and aspirations. . . ."

With all these dehumanizing influences at work in our times, it is all the more vital that we recall the teaching of our tradition which underscores the uniqueness of each of us.

Our sages dramatize this point in a vivid parable. A mortal king, they said, when he wishes to make many coins, creates one mold and with that mold he stamps out all the coins he needs. Each coin is exactly like every other coin. God, however, created all men from but one, and yet no two individuals are exactly alike.

Judaism reminds us that there is no common man. Each one of us is uncommon. There has been nothing like us ever, nor will there ever be. There is no such thing as an average man except on the graphs and the charts of the statisticians.

The railroad porter in the old anecdote stumbled on this truth quite by accident. When he deposited the two pieces of luggage on the train he was asked by their owner what the average tip was for carrying a suitcase. "One dollar each," he answered. The man gave him $2. "Thank you, sir!" the porter exclaimed with grateful enthusiasm. "You're the only one who ever lived up to the average."

The "average" person knows in the depths of his being that he is not average. He is someone special, someone apart, someone solitary and individual, with his own sad secrets, his own bundle of hopes and dreams, fears and fantasies, drives and desires. Each one of us is an original, even though we sometimes forget that and try to make of ourselves carbon copies.

"Every single man is a new thing in the world and is called upon to fulfill his particularity in the world." Thus taught the Hasidic rebbe, Yechiel Michael of Zlotchov.

In each of us all the past centuries coalesce. In each of us all the future centuries have their beginnings. In each of us there are found very special endowments. "It is a pleasant fact," said Henry Thoreau, "that you will know no man long, however low in the social scale, however poor, miserable, intemperate and worthless he may appear to be, a mere burden to society, but you will find at last that there is something which he understands and can do better than any other."

Earlier in the service we read in the *Unsaneh Tokef*: "All who enter the world You cause to pass before You, one by one, as a flock of sheep. As a shepherd counts his sheep and causes them to pass beneath his staff so do You review and record and count and remember, every living soul."

In the eyes of our Creator we are not statistics. We are each the object of God's care and compassion. We are each counted. We are each remembered. We are each one – one unique man, one special woman, one precious little boy.

There is a second vital lesson in Rosh Hashanah's preoccupation with the lone human being. It drives home to us not only the uniqueness of each person but also the sanctity of each person. Every human being is a whole world in himself.

This thought is found explicitly in the Mishnah. There we read that witnesses who appeared before a Jewish court to testify in cases involving capital crimes were given strictest admonition concerning the enormity of their responsibility. It was pointed out to them that God did not begin the human family by creating many people at once. Instead, He created a single human being in order to impress upon us that he who slays a single soul is as though he caused the whole world to perish, and he who saves a single soul is credited with saving the whole world.

In a world where we have become aware of so much poverty, hunger, and human need, it is easy to develop what has been called "compassion fatigue." We just can't embrace the whole world and we can't worry about every needy Israeli and every homeless Asiatic and every illiterate African and every hungry Indian.

The mind staggers in the face of the magnitude of the task of human salvation and redemption which cries out to us, and so we are very likely to do nothing at all, to grow weary of caring, to shut the world out and to focus upon me and mine.

To us, Rosh Hashanah says—no! Because you cannot help everyone is no excuse for helping no one. He who saves one life has sustained the whole universe. One life is sacred, and we must never forget that.

After hurricane Betsy had paid a violent visit to Miami, a newscaster was reporting on the damage left in its wake. "Damage to property," he said, "is estimated in the millions, but there was only one life lost." The word "only" bothered me very much when I heard the newscast. If that one victim were the broadcaster's child, would he have said "only"? To the family of that victim it wasn't "only." A whole universe perished with that solitary person.

Horace Mann, the famous 19th-century educator, once spoke at the dedication of a building which was designed as a corrective institution for boys who had gotten into trouble. In the course of his address, he referred to the many thousands of dollars the building had cost, and he went on to say, "If all this which has been spent upon this building results in the reformation of one boy, it is money well spent."

After he finished speaking, a member of the audience approached him privately and asked him, "Mr. Mann, do you really think that one boy is worth all that money?" "Yes," he said, "if he is my boy or yours." One little boy.

There is a third implication in what we have been saying. By focusing upon the single individual, Rosh Hashanah reminds us not only of our uniqueness, not only of our sanctity, but also of our power. You and I have extraordinary capacities and all kinds of latent force. We each have the power to transform our lives. We can each make a decisive difference in the world.

There is a desperate need in Jewish life today for men and women who grasp the basic truth that the future of American Judaism is in their own hands. The verdict is not with those who write articles about "The Vanishing American Jew." We have been vanishing for 2,500 years – according to the social scientists. If we are still very much in evidence today and more alive than ever before, it is because the individual Jew always declared: "*Lo Amut Kee Ech-yeh* – I shall not die but live*." And he translated that life affirming boast into daily personal acts of consecration and devotion.

On Rosh Hashanah, when we are properly concerned with the Jewishness of our lives, our homes, our synagogue, and our community, it is so important that we learn to look upon ourselves not as helpless pieces of driftwood afloat on the turbulent currents of our time. We have to learn to see ourselves as persons endowed with the capacity to will and to shape and to mold circumstances.

We must look upon the world, our tradition teaches us, as being in a state of delicate balance between good and evil, and our very next deed can be decisive in tipping the scales to one side or the other.

We can profoundly influence the Jewish character of our homes and the Jewish quality of our lives. And if we do, and we send out into the world one little boy and one little girl a little prouder of our heritage, a little better informed of our past, a little more in love with the Jewish present and a little more hopeful of the Jewish future, is that a mean contribution?

Nobody asks of us spectacular victories. The greatest things in the world are never spectacular. Hurricanes are spectacular but soft rain makes things to grow. Day by day loyalty to convictions, to principles and to mitzvot, this is the kind of undramatic faithfulness which Jews have always needed to stay alive and to keep alive that which Rosh Hashanah is all about.

This then is our answer to history's most bestial assault on the dignity of the human being. Despite all that was done to cheapen life, we insist that each life is unique, each is sacred, each is capable of making a vital difference in the world. This is the ultimate, reassuring, challenging truth about your life and mine.

A new venture in recorded music was launched entitled "Music Minus One." The finest chamber music is reproduced, but in each recording one instrument is deliberately omitted. The owner of the record is supposed to supply the missing instrument by playing along with the record.

The orchestra of humanity plays for each of us Music Minus One. If we fail to play our unique part, something vital will be missing. Each of us has the welcome opportunity and inescapable responsibility to supply the missing instrument. In the New Year that trembles with so many hopeful possibilities, may each of us contribute our own harmonies to the music which is the gladness of the world.

God Was Present

We were moving serenely along the New York Thruway when suddenly, whether due to human or mechanical failure, we found ourselves careening out of control over a ditch that lined the right side of the road. After an eternity of bouncing, the car ground to a halt on an embankment, tilted at a precarious angle. Within moments, we were surrounded by passing motorists who extricated Hilda and me from the wreckage, placed us on the grass and summoned help. Minutes later we were en route, via ambulance, to the Benedictine Hospital in Kingston, N.Y.

Among the myriad of questions we were asked in the emergency room, I remember the following:

"Where were you coming from?"

"Skidmore College."

"What were you doing at Skidmore?"

"I had come to deliver a lecture."

"What was your subject?"

"Where Is God When We Suffer?"

To this my interviewer commented wryly, "After this accident, you might want to take another look at the subject."

Well, I had some long days and nights in the hospital to take another look at that subject. Where was God when Hilda and I suffered this totally unnecessary accident? Let me say very emphatically that I do not believe that God was punishing me or Hilda for any wrong that either Hilda or I had committed. Not that I pretend for even the slightest moment that I am incapable of doing wrong. Jewish teaching reminds us, and my own conscience convinces me, that "there is none so righteous as to be without sin." But if God wanted to punish me for the things I have done wrong in my lifetime, He didn't have to involve so many other people.

This matter of "punishment" can never be neatly contained or confined. When my good wife suffered a broken arm and nose and a fracture of a spinal vertebra, a host of people who heavily depend on her were also disadvantaged. Her mother and father, to whom she has been ministering several hours daily for the past five years, lost their most constant source of solace, support, and devotion. Our whole family felt her pain, and hundreds of people in our congregation and elsewhere, who love her dearly, suffered along with her. And one most deserving 13-year-old in Jerusalem will probably be deprived of having his insanely devoted grandmother attend his Bar Mitzvah celebration. If punishment were indeed in order for either Hilda or me, why involve the whole immediate world? No, I don't believe for a moment that God "wanted" us to have this accident. We are grown people, and must not hold God responsible for our own carelessness or negligence. But where was He when the accident took place?

Here's where I think He was. God was in the hearts of those wonderful strangers who interrupted their journeys to come to the aid of two wounded travelers they did not know. God was in the ambitions of the paramedics who had dedicated themselves to help people when their lives are threatened. God was in the emergency room, ministering through the trained minds, the caring hands, the consoling words of all the people who were there to attend to us quickly and effectively. God was in the hearts of the generous people who had built the hospital because they knew that hospitals spell the difference between life and death. God was in the healing that began as soon as we were bruised. God was in the Niagara of love, prayer and concern that came cascading toward us from an incredible number of friends and colleagues, and even remote acquaintances who reached out to us from near and far.

If ever I needed an answer to the question, "What does one have to show for 41 years in the rabbinate," the answer came with unmistakable clarity. "There is indeed reward for your labors." In no other life's calling could Hilda and I have made so many friends as we did while trying to do God's work. So now I believe I know where God was when we suffered. He was there showing us through the massive kindness and affection that enveloped us, that even in the darkness His light glowed tenderly, held firmly by faithful hands who protected it against the winds of despair and desolation.

And there is one other gift God has given us for a time like this. He has enabled us not only to endure suffering but to use it, to learn from it, to become enlarged by it. Despite its forbidding countenance, suffering possesses great potential power to expand our lives and to widen our compassion. It can help to purge us of pettiness and selfishness.

Our own suffering can make us more sensitive to the suffering of others. When we remember how we called for the nurse to relieve our pain in the middle of the night, we cannot help but become more aware of the others for whom pain is a constant companion.

I recall now the parable of the man who complained to God: "How come, in times of joy when I walked in the sand, I found Your footprints alongside mine. But in the time of trouble, I only saw a single set of footprints. Why did You abandon me in my time of need?" "My child," came the tender reply, "I never forsake those in need. When in your suffering you saw only a single set of footprints, those footprints were Mine. It was then that I carried you."

On the Sabbath following our accident, the prophetic portion read in the synagogue concluded with the prayer of Jeremiah: "Heal me, O Lord, and I shall be healed, save me and I shall be saved, for You are my praise."

The God We Must Keep Alive

There is a story about a young boy who concluded his bedtime prayer with this afterthought:

"And O yes, dear God, please take care of Yourself because if anything happens to You, we're all sunk."

Well, if some of our contemporary Christian theologians are to be believed, the boy's worst fear has come true. Something terrible has happened to God. We have been told that "God is dead."

Normally what theologians say and write is rather widely disregarded by the rest of the population. What is noteworthy about the assault upon God is the fact that the theme has been treated in popular magazines. There is scarcely a magazine that hasn't dealt with it. The question has been on the cover page of *Time,* explored by *Look* and *Red Book* and the others. The theologians who advocate this point of view are enjoying national prominence. Their lectures attract thousands. Their books sell in the tens of thousands. What we are talking about are not the sentiments of a few obscure ivory-tower thinkers. We are discussing a question which is on the lips of multitudes of Americans. In a special issue of *Commentary* magazine containing a symposium on the state of Jewish belief, some forty religious leaders of American Jewry were asked to react to five specific questions. One of them read: "Does the so-called 'God is dead' question which has been agitating Christian theologians have any relevance to Judaism?"

This is a question which we cannot evade because it is all around us. It goes to the very heart of Rosh Hashanah, when we proclaim the kingship of God and we blow the shofar to suggest the coronation of the King of kings.

The phenomenon of disbelief in God is not new. Long ago the psalmist declared "The fool says in his heart 'there is no God.' " What is new today is that it is no longer the fool who is saying this. Theologians ostensibly committed to a belief in God are today writing God's obituary and, may I add, they are doing it with dry eyes.

A number of observations on the death of God are in order. In the first place it should be noted that the statement, to a Jew, is both blasphemous and self-contradictory. If He is God, He cannot die. If He can die He is not God.

To the Christian the phrase is not quite as shocking because at the heart of Christian theology is a God who was killed. The image inevitably associated with Christianity is the crucifix which pictures the Christian God bleeding to death. That God died because He was born. Among Jews, God has no birth and therefore is incapable of death.

It is more than a little ironic that for centuries Christians have been teaching that Jews killed God. Now it is the Christians who are proclaiming the death of God.

Should we as Jews be distressed by this movement?

Henrich Heine once declared: *"Vee es Christelt sich, zo Yudelt es sicht –* as Christianity goes, so goes Judaism." Inevitably we are caught up in a Christian culture. Jews read the same magazines that Christians read and the same books and listen to the same programs. Inevitably, when the Christian says Kaddish for God, the Jew will be tempted to answer Amen. To that extent of course there is a great danger that Christian moods and doctrines will have an impact upon Jews. However, for the Christian, the problem is a lot more serious than it is for the Jew. The Jew can stop believing in God and still declare himself a Jew and feel part of the Jewish people. We do have the phenomenon of irreligious Jews or even atheistic Jews. But what remains for the Christian when his belief in God goes? The new theologians are therefore trying to proclaim the paradoxical doctrine: There is no God and Jesus is His son. So that what emerges is this historical paradox. Traditional Christianity has always taught that on the cross the son died to glorify the Father. Now what is being said is that the Father has died, and the son is to be glorified.

As far as I am concerned, the crucial question in this whole discussion is – which God is dead? It is sobering to recall that Judaism began with the cry, "The gods are dead but God is alive." Abraham, according to our tradition, was the first iconoclast. He was a breaker of idols in the home of a maker of idols. Throughout history our traditional role was to deny the gods whom others worshipped – the multiple gods of the pagans, the double gods of the Zoroastrians, the Trinity of the Christians. Which God is dead?

Is He the God who is expected to intervene miraculously to save us from the fruits of our own folly, the consequences of our own evil, and suspend the laws of nature for our convenience? (During my chaplaincy days I remember talking about the soldier who sowed wild oats and then prayed for a crop failure.) Is He the God whom we expect to cater to us, to serve us, to do for us what only we can do for ourselves? Is He, in brief, the God whom we want to be alternately our universal magician and bellhop? Then we might be better off without Him.

Is He the God in whose name the hungry and the oppressed were so often in history offered "pie in the sky" so that they would not rebel against those who denied them bread on earth? Then we would be better off without Him.

Is He the God in whom the assassinated Prime Minister of South Africa fervently believed – the God who made the black man to serve the white man in perpetuity as a "hewer of wood and drawer of water"? If so, we would be infinitely better off without Him.

Is He the God who permitted His worshippers to stand idly by the blood of their neighbors during the most frightful holocaust in history – a holocaust made possible by 19 centuries of preaching in the name of that God – then we would be better off without Him.

If the God whose death is being proclaimed is the God who was alleged to have rejected the Jews as an accursed race, then we would surely be better off without Him.

What kind of a God do we in fact affirm on Rosh Hashanah? What kind of a God do we have in mind when we declare: "You are our God, O King who lives and is."

He is the God who gives meaning and purpose to life. "Remember us to life, O King who desires life." God wants us to live. Our lives are willed by Him. It is He who rescues us from the absurdity to which the pessimist and the morbid existentialist have reduced life. One of the high priests of existentialism, Sartre, has declared, "The only logical question is why should I not commit suicide?" For him there is no meaning and no purpose to life. Then why indeed go on living at all? Dr. Carl Jung, the Swiss psychiatrist, quotes one of his patients: "If only I knew that my life has some meaning and purpose there would be no silly talk about my nerves." The Jew who believes in God looks upon his life as the handiwork of a Creator. That God we must keep alive because He gives meaning to our lives.

God, our God, not only gives meaning to our lives; He also gives direction to our deeds. He is the God in whose name the prophets of Israel cried out for justice and righteousness. In his name, Isaiah called upon the people of Israel "to loose the fetters of wickedness, to undo the bands of the yoke, to let the oppressed go free, and to deal your bread to the hungry, to bring the homeless to your house. When you see the naked that you cover him and that you hide not yourself from your fellow man."

It was in His name that the prophets dreamed of the day when "nation shall not lift up sword against nation; neither shall they learn war any more."

The God who urges us to enter into the struggle against poverty and inequality and discrimination, the God who encourages us to dream of a better day and not to despair while we work for that day, that God is more needed today than ever before.

The God whom we affirm is the God whom we are called to imitate. "Notice, " our Sages said, "that on the first page of the Torah, God clothed the naked–Adam; and on the last page He buried the dead–Moses. As He is compassionate, you be compassionate; as He is merciful, you be merciful."

In a world blighted with poverty and scarred with hunger, in a world where two-thirds of humanity goes to bed hungry every night, we need that God more than ever.

"By all that He requires of me, I know what God Himself must be."

The God we affirm on this day is the God who endows man with sanctity. Because in each of us there is a spark of His divinity, we carry the signature of the King impressed upon our very being.

So many factors conspire to cheapen human life today. Eric Fromm has pointed out that the problem is not so much that God may be dead, but what we confront now is the possibility that man is dead, transformed into a thing, a producer, a consumer, an idolator of other things.

It is our belief in God which elevates and ennobles us. "What is man that You are mindful of him?" asks the psalmist. And he answers, "Yet You have made him but little less than divine and have crowned him with glory and honor."

It is a great privilege to be human. It is a great challenge to be human. If we believe in the power of man to grow, to repent, to improve, to reach beyond himself and into the lives of others, it is because we are not machines but children of God. Man is not, as one modern writer declared, "a small but boisterous bit of organic scum that for the time being coats part of the surface of one small planet." Man is the bearer of the *"Tzelim Elohim,* the divine image."

It is noteworthy that in our Ten Commandments the first word is *"Anochee*–I–am the Lord thy God." The last word is *"L'rayacha*–Your neighbor." The commandments begin with God and they end with man. Man derives his sanctity from God's divinity. The God who raises us to high honor is the God whose existence we affirm on this day.

Whether God is dead for us or not is determined not by what we say but by what we do. The answer is to be found in our lives. There are so many who in speech are theists but who in practice are atheists. They act as if there were no God; no reverence, no commitment, no obligations.

There is an old story about a wise man who was reputed to be able to read the thoughts of every man and to fathom even things he could not see. A young man decided that he would reveal the wise man's limitations through a ruse. He appeared before him with a live bird clutched in his hand which he held behind his back. "What do I have in my hand?" he asked. "A bird," answered the wise man. "Is it alive or is it dead?" he asked: saying to himself, "If the wise man answers 'dead' I will produce the live one; and if the wise man says that the bird is alive I will instantly squeeze it to death." The wise man reflected briefly, and the young man repeated the question, "Is it alive or is it dead?" The wise man answered, "As you will, my son, as you will."

In a sense this is true of God too. Whether God lives or not depends upon us – not on what we say but on what we do. " 'You are My witnesses,' says the Lord." And the Sages give a very daring interpretation of this verse. "If You are My witnesses, then I am God. If You are not My witnesses, then I am not God."

Alive or dead? As you will. As you will, my son, as you will.

On Rosh Hashanah we affirm that our destiny is in the hands of God. Perhaps the more daring thought is that God's destiny is in our hands. Whether or not God is alive is demonstrated by how we live.

"The best argument for the existence of God," says Dr. Mordecai M. Kaplan, "is a God-like human life." Let us each make of our lives convincing arguments that God truly lives.

Where Is Holiness?

The words "holy" and "holiness" are dead tired from overwork in sermons and prayers, but they are almost completely unemployed in our everyday speech. If these words are not part of our daily vocabulary, it is because the ideas they conjure up are remote from our thinking. Perhaps if we understood them better we would see a closer connection between these words and our lives. What does holiness mean?

First, let us say what holiness is not. It is not something available to the few, to the select, to spiritual leaders. It is accessible to all. Nor is holiness achieved by turning one's back on society and the world. It is achieved in the midst of daily living. Holiness is not something apart from life, it is a part of life.

The Jewish conception of holiness is revealed most clearly in the nineteenth chapter of Leviticus. There we read: "Speak to the whole congregation of the children of Israel and say to them: 'You shall be holy; for I, the Lord your God, am Holy'" (Leviticus 19:2). Notice that the whole congregation, every Jew, is summoned to holiness.

The Bible then proceeds to teach us that holiness is not an abstract or mystic idea; it is meant to be a principle which regulates our daily lives. How is holiness attained? By honoring parents, observing the Sabbath, showing kindness to the needy, paying wages promptly, dealing honestly in business, refraining from talebearing, loving one's neighbor, showing cordiality to the stranger, and acting justly.

Holiness is a crucial dimension of daily living. One employer caught some of this spirit when he said to a prospective employee: "I see that you have references from three ministers. We don't work here on Sundays. Do you have a reference from someone who sees you on weekdays?"

Prof. Solomon Schechter, one of the great Jewish scholars of the twentieth century, once asked: "Where are the Jewish saints? In other communions, you have a long list of saints. Churches are named after saints. Where are the Jewish saints?"

Schechter answered his own question: "Jewish saints do not form a sect apart. You find them in the very midst of the community. They are not raised on a special pedestal, because a man who works as a doctor can be a saint, a man who works as a laborer can be a saint. It is sometimes possible even to achieve a degree of holiness in the pulpit—surprising as that may be."

It is this Jewish conception of holiness which found expression in the following passage included in the High Holy Day Prayer Book, *Mahzor Hadash*:

> "There is holiness when we strive to be true to the best we know.
> There is holiness when we are kind to someone who cannot possibly be of service to us.
> There is holiness when we promote family harmony.
> There is holiness when we forget what divides us and remember what unites us.
> There is holiness when we are willing to be laughed at for what we believe in.
> There is holiness when we love—truly, honestly, and unselfishly.
> There is holiness when we remember the lonely and bring cheer into a dark corner.
> There is holiness when we share—our bread, our ideas, our enthusiasms.
> There is holiness when we gather to pray to Him who gave us the power to pray."

"In our time," wrote Dag Hammarskjöld, "the road to holiness necessarily passes through the world of action."

For us Jews that is where the road to holiness has always been.

Dear David

I have before me the melancholy clipping from the *New York Times* of June 10, 1971.* The headline proclaims: "At Graduation, Top Princeton Senior Voices Despair." You were that senior. You were the

---

*The date of the commencement, the name of the school, and the number of graduates have been deliberately altered to preserve the anonymity of the graduate involved.

highest ranking student among the 950 graduates. You had majored in mathematics and you were a computer expert. Your position at the top of the class won for you the right to deliver the Valedictory address at the commencement exercises.

I am sure that never before were such gloomy words heard at any commencement as the words you spoke on the morning of June 10. Your sentiments contrasted sharply and darkly with the festive air that prevailed at the exercises.

You are quoted as saying:

"I have rejected graduate school offers because I could not worship black ink on white paper. I have made no plans because I have found no plans worth making.

"Take pity on me. Those of you who can justify the air you breathe, send me letters and tell me why life is worth living. Rich parents, write and tell me how money makes your life worthwhile. Princeton alumni, tell me how the Princeton experience has given value to your existence.

"And, fellow graduates, fellow members of the class of 1971, take pity on a student who did not think but only studied. Tell me how you have justified your existence to yourself. Or perhaps why you have not felt the need to do so."

These are the bitter words you spoke, David, and they have bothered me since I read them. I have re-read the newspaper clipping several times since June and I am reacting to your sentiments on Rosh Hashanah day because this is the time when we deal with life's basic issues, the kind of gut issues which you dared to raise at a time more generally reserved for pleasant platitudes and shallow optimism. You asked harsh questions and, by implication, issued some severe judgments. I can understand why the parents and guests, according to the newspaper report, greeted your remarks mostly with silence.

What I can't altogether understand is why your classmates applauded you so warmly. Perhaps it is because they, like I, admire your frankness and your courage. You dared to lay bare your own naked, tormented soul. You were brave enough to put into words a condition which so many endure but few recognize and fewer admit – especially in public.

I think that John Truslow Adams was thinking of precisely this widespread human predicament of which you complain when he whimsically suggested, "Perhaps it would be a good idea, fantastic as it sounds, to muffle every telephone, stop every motor and halt all activity for an hour some day to give people a chance to ponder for a few moments on what it is all about, why they are living and what they truly want."

As a matter of fact, his suggestion isn't really as fantastic as he thinks it is. This is exactly what we Jews do on the Days of Awe – for much more than an hour. On Rosh Hashanah and Yom Kippur, we Jews muffle the telephones, stop the motors and we come together to ponder on what it is all about, why we are living and what we truly want. And that is why I am dealing precisely on this day with the challenge you hurled to the thousands in your audience and the hundreds of thousands who read your words in the press.

Twice in the course of your quoted remarks you asked for pity. It's the easiest thing I can give you. Who can fail to be moved by your pain, your bewilderment? Here you are, so magnificently endowed in mind and so tormented in spirit! Your future could be so bright but your horizon is so ominously bleak. You have everything *with* which to live but nothing *for* which to live. If it makes you feel better – here is the coin of pity for your outstretched beggar's cup.

I can give you more than pity. I can offer you also the coin of solace. If, as the old saw has it, misery loves company, then I suppose you might be consoled by the knowledge that you are not alone in your anguish. The applause of your fellow graduates may be one indication of it. There are many, many more on all sides.

The thousands of cop-outs in our time are largely made up of people who have found no answers to the shrieking questions you flung at us. A magazine cartoon shows a bearded, long haired young man in his bare feet and tasseled poncho standing in front of an information booth in some railway station. He turns to the man behind the desk and asks, "Who am I and where am I going?" Need I add that neither the man behind the desk nor the computer which you mastered so well can provide the answers to the young man's poignant haunting questions – so closely related to the ones you ask.

Nor is it only among your contemporaries that you will find those who have not been persuaded that life is worth living. More than ever before in this country, people are undergoing voluntary sterilization to keep themselves from inflicting upon others the burden of existence which their parents inflicted upon them. In unprecedented numbers married couples are today deliberately planning to have no children. Some time ago a new book appeared, *The Case Against Having Children*. Childlessness, which used to be viewed as a great deprivation, is to many today a preferred status. And I wonder how many people's feelings are reflected in the poem Dilys Laing addressed to her son. She calls it "Forgive Me."

> "Forgive me for neglecting to show you that the world is
>   evil.
> I had hoped your innocence would find it good
> and teach me what I know to be untrue.
> Forgive me for leaving you open to persistent heartbreak
> instead of breaking your bright heart with medicinal blows.
> I had hoped your eyes would be stars
> dispelling darkness wherever you looked.
> Forgive me for a love that has delivered you
> unwarned to treachery. Now I confess that the world,
> more beautiful for your presence, was not fine enough
> to warrant my summoning you into it.
> My beloved."

While I am assembling the company to share your misery, let me add that it is not only among the living that you find those who doubt the worthwhileness of life. This malaise is not a 20th-century phenomenon. We usually think of the Bible as a great medicine chest of faith, but it does contain the Book of Koheleth whose weary white-flag refrain is "Futility of futilities, all is futility." It also contains the lament of Jeremiah, "Cursed be the day wherein I was born. Cursed be the man who brought tidings to my father, saying, 'A man child has been born to you.'" Job lamented his birth in virtually the same words.

Moreover, the Talmud records a running discussion that lasted 2½ years between the two greatest schools of Sages of their time, the academies of Shammai and Hillel. They "rapped" on this very question, whether it is better for man to have been born than not to have been born at all. Ultimately, they took the matter to a vote. The majority verdict was that it would have been better if man had not been born at all. Weighing the pain against the gain, the joys against the

---

"FORGIVE ME" from the collected poems of Dylis Laing, published by Case Western Reserve University, used with permission.

jolts, the blessings against the bruises, the ecstasy against the agony, perhaps non-being is to be preferred over being.

So you see David, you have some very impressive company in your misery. And for whatever that company is worth, I summon them to share your aching yearning and join your flaming protests.

So now you have my pity and you have some solace. Is there something else more sustaining than pity and more substantial than solace that I can offer you? I believe there is. The first thing I would like to offer is a reaction to some of the questions you ask.

Let us start with the question which you put to the "rich parents": "Write and tell me how money makes your life worthwhile." Do I detect a note of rebuke or snobbishness in your question to the *rich* parents? Is there anything wrong with being a rich parent? Are you trying to suggest that because parents have accumulated wealth that there is something immoral, or unethical about them? Perhaps your fellow graduates who are having so much trouble finding jobs this year may be less inclined to look down their noses upon their parents who struggled through a mammoth depression and fought back to win the rewards of service and enterprise. My own observations lead me to conclude that in the overwhelming majority of instances, the so-called rich are people who have brought to society greater industry, greater initiative, greater ability. Their wealth is not something for which they should be rebuked.

But that is not to say that it is money which makes life worthwhile. Who has ever seriously made such an inflated claim? Money does enable people to do many worthwhile things. There are not too many significant communal goals which can be accomplished without money. Whether we are trying to build a synagogue, protect the security of Israel, discover a cure for cancer, eliminate slums, fight drug addiction, provide jobs for the unemployed, cut down on air and water pollution – whatever commendable social objective we set for ourselves will require money. In our tradition, David, the mere possession of wealth does not render a person suspect. The crucial questions are how did he amass it and how does he spend it. Judaism never extolled poverty nor denigrated wealth.

By the same token, however, it recognized the limitations of wealth. There is much, as we said, that money can buy. But very many precious things simply have no price tags. A sense of life's worthwhileness is surely not up for sale. How one develops that is another question which I will leave for a little later.

You also cry out to the Princeton alumni, "Tell me how the Princeton experience has given value to your existence." Again I submit, David, that your question is loaded. You imply that someone has seriously claimed that a college education gives value to one's existence. No, it doesn't. A college education has great value. It does not give value to existence. It enriches it. It should broaden one's perspectives and deepen one's understanding. It should equip one to make a more effective use of his life and to make a more worthwhile contribution to his community. But it doesn't give value to existence.

This leads me to the question which you put to your fellow members of the class of 1971: "Tell me," you challenge them, "how you have justified your existence to yourself. Or perhaps why you have not felt the need to do so." No human being, David, has to justify his existence. Life itself is a supreme value. *The* supreme value! It needs no further validation. To whom should one justify one's existence? To the state? To the United Nations? To the policeman on the corner? Why do you feel so guilty for taking up room on this earth?

The framers of the American Constitution intuitively grasped one of the bedrock truths of the human race when they affirmed, "We hold these truths to be self evident; that all men are created equal and are endowed by their Creator with certain unalienable rights. Among these rights are life. . . ." This is the prime unalienable right. It is self-evident. It requires no defense, proof, justification, validation. "I am, therefore I am." You are, therefore you are. There is no point, David, in trying to put anybody on the spot to justify his existence. He is alive and the fragile, slender thread of life must be protected, nourished and sustained.

And now we come to the heart of the whole business, the question which you addressed to "those of you who can justify the air you breathe." "Send me letters," you plead, "and tell me why life is worthwhile."

Would you be very disappointed if I tell you that the question has no answer? No one can tell anyone else why life is worth living. Life poses that question to each of us and each of us must spell out the answer with his very life.

The most magnificent insight into this whole problem was

captured by George Santayana, the American philosopher, who condensed a great truth into one sentence: *"That* life is worth living is the
most necessary of assumptions, and were it not assumed, the most
impossible of conclusions." Read this sentence again, David, before
you go on. Life isn't like a neat mathematical equation in which you
add up all the components and come out with a precise sum, a neat
total whose validity can be checked. Life isn't like a theorum in
geometry which flows as the logical consequence of a series of axioms
and corollaries. No computer has yet been discovered which can even
begin to digest the impulses, the symbols, and the markings which are
punched into the card of every human being's life. That life is worth
living is an assumption, an act of faith which defies proof.

And it is a most necessary assumption. Without it, unless I
assume that my life is worth living, I will wallow in self pity, as you
seem to be doing, I will be gripped by paralysis and yield to despair.

Now, if I am confronted by two principles, one which leads to
despair and the other to hope, one to self pity and the other to self
motivation, one to passivity and the other to action, and if both
principles are equally not susceptible to proof, then there is no question
which is to be preferred. It is for this reason that Santayana calls the
life-affirming choice as the most necessary of assumptions. It is an
assumption, to be sure, but a most necessary one. Without it even the
most brilliant Princeton senior can only wring his hands in the
morning of his life, sobbing for pity when he should be summoning us
to get going, to tackle the multitude of problems which cry out for
solutions.

No, David, I can't tell you *why* life is worth living. Nor can
anyone else prove life's worthwhileness. But for that matter some of
the most beautiful things in life can't be proved. The magnificence of a
purple and orange sunset cannot be proved. The warmth of a child's
smile, the tenderness of a mother's soft embrace, the transforming
power of love, the glow of mercy, the white loveliness of untrampled
snow, the strength of forgiveness, the power of kindness, the compelling majesty of truth – none of these things can be proved. And yet we
affirm these things because we know them to be so, with a special kind
of knowing which does not depend on balanced mathematical equa-
tions or computer validations.

In the same way we affirm the worthwhileness of life. This is
indeed"the most necessary of assumptions." For it is this assumption

that makes possible all human accomplishment. It is this assumption which can translate your enormous potential into solid and perhaps even spectacular achievement.

And as you make this most necessary assumption – that life is worth living – the whole tradition and the whole history of your people are behind you and encourage this act of faith. To be sure, the voices of Koheleth and Jeremiah and Job sound more like cries of surrender than orders to march. But these are minority voices; and even Koheleth's refrain that all is futility is not the last word in the book. His pessimism is canceled out by the concluding lines which summon man to a full life. "To sum it all up, in conclusion, stand in awe of God, obey His commandments; that is everything for every man." Jeremiah and Job cried out under the impact of life's relentless pounding when they expressed the hope that they had never been born. But these were passing moods – which none of us escapes. Even the sun has a sinking spell every day. Both of them fundamentally affirmed life's worthwhileness. Jeremiah found meaning in service to his people, and Job in the anguished, stubborn pursuit of truth. And the schools of Shammai and Hillel did not stop with their melancholy verdict that it were better for man not to have been born. They went on to add – "having been born, let him look well to his deeds." In other words, now that we are here, we have to affirm and accept the validity of the human enterprise and act responsibly.

Beyond what we say to explain away the cries of Koheleth and Jeremiah and Job and the verdict of the schools of Shammai and Hillel, we ought to be aware that they were subdued voices in the Jewish tradition. The predominant mood was shaped by such Biblical verses as "God saw everything that He had made and behold, it was very good." And God created man in His own image, in the image of God He created him, male and female. He formed both and God blessed them and said to them, 'Be fruitful and multiply. Fill the earth and subdue it.'" This command to Adam and Eve became the first and paramount mitzvah of Judaism, to have children, to be fruitful, to pass along the gift of life. Another of the towering Biblical verses which shaped the Jew's values and fed his passion for life came from Deuteronomy. "I have set before you life and death, the blessing and the curse. Therefore choose life that you may live, you and your seed."

We Jews are a life-affirming people. In the presence of death we recite Kaddish, which is a majestic hymn to God and an Amen-saying to creation. Our favorite toast is *"L'chayim."* The Fiddler on the Roof, precarious as his very existence is, nevertheless sings "To life, to life, *l'chayim."* And in doing so, he strikes the most genuine chord of Jewish experience. For we are a people whose Sages have taught: "Each human being is obliged to say: 'The whole world was created for my sake.' "

Now, if any people is entitled to the luxury of self pity and to the questionable privilege of despair, it is your people, David, the Jewish people. Which people has been pounded more heavily and more persistently by the hammer of prejudice? Which people has been more frequently victimized by man's malevolence? Which people saw more clearly how brutal man can be to his fellow man? Which people earned more justly the right to declare its ideals an illusion, its hopes a snare? And yet it is your people which walked into the crematoria singing, *"Ani Ma'amin* – I believe in the coming of the Messiah. And even though he tarry, yet will I wait for him, because I believe." It is your people which on one this day of Rosh Hashanah prays, "May all Your children unite in one fellowship to do Your will with a perfect heart." "Therefore the righteous shall see and be glad, the just exult, and the pious rejoice in song while evil shall close its mouth and all wickedness shall vanish like smoke, when You remove the dominion of tyranny from the earth."

Professor Abraham J. Heschel is one of the most authentic voices of the Jewish people in our time. He has marched in the civil rights protests. He has demonstrated against the tragedy of Vietnam. He is involved in every worthy contemporary endeavor. His words therefore, deserve a special hearing.

"I as a Jew do not know what despair is. Despair means utter futility, being utterly lost. I will never be lost. I know where I came from, I know where I am going. I am the son of Abraham. Despite all my imperfections, deficiencies, faults and sins, I remain a part of that Covenant that God made with Abraham; we are going toward the Kingship of God and the Messianic Era. This is the preciousness of being a Jew."

Life has spoiled you, David, because it has given you so much, endowed you so extravagantly. And so you expect to be always on the receiving end. But you are being unreasonable. You want someone else to give you the answer which only you can and must provide for yourself.

What makes life worth living for one person may not be the same for the next person. For some of us, it is our families whom we love, it is the child we want to raise, it is the grandchild in whom the supreme miracle of life unfolds once more as we are given the greatest possible encore. For some, it is being needed by a person, by a cause. For some it is the privilege of being co-workers with God in the on-going act of creation by planting a garden, composing a song, writing a poem. Emily Dickinson found the worthwhileness of life in small acts of goodness.

> "If I can stop one heart from breaking
> I shall not live in vain.
> If I can ease one life the aching
> Or cool one pain
> Or help one fainting robin
> Into his nest again,
> I shall not live in vain."

Among the sign-posts to a worthwhile life most frequently invoked by our people has been the challenging wisdom summed up in the three brief rhetorical questions Hillel asked. In them you may find the answer to your own.

> "If I am not for myself who will be for me?
> But if I am only for myself what am I?
> And if not now, when?"

For you, David, at this time of searching, the middle question may be the most reliable answer. Avoid getting hung up on yourself. A person all wrapped up in himself makes a very small package, and paradoxically a very heavy one to carry. Your life will become most worthwhile when you find a cause or purpose or person to which to dedicate a vital portion of yourself. Your life will be as worthwhile as the things to which you dedicate it.

And as a member of the Jewish people with its perplexing problems in America, its threats to its survival in Israel and its special agony in the Soviet Union, there is no shortage of causes which can benefit from your allegiance and in turn help you find high purpose and exhilarating adventure in the privilege of being alive.

I have invited a number of people to talk to you today, David. And I am going to conclude with the words of still another American philosopher, William James: "Be not afraid to live. Believe that life is worth living and your belief will help create the fact." You want to know why life is worth living. Bet your life that it is, and because you believe it, you will help to make it so.

Believe me,
Rabbi Sidney Greenberg

Things That Do Not Change

Someone has objected to the popular adage that "love makes the world go round." He insists that love only keeps the world populated. It is change that makes the world go round.

I believe it was the ancient Greek philosopher Heraclitus who emphasized the idea that things are always in a state of flux. Change is the only constant. Therefore, he said, a man cannot step into the same stream twice. By the time he steps into the stream a second time, both he and the stream have changed.

One of the most striking characteristics of our century has been the intensified rate of change in almost every aspect of our lives. My grandfather grew up in the oxcart age. His grandson is living in the space age. Some years ago, Robert Oppenheimer, the atomic scientist, declared that 90 percent of today's scientific knowledge has been discovered since he left college.

It is exciting to be alive in a time of change. All sorts of wondrous possibilities lie before us. But it is also bewildering to be living in a time of revolutionary change. Familiar landmarks are obliterated and with them there is lost, too, a sense of orientation.

What happens to the old standards of decency? Are they now outmoded? What happens to the ancient teachings about honesty, morality, and human responsibility? Have they become archaic? What value do the old signposts have if people now fly at thirty thousand feet above the roads?

The prophet Isaiah seemed to be pondering such questions even in his day. To be sure, his age was scarcely as volatile as our own. To him, however, it must have seemed to be a time of radical transformation. And so he said to his people, in the name of God: "For the mountains may depart and the hills be removed; but My kindness shall not depart from you, neither shall My covenant of peace be removed, says the Lord who has compassion on you" (Isaiah 54:10).

To the prophet, the mountains and the hills represented the most enduring of physical things. But more enduring than the physical things, he said, are the spiritual values of life – God's kindness and God's promises. These are the changeless realities in a changing world; these are the things one could cling to in a slippery time, the things that the teeth of time would not chew to pieces.

What are some of these things? The redeeming power of compassion, the healing power of forgiveness, the transforming power of love – these things do not change.

The purifying power of repentance, the energizing power of prayer, the sustaining power of faith – these things do not change.

The nourishment that comes from beauty, the strength that comes from adversity, the joy that comes from generosity – these things do not change.

The supreme value of character, the ultimate worth of human life, the permanent perpetuation of personality – these things do not change.

Our capacity to change and improve ourselves, our ability to change the world for the better – these things do not change.

Living at a time of accelerated change, we need desperately the wisdom to cling to the things that do not change.

Living Up to Our Masks

During the eighteenth and nineteenth centuries, a favorite form of social entertainment for European aristocrats was the masqued ball. The guests would each come in costume and wear some disguise. When the midnight hour struck, off came the masks and each guest stood revealed in his or her true identity. A Swedish theologian was

thinking of these masqued balls when he said something which applies
not only to the aristocracy. "There comes a midnight hour when all
men must unmask."

For us Jews, the night of *Selihot* is such a midnight hour when we
usher in the season when we are summoned to appear before God
without masks or disguises. We stand stripped of all pretense before
Him Who, in the words of our Bible, "does not look as man looks; for
man looks with the eyes but God looks into the heart." He is the
"searcher of hearts" and the "revealer of all hidden things." Masks are
not much help.

The habit of wearing masks is one which all of us have cultivated.
The very word "person" in English comes from the Latin "persona"
which means "a mask." In the theatre of ancient Rome each character
wore a distinctive mask and his identity was reflected in his "persona."
To be a person is to wear a mask.

Gilbert and Sullivan put the matter in poetic form:

> "Things are seldom what they seem,
> Skimmed milk masquerades as cream."

Masks, it would seem, are instruments of deception and whether
we delude ourselves or others is immaterial. To attempt to live our lives
behind masks is as treacherous as erecting a skyscraper on a foundation
of sand. John Erskine gave eminently sound advice when he urged,
"Put on what man you are; put off the mask."

And yet, after we have said all this there is a lingering feeling that
we have not explored this truth completely. The fact is that certain
masks are quite indispensable for living. Were we entirely incapable of
masking our true feelings, we often could not perform our assigned
tasks.

The salesman soliciting an order may be quite worried about his
sick little boy at home, but unless he can put on the mask of enthusiasm over his product, he will not be able to provide for his sick child.
The restaurant hostess may be heartsick over a shattered marriage, but
unless she can wear the mask of radiant good cheer she may soon find
herself without a job. The professional counselor may have a host of
personal problems gnawing away at him, but unless he can put on the
mask of certainty and composure he will soon lose his usefulness to
those who seek his aid. The grieving widow may feel an awesome

burden of sorrow oppressing her heart, but if she cannot manage to mask her true feelings, she may find friends hard to come by. And any one of us may find ourselves at the bedside of a dear friend or a loved one suffering from a fatal disease, and unless we can put on the mask of hopefulness and confidence we will betray our mission of mercy. All of us, at one time or another, must play Pagliacci wearing the mask of the carefree, laughing clown over a face distorted by pain and twisted in agony. As a temporary facade behind which to conceal untimely emotions, masks are not only permissible, they are priceless.

Moreover, we could all grow into finer human beings if we learned to wear the mask of the finest human being we know–not in order to pretend to be what we are not, but rather as a means of aspiring to be what we can become. If we would become kinder and more sympathetic, we would do well to assume the pose and strike the attitude of the kindly and sympathetic person. If we would become more understanding and more merciful, we could profitably don the masks of understanding and mercy. Someone has said with fine insight, "Act human and you will become human." In the very process of playing the role of a better person, we can take an impressive forward stride in actually becoming better. All aspiration is partial realization.

One of the most dramatic illustrations of this truth was provided by the actor Richard Berry Harrison, who played the role of "De Lawd" in the original production of *Green Pastures*. Harrison was chosen for the role because of his powerful build and deep resonant voice, not necessarily for any spiritual qualities. People who watched him perform in the play testified, as did Harrison himself, that after 1,700 performances as the Lord, he had become a highly spiritualized individual. As he himself explained it, he strove to become godlike, to be worthy of the role he played. He tried with conspicuous success to live up to his mask. He demonstrated the truth of Professor Hocking's assertion: "There is a deep tendency in human nature to become like that which we imagine ourselves to be."

Let us select our masks carefully, and then let us live up to our masks.

VIII

A SHEAF OF PRAYERS

If we have forgotten how to pray, remind us.

Bless Us Enough

Source of all goodness, as we join in Shabbat worship,
We ask Your blessings.

Grant us health enough to perform our daily tasks,
Wealth enough to answer our needs,
Compassion enough to feel the needs of others.

Give us strength enough to recognize our future,
Wisdom enough to understand Your laws,
Loyalty enough to discharge our duties.

Give us courage enough to be true to the best within us,
Charity enough to see the best in others.

Give us patience enough not to become discouraged,
Hope enough to overcome all fears for the future,
And faith enough to feel Your presence.

Amen.

A Prayer for Life

Source of all life, we pray for life. Bless us, once more, with a year of life so that we may be privileged to complete the year we have just begun.

Despite the burdens and the heartbreaks, the pains and perils, we want to live; we ask to be inscribed in the Book of Life.

But even as we pray that years may be added to our lives, we ask, too, that true life may be added to our years.

May the new year be for us a time for enhancing the quality of our lives, enriching their content, deepening their meaning.

Help us to keep our minds alive. May we be open to new ideas, entertain challenging doubts, reexamine long-held opinions, nurture a lively curiosity, and strive to add to our store of knowledge.

Help us to keep our hearts alive. May we develop greater compassion, be receptive to new friendships, sustain a buoyant enthusiasm, grow more sensitive to the beauty which surrounds us.

Help us to keep our souls alive. May we be more responsive to the needs of others, less vulnerable to consuming greed, more attentive to the craving for fellowship, and more devoted to truth.

Help us to keep our spirits alive. May we face the future with confidence, knowing that every age has its unique joys and satisfactions, each period in our lives a glory of its own.

Help us to keep our faith alive. May we be sustained by the knowledge that You have planted within us life eternal and have given us the power to live beyond our years.

Whether our years be few or many, help us to link our lives to the life of our people and to our eternal faith.

Inspire Us

Heavenly Father,
We have come together to pray as a congregation;
Yet each of us is strangely solitary in Your presence.

Each of us comes before You with special hopes and dreams;
Each of us has personal worries and concerns.

Each of us has a prayer no one else can utter;
Each of us brings praise no one else can offer.

Each of us feels a joy no one else can share;
Each of us has regrets which others cannot know.

And so, we pray:
If we are weary, give us strength;
If we are discouraged, give us hope.

If we have forgotten how to pray, remind us;
If we have been careless of time, forgive us.

If our hearts have been chilled by indifference,
Warm them with Your mercy, and inspire us
With the glowing spirit of Your holy Shabbat.

Amen.

Each Of Us Is an Author

"You open the Book of Remembrance, and it speaks for itself,
For each of us has signed it with deeds."
This is the sobering truth,
Which both frightens and consoles us:

Each of us is an author,
Writing, with deeds, in life's Great Book.
And to each You have given the power,
To write lines that will never be lost.

No song is so trivial,
No story is so commonplace,
No deed is so insignificant,
That You do not record it.

No kindness is ever done in vain;
Each mean act leaves its imprint;
All our deeds, the good and the bad,
Are noted and remembered by You.

So help us to remember always,
That what we do will live forever;
That the echoes of the words we speak,
Will resound until the end of time.

May our lives reflect this awareness;
May our deeds bring no shame or reproach.
May the entries we make in the Book of Remembrance
Be ever acceptable to You.

For These Gifts We Give Thanks

O God, to whom we come so often with needs to be satisfied, we come to You now in gratitude for what we already have and are.
For gifts beyond deserving or counting, we give thanks.

You have given us the ability to become more than we have been, the urge to be more than we are, and a gnawing hunger to attain heights only dimly imagined.
For the power to grow, we give thanks.

You have endowed us with the capacity to discern the difference between right and wrong; and You have enabled us to follow the right, to avoid the wrong.
For the power to choose, we give thanks.

You have blessed us with the ability to fashion things of beauty, to sing new songs, to spin new tales, and to add to the treasure-house of human civilization.
For the power to create, we give thanks.

You have equipped us with the yearning to commune with You, to bring You our fears and our dreams, our hurts and our joys, our guilt and our gratitude; to share hopes and concerns with You and with others.
For the power to pray, we give thanks.

You have fortified us with the ability to rise above disappointment and failure, to go on after we have been bruised and bereaved, to refuse to submit to defeat and despair.
For the power to hope, we give thanks.

You have enlarged us with the ability to cherish others, to make their lives as dear to us as our very own, to share their hopes, to feel their hurts, to know their hearts.
For the power to love, we give thanks.

You have ennobled us with the strength to abandon our sins, to overcome our faults, to mend our ways, and to answer the summons of this day "to turn to You with all our heart and soul."
For the power to repent, we give thanks.

The Synagogue – The Doorway to a Richer Life

May the door of this synagogue be wide enough
to receive all who hunger for love,
all who are lonely for fellowship.

May it welcome all who have cares to unburden,
thanks to express, hopes to nurture.

May the door of this synagogue be narrow enough
to shut out pettiness and pride, envy and enmity.

May its threshold be no stumbling block
to young or straying feet.

May it be too high to admit complacency,
selfishness, and harshness.

May this synagogue be, for all who enter,
the doorway to a richer and more meaningful life.

Amen.

Thanks for Your Precious Gifts

O God, who revealed Yourself to a lonely shepherd
in a lowly thorn-bush enveloped in flames
which marvelously was not consumed,

We thank You, for Your precious gifts
which stubbornly defy the fires that would consume them:

For the yearning for liberty
which will not be strangled by the cold chains of tyranny.

For the striving for truth
which will not be discouraged by the persistent clamor of
falsehood.

For the struggle for justice
which will not be defeated by the cruel powers of malice.

For the urge to love
which will not be stifled by the cynical call to hate.

For the belief in tomorrow
which will not be crushed by the heavy burdens of today.

For the will to live
which will not be choked by the rude hands of sorrow.

For the power of the spirit
which will not be conquered by the brute spirit of power.

For the faith in You
which will not be uprooted by the chilly winds of despair.

For all these precious gifts
we offer thanks to You who first spoke to Moses
from the bush that burned, but was not consumed.

The Prayer of Our Lips

"Areshet sefateynu ye-erav lefaneha . . ."
"May the prayers of our lips be pleasing to You, O God."

May our prayers be pleasing to You because they are spoken with sincerity and with truth.

May our prayers be pleasing to You because they are uttered in humility, as we acknowledge our frailty and our need for Your sustaining strength.

May our prayers be pleasing to You because they are offered in gratitude for Your manifold blessings, too numerous to be counted, too constant to be deserved.

May our prayers be pleasing to You because we firmly resolve to take these noble words with us and to permit them to guide our actions in the year ahead.

May our prayers be pleasing to You because the lips which speak them also speak words of hope to the discouraged, cheer to the distressed, solace to the bereaved, and kindness to all.

May our prayers be pleasing to You because they reflect not only our own needs but also the needs of others, and the needs of our people.

May our prayers be pleasing to You because they remind us of what You expect of us, and because they challenge us to become all that we are capable of being.

A Protest . . . A Prayer

Dear God, so much innocent bloodshed!
We are supposed to be created in Your image,
But O how we have distorted it.

When we recall the beastly acts of people,
We are ashamed to be human.
When we read of the nobility of their victims,
We are proud to be Jews.

Teach us, O God, to honor our martyrs,
By being vigilant in defense of our people everywhere,
And by fighting cruelty, persecution, and hate.

But must cruelty always be?
Must viciousness ever be the signature of humanity?
No! No! We refuse to accept that!
We refuse to give hatred the last word,
Because we have known the power of love.

We refuse to believe that cruelty will prevail,
Because we have felt the strength of kindness.
We refuse to award the ultimate victory to evil,
Because we believe in You.

So help us, O God, to draw strength from our faith,
    And help us, our Father, to live by our faith.

Where there is hatred, may we bring love.
Where there is pain, may we bring healing.
Where there is darkness, may we bring light.
Where there is despair, may we bring hope.
Where there is discord, may we bring harmony.
Where there is strife, may we bring peace.
Make this a better world and begin with us.

Have Compassion upon Us

Have compassion upon us, Your handiwork;
We are so frail and so weak.

Disease and misfortune come without warning.
The wrath of nature can sweep us away.

Trouble and tragedy are our common lot.
Disappointment and heartbreak visit us all.

The good for which we strive often eludes us,
Confusion and uncertainty frequently torment us.

We stand in need of Your mercy, O Lord,
Watch over us and protect us.

Keep us from yielding to bleak despair.
Keep shining before us the gentle light of hope.

Help us in all our worthy endeavors.
Bless and "establish the work of our hands."

Keep us firm and steady and true,
Whenever we labor for what is just and right.

May our lives daily proclaim the truth,
That You have fashioned us in Your image,

And endowed us with the ability to grow,
In heart, in mind, and in spirit.

To us, You have entrusted Your holy name;
You have given us the power to sanctify it.

May our every deed bring joy to You,
O merciful God, our Creator.

And may our lives in the year ahead
Bring glory to Your holy name.

Amen.

A Family Prayer

We thank You, O God, for Your gift of Shabbat,
For the home in which we observe it,
And for the dear ones with whom we share it.

May the joy of Shabbat gladden our hearts,
And may its peace quiet our spirits.

As we observe Shabbat together,
May we understand its meaning and capture its mood.

Bring us closer to one another in love;
With laughter and soft words,
With shared concerns and mutual respect.

Help us to make our home a sanctuary,
Warmed by reverence, adorned by tradition,

With family bonds that are strong and enduring,
Based on truth, trust, and faithfulness.

Keep us far from strife and anger;
May we be spared shame and reproach.

Help us so to live in the week ahead
That You may look upon all we have done
And find it good and worthy of Your blessing.

You Reach Out

"You reach out Your hand to transgressors
And Your right hand is extended to accept the penitent."

When we are heavy with guilt and remorse,
God's forgiveness can lighten our burden.

When we feel trapped by fear or habit,
God assures us and moves us to action.

When, in despair, we have no place to turn,
We can turn to Him and be welcomed.

When we feel lonely, abandoned, or forsaken,
The words of His Psalmist bring us comfort:

"The Lord is near to all who call upon Him —
To all who call upon Him in truth."

When the voice of cynicism denies life's meaning,
We can "hope in the Lord and take courage."

When repentance and change seem too hard,
We draw strength from the divine promise;

For on the road to true repentance,
We are met by God's love and compassion.

For Everything There Is a Time

FOR EVERYTHING THERE IS A SEASON, AND A TIME FOR EVERY PURPOSE UNDER THE HEAVENS.

A TIME TO BE BORN, AND A TIME TO DIE. (Ecclesiastes, Chapter 3)

We do not choose to be born, we do not choose the time to die. But we can choose our way of life. We are fully born when we choose to live nobly. We cannot hope to avoid death, but we can invest a part of ourselves in the things that never die, and thus live on beyond our mortal span.

A TIME TO PLANT, AND A TIME TO HARVEST WHAT HAS BEEN PLANTED.

We harvest what others have planted before us. The harvest of a life sustains and nourishes those who survive. May we so plant that those who come after us will enjoy a rich harvest that nourishes life and hope.

A TIME TO BREAK DOWN AND A TIME TO BUILD UP.

In the presence of death we are reminded that now is the time to break down the walls of estrangement that separate brother from brother, parents from children, husbands from wives, each of us from God. This is the time to build up the bonds of caring that draw us closer to one another in tenderness and in love.

A TIME TO WEEP, AND A TIME TO LAUGH.

At this time of mourning, we weep for the dead. We weep also for the days we have wasted, for the thanks we did not offer, for the tears we did not wipe away, for the gifts we did not use, for the good we left undone. Let us laugh with the hope that sorrow will teach us to do better and live more wisely in the days ahead.

A TIME TO MOURN AND A TIME TO REJOICE.

At this time we mourn the death of a loved one. When the pain subsides and the wounds heal may we rejoice in gratitude for the years we shared, for the memories which death can not rob from us.

A TIME TO CAST AWAY STONES, AND A TIME TO GATHER STONES TOGETHER.

Now is the time to try to cast away the heavy rocks of remorse and regret that lie on many hearts, the rubble of blasted dreams and collapsed hopes. May the time not tarry when the mourners will find the courage and the strength to rebuild their lives in confidence and in hope.

THERE IS A TIME TO SEEK, AND A TIME TO LOSE.

Death reminds us that it is always time to seek the good in each other and for each other. It urges us also to lose the pettiness and callousness that diminish our stature and shrink our horizons.

THERE IS A TIME TO KEEP, AND A TIME TO CAST AWAY.

This is the time to keep in treasured possession our faith in the God who heals the broken hearted and binds up their wounds. This is also the time to try to cast away the bitterness, resentment and anger death leaves in its wake.

A TIME TO LOVE, AND A TIME TO HATE.

The time for love is always, for to love is to expand life to its fullest dimensions. Let us remember that it is also time to hate malice and bigotry, meanness and selfishness, and all things that deprive life of its beauty and joy.

A TIME FOR WAR AND A TIME FOR PEACE.

Now is the time for the mourners to fight against despair and hopelessness. May they do so in the stubborn hope that the time will surely come when they will again know serenity of spirit and inner peace.

Peace Means More than Quiet

Help us, O God, to lie down in peace;
But teach us that peace means more than quiet.

Remind us that if we are to be at peace at night,
We must take heed how we live by day.

Grant us the peace that comes from honest dealing,
So that no fear of discovery will haunt our sleep.

Rid us of resentments and hatreds
Which rob us of the peace we crave.

Liberate us from enslaving habits
Which disturb us and give us no rest.

May we inflict no pain, bring no shame,
And seek no profit by another's loss.

May we so live that we can face
The whole world with serenity.

May we feel no remorse at night
For what we have done during the day.

May we lie down in peace tonight,
And awaken tomorrow to a richer and fuller life.

                                                        Amen.

A Prayer for Graduates

Lord of the Universe, Dean of the University of Life:

You have given us minds that can stretch with knowledge, spirits that can deepen with understanding and hearts that can overflow with gratitude. We thank You for our sons and daughters who have grown in mind and in spirit, and we are abidingly indebted to their teachers who have patiently and hopefully nurtured that growth.

As our graduates go forth from this school into Your University of Life, keep them ever mindful that among the required courses in Your curriculum are firm loyalty, constant kindness, soft compassion and wide tolerance.

Teach them the lessons they must learn by heart and the lessons the heart must learn.

May they never forget that it is important to know not only how to make a living, but also how to make a life. We make a living by what we get; we make a life by what we give.

May they always remember that the harvest of happiness is reaped by the hands of helpfulness, and the City of Contentment is located in the State of Mind. The whole world was not enough for Alexander the Conqueror, but a tub was sufficient for Diogenes.

Keep them from any enterprise for which they would hesitate to ask Your blessings.

Help them to become all that they are capable of being.

May they live up to their own highest expectations and make the most of their native endowments.

Help them to understand that more important than mastering any skill is mastering themselves; more crucial than controlling others is self-control.

May they learn to prize integrity above luxury, principle above expediency, value above valuables, worth above wealth.

When life tests their courage and their character, may they pass with highest grades. Impress upon the tablets of their minds that service is the tuition they must pay for the seat they occupy in life's classroom. May they measure the rewards of service not by what they get for it, but by what they become through it.

Help them, O God, so to live that their names may be worthy of being on Your Roll of Honor.

Amen

V'al Yerushalayim: A Prayer for Israel

O Guardian of Israel, we ask Your blessings
Upon the People of Israel and the Land of Israel.

> *Bless them with peace, tranquility, and achievement,*
> *Bless them—even as they have been a blessing to us.*

For they have nurtured our pride,
And renewed our hopes.

> *They have gathered in our homeless;*
> *They have healed the bruised and the broken.*

Their struggles have strengthened us;
Their sacrifices have humbled us.

> *Their victories have exalted us;*
> *Their achievements have enriched us.*

They have translated into fulfillment
The promises of Your ancient prophets:

> *"They shall build the waste cities and inhabit them;*
> *They shall plant vineyards and drink their wine."*

Truly, they have made the wilderness like Eden,
And the desert like the garden of the Lord.

> *Watch over the Land, we pray;*
> *Protect it from every enemy and disaster.*

Fulfill the prophetic promises
Which still await realization.

> *"Violence shall no more be heard in your land,*
> *There shall be no desolation within your borders."*

"Zion shall be redeemed through justice,
And they that dwell therein through righteousness."

Al Het: For These, Too, We Repent

We have sinned against You
by forgetting that we are made in Your image;

> *And we have sinned against You*
> *by forgetting that others are also made in Your image.*

We have sinned against You
by sacrificing conscience on the altar of comfort;

> *And we have sinned against You*
> *by surrendering abiding values for fleeting pleasures.*

We have sinned against You
by meeting petty irritations with fierce anger;

> *And we have sinned against You*
> *by greeting massive wrongs with cool indifference.*

We have sinned against You
by remembering too long the hurts we have suffered;

> *And we have sinned against You*
> *by forgetting too soon the hurts we have inflicted.*

For these sins,and others for which we also repent,
forgive us, pardon us, grant us atonement.

V'al kulam Elo-ha selihot, s'lah lanu, m'hal lanu, kaper lanu.

We have sinned against You
by squandering the riches of our heritage;

> *And we have sinned against You*
> *by neglecting to study and to teach Torah.*

We have sinned against You
by abandoning our noblest ideals;

*And we have sinned against You
by clinging to old prejudices and evil habits.*

We have sinned against You
by neglecting the needs of our families;

*And we have sinned against You
by evading our responsibilities to our people.*

We have sinned against You
by ignoring the weak and the suffering;

*And we have sinned against You
by forsaking the lonely and the oppressed.*

*For these sins, and others for which we also repent
forgive us, pardon us, grant us atonement.*

**V'al kulam Elo-ha selihot, s'lah lanu, m'hal lanu, kaper
lanu.**

We have sinned against You
by emptying our lives of sacred rites and holy days;

*And we have sinned against You
by filling our days with trivialities and seeking status.*

We have sinned against You
by speaking words of gossip and harsh rebuke;

*And we have sinned against You
by withholding words of encouragement and praise.*

We have sinned against You
by failing to do our utmost in our work;

*And we have sinned against You
by not "serving God in joy."*

We have sinned against You
by not becoming all that we could be.

*And we have sinned against You
by not permitting others to become all that they could be.*

*For these sins, and others for which we also repent,
forgive us, pardon us, grant us atonement.*

**V'al kulam Elo-ha selihot, s'lah lanu, m'hal lanu, kaper
lanu.**

Draw Us Closer

Eternal God, in whose service we are enlisted and in whose name we have gathered, lift our thoughts that we may renew our minds; and lead us beside the still waters so that we may restore our souls.

We thank You, O Lord, for our hallowed memories and for our abiding hopes.

Help us to show that we are Your children by giving ourselves faithfully to Your tasks.

Help us to convert our convictions into conduct and commitment.

Help us to narrow the gap between our principles and our practices, between our aspirations and our actions.

Keep us from blaming others for our own faults; help us to heal the wounds we have thoughtlessly inflicted.

Help us to face our defeats with courage and to carry our successes with humility.

Keep us from the pride that blinds the mind and from the anger that locks the heart.

Make us loyal to our convictions in the face of falsehood; but help us to speak the truth in love.

Draw us closer to Your teachings, closer to each other, and closer to You.

Amen.

What Death Cannot Take from Us

Death has cast its dark shadow over this home,
And it has left us all deeply bereft.

> *A voice has been stilled, a heart has been stopped,*
> *Laughter has departed, joy has fled.*

Gone are the warmth and the glow of a loved one's pres-
    ence;
The chain of love has lost a vital link.

> *Death has taken a life which was precious;*
> *It has brought pain, loneliness, and sorrow.*

And yet there is so much which death cannot touch,
So much over which it has no dominion.

> *Death cannot rob us of our past:*
> *The years, the dreams, the experiences which we shared.*

Death cannot take from us the love we knew;
It is woven into the tapestry of our lives.

> *The lessons we were taught we shall continue to cherish;*
> *We shall cling to the wisdom which lives on.*

What we have had, we shall always possess;
What we have known, we shall always hold dear.

> *Death cannot take from us our abiding trust,*
> *That God will give us strength to endure what we must.*

Death cannot take from us our sustaining hope,
That darkness will yield to light, and hurt give way to
    healing.

> *Death cannot take from us the comforting faith,*
> *That with God every soul is precious; none is ever lost.*

Thus, even in sorrow, we thank the Lord our God,
For our memories and our hopes, for our trust and our faith.

For these, we believe, need never be lost;
These, and so much more, death cannot take from us.

GREENBERG, SIDNEY

AUTHOR

WORDS TO LIVE BY

TITLE

DATE DUE		BORROWER'S NAME

190
SG

190
SG